THE MEANING OF DISABILITY

Sociology of Social and Medical Care Series
General Editors Raymond Illsley and Gordon Horobin

THE MEANING OF DISABILITY

A Sociological Study of Impairment

MILDRED BLAXTER

HEINEMANN
LONDON

Heinemann Educational Books Ltd
22 Bedford Square, London WC1B 3HH

LONDON EDINBURGH MELBOURNE AUCKLAND
HONG KONG SINGAPORE KUALA LUMPUR NEW DELHI
IBADAN NAIROBI JOHANNESBURG
EXTER (NH) KINGSTON PORT OF SPAIN

ISBN 0 435 82032 X

First published 1976
First published as an HEB Paperback 1980

Printed in Great Britain by
Richard Clay (The Chaucer Press) Ltd,
Bungay, Suffolk

CONTENTS

ACKNOWLEDGMENTS

This work was supported by the Social Science Research Council, as part of a programme of studies on *Objectives and Needs in Medical and Social Care Systems* carried out at the Centre for Social Studies, Aberdeen.

I gratefully acknowledge the invaluable help of Isobel Morrison, Research Assistant, who shared the task of interviewing.

Thanks are also due to Professor Raymond Illsley, Gordon Horobin, and Alan Davis, and my other colleagues at the M.R.C. Medical Sociology Unit and Centre for Social Studies, for their unstinting encouragement and advice, and to Jeanette Thorn for her secretarial work.

This study could not have been undertaken without the co-operation of doctors, administrators and other professional workers, too numerous to name, to whom I am very grateful. The greatest debt, however, is to the people of the survey, who suffered our intrusion into their homes and lives with such patience and friendliness. I should like to thank them very much.

INTRODUCTION

To be disabled is to be presented with problems. In commonsense terms, this is what disability means: to be less able, to be at a disadvantage in earning one's living or in the ordinary activities of daily life. But the concept of disability itself also *presents* problems to those who wish to help, and the two levels of problem are interrelated. These interrelations are the theme of this study.

Who are the disabled? Most people are impaired at some time or to some degree: like health and sickness, disability and 'normality' form a continuum. Where an individual is placed on this continuum depends on many factors of social and family environment, individual characteristics, and cultural concepts of what it is to be normal, as well as on clinical facts describing an impairment. Even among those clearly identified as 'the disabled' there is great diversity. Impairment may be congenital, or a harbinger of approaching age; it may occur by sudden accident or slowly and insidiously over many years. It may be visible or invisible, a common or a rare condition, handicapping in only one area of activity or affecting the whole of life.

Society has defined 'the disabled' as a group whom it wishes to help, and an elaborate structure of services has been established. Yet the provision of services obviously depends upon the specific definition of the client and his needs, and ambiguity remains about who the disabled are. Currently, attempts are being made to extend the scope of help offered through the health and welfare systems to the physically impaired, but in attempting to widen services the problem has to be faced that although handicap is obviously relative and dependent upon individual circumstances, formal categorizations still have to be found for the disabled person before help can be made available to him.

This study does not attempt to offer definitions of 'the disabled' or recipes for helping services. Rather, it explores some of these processes of categorization, at the same time demonstrating, from the disabled person's point of view, the nature of his problems. Since processes of definition are a central focus of the study, it was obviously not appropriate to study any group of people already defined as disabled. The sample, therefore, consisted of all those people discharged during a four-month period from four wards of a large teaching hospital, whose illness or accident was neither trivial nor expected to be soon fatal. The two extremes were excluded not on logical grounds – for in some cases a very trivial illness may prove disabling, and helping services may certainly be relevant in cases where the prognosis is very poor – but simply on practical grounds, in order to concentrate attention in the area most likely to be of interest. Obviously the categories of 'trivial' and 'poor prognosis' used could not be clear-cut and exclusive; even the most scientificially based clinical diagnosis and prognosis must in fact contain an element of opinion. Thus, some patients were included whose illness eventually proved to be less serious than it first seemed, and others did die during the course of the survey. The intention was to select a sample of people with varying degrees of seriousness of clinical condition who were potentially *likely* to be impaired to a greater or lesser degree either permanently or for a considerable time, and so were likely to have some problems of adjustment. The four wards, chosen simply to offer a wide spectrum of clinical conditions, were those of general medicine, general surgery, neurology and orthopaedic surgery.

The study was restricted to people of 'working' ages, 16–65. The welfare and education of disabled children, and the rehabilitation of the elderly, are equally important but different subjects. They were, of course, sometimes relevant: part of the explanations for the current 'careers' of congenitally disabled adults might lie in their childhood experiences, and the vexed question (for administrators) of distinguishing 'disability' and 'old age' raised shadowy queries as early as the mid-fifties.

These criteria produced a potential sample of 205 people. One could not be traced and four were excluded at the request of their general practitioner. Of the remaining 200, only six did not wish to take part in the study. The resulting 194 people were first interviewed soon after their discharge from hosptial, and at two- to three-monthly intervals throughout the succeeding year. Their families, and as far as possible all those agencies with whom they were in touch, were also interviewed, in an attempt to trace out the events of the year. In all, about a thousand interviews were conducted.

The 'career' perspective which is used examines the happenings of this year, in Lemert's[1] terms, as the 'recurrent or typical contingencies and problems awaiting patients' as they adjust to the sequelae of illness; in particular, their need-perceiving and help-seeking careers are traced and the processes explored by which they come to define themselves as having problems to be solved. Recovery (clinical and/or self-perceived improvement in physical condition) and rehabilitation (restoration to the best possible level of functioning in social and working life) are not 'outcomes' of themselves, but are both components of careers.

In this wide sense a 'career' has no ending during a lifetime, and the idea of an 'outcome' is avoided because the whole emphasis of the study is on a continuing process. Many studies of the rehabilitation of the disabled have analysed outcomes in terms of a successful/unsuccessful dichotomy at one point in time, to conclude at some arbitrary date that this man is rehabilitated, this man not. Such an approach usually means viewing one area of life (usually the area of employment) in isolation from others. The assumptions of the present study are that all areas of life are connected, and that it is never possible to say that a final outcome has been reached at a given moment of time.

The point of time at which the patient was discharged from hospital was obviously not the beginning of his impairment, which might have been weeks, months, or even many years before. In most cases (injury is an obvious exception) it was found to be indeterminate in any case, and the patient's or his family's ideas about 'the beginning' might be very different from those of clinicians. Nor was treatment usually completed at discharge from hospital, or necessarily even a year later. The point of time when some medical event necessitated hospitalization is, however, justified as a point of clinical definition or re-definition, and hence as a useful starting point. The following year is regarded simply as a sample in time of the lives of some physically impaired people.

The presentation of this material falls into three parts: a discussion of the structure of the relevant services (Chapters 1 and 2), the detailed evidence about what happened to the people of the sample (Chapters 3–9), and a general conclusion (Chapter 10) in which the themes are brought together. The central chapters deal in turn with four categories of 'problem' relating to different areas of life, and certain of the themes raised in Chapters 1 and 2 run throughout. An appendix discusses some of the problems of this type of research.

No attempt is made to measure the 'efficiency' of service-provision in any quantitative way. Rather, the study seeks to demonstrate and if possible to explain a range of processes which may be involved in defining oneself as 'disabled', in being so defined by others, in definitions of need for help and eligibility for services, and in finding or not finding the solution to problems of physical impairment. In particular, it is suggested that there will be interactions between three sets of definitions: the medical labels applied to a patient's condition, the administrative categories into which he necessarily has to be put, and the definitions – not perhaps congruent with either or both of the others – which he and his family make of his own state. It is suggested that the definitions in use in the various relevant systems of society, which may bear little relation to the reality of the individual's situation as he sees it, are likely to be crucial to his pathway through the services designed to help him.

Deliberately, an attempt is made to combine several levels of analysis. The 'pathway' or 'career' approach facilitates this, for as Goffman said:

> One value of the concept of career is its two-sidedness. One side is linked to internal matters held dearly and closely, such as image of self and felt identity; the other side concerns official positions, jural relations, and style of life, and is part of a publicly accessible institutional complex. The concept of career, then, allows one to move back and forth between the personal and the public, between the self and its significant society, without having to rely overly for data upon what the person says he thinks he imagines himself to be.[2]

The intention is to include both 'the personal and the public': to analyse situations and interactions, but also to attempt to account for the societal structures within which these encounters take place. The details of these patients' help-seeking careers may often be trivial, but cumulatively they make up a complex pattern representing the mutual adjustment of the individual and society. Increasing complexity of social organization and increasing wish to provide for social need, both involve the individual in more frequent interaction with institutional structures. The two major systems which are relevant to this study – the system of medicine, and the administrative and legal structure of welfare, social security and employment – are perhaps particularly important from this point of view. The subjects are an interesting group to consider, in part because they are being examined at a point when, as individuals, they are especially vulnerable to the pressures of the systems around them, and in part because, as a large but vaguely defined group, they are people whose help has been the object of a very long and complex history.

REFERENCES

1. Lemert, E. M., *Human Deviance, Social Problems and Social Control,* Englewood Cliffs, N.J., Prentice Hall, 1967.
2. Goffman, E., 'The Moral Career of the Mental Patient', in *Asylums*, N.Y., Doubleday, 1961.

1
DEFINITIONS OF DISABILITY

The current welfare provision for the disabled is still conspicuously full of legacies of earlier definitions of disability. The history of legislation in Britain, as in most Western industrialized countries, shows clearly the interaction of two, not always compatible, social movements: humanitarian concern and economic pressures. The earliest sympathy, expressed initially in the activities of voluntary charity, was for the most visible and 'innocently' disabled, and particularly for those whose needs could be clearly defined within the welfare ideologies of the time, and who could be presented as having a potentially hopeful future – crippled children, the blind and the deaf. These were groups with an immediate emotional appeal to the public whose charitable money was sought, and groups whose social welfare could be seen as a measure of a society's progress.

Thus, these were also the first groups for whom any general welfare legislation was enacted. Powerful voluntary societies, such as those for the blind, became pressure-groups demanding provision as of right rather than as charity, while at the same time guarding their own spheres of interest. A dual provision – statutory and voluntary – is now firmly established in the welfare system, and is formally presented as a partnership. It may well be, however, that early conflicts will still be found to leave an echo. Certainly, these first definitions of who the disabled are have left their mark on the structure of services: for instance, the blind – whose welfare was the concern of the first legislative measure specifically for the disabled in this country, the Blind Persons Act of 1920 – are still statutorily a class apart.

The second thread woven into the history of legislative provision is the economic, given impetus by the need during two world wars for maximum use of manpower, and by the post-war concern for disabled ex-servicemen. Early legislation in Britain (as in most other developed countries) selected out the war-disabled and the industrially disabled as the groups for whom special provision should be made: their needs were similar (principally for aids to mobility and dexterity, and training and employment) and the same principles of compensation could be seen to apply. Thus, the first practical provision of official rehabilitation help was the setting up of Government Instruction Factories for ex-servicemen of the First World War, a programme which was later extended to the industrially injured.

Ever since the days of the Poor Law, these two principles of social policy have been to some extent separate: a division has existed between those 'outside' the economic system, to whom only charity is owed, and those who are economically active and potentially valuable, whom society must help in its own interest and as a matter of social justice. When in 1942 the Beveridge Report offered its comprehensive plan for ensuring that all members of the community would at all times be free from want, the new concept of rehabilitation services as a right 'for all disabled persons who can profit from it irrespective of the cause of their disability' still used economic factors as the paramount argument. Rehabilitation was defined as the process by which the disabled became 'producers and earners', and when the National Insurance Act, 1946, became part of the implementation of the Beveridge recommendations, the differences between 'workers' and 'others' and between 'industrial' disease or injury and that produced by other causes was perpetuated and solidified.

The disabled 'producers and earners' are defined by the Disabled Persons (Employment) Acts, 1944–58; an individual must be 'a person who on account of injury, disease or congenital deformity, is substantially handicapped in obtaining or keeping employment, or in undertaking work on his own account, of a kind which apart from his injury, disease or deformity would be suited to his age, experience and qualifications.' He must also 'desire to engage in some form of remunerative employment or work' and 'have a reasonable prospect of obtaining and keeping such employment or work'. The welfare of those for whom vocational rehabilitation is assumed not to be applicable was originally legislated for in the National Assistance Act, 1948. Here the definitions were wider: the handicapped are 'those persons who are blind, deaf or dumb, and other persons, who are substantially and permanently handicapped by illness, injury or congenital deformity, or such other disabilities as may be prescribed by the Minister'.

Thus, the earlier provision for the disabled tended to define them either by their specific handicap or by its cause, with a division between those in the labour market and those outside it. Despite current ideologies of welfare stressing the nature of needs themselves, rather than categorizing them by causes, this too may have left a legacy in the formal structure of services.

The more recent history of legislation for the disabled again shows the influence of two social movements. The first is the movement towards an holistic approach to social welfare, recognizing that all the various areas of life are interconnected, and that health and welfare, in particular, affect each other closely. This is, of course, hardly a new idea: since the end of the last century, when the surveys of Booth and Rowntree demonstrated that sickness, old age and disability were major causes of deprivation, all the major movements of social policy (the Liberal legislation of 1906 onwards, the erection of the 'welfare state' from 1944 onwards) have been towards a closer connection between health and social welfare. Of more recent years, a new impetus towards 'integrated care' has been provided by the many studies showing that comprehensive medical care may be wasted unless it is co-ordinated with social and vocational help, and that poverty and unemployment are still correlated with chronic sickness and disability.

Thus, in Britain as in most other developed countries, the legislation for the assistance of the sick and disabled has widened in its scope. Whereas the earlier provisions dealt with isolated problems – the problems of mobility, or of vocational help – or with specific disabilities, the present tendency is to legislate for all disability groups and to cover as many areas of life as possible. Many official reports have appeared since the 1940s, all urging integration of services to achieve more effective rehabilitation of the disabled.[1]

The second, and parallel, movement has been towards the loosening and widening of definitions of disability. Whereas the earlier provision tended to use categorizations based on the specific handicap (blindness) or its cause (war injury), it is now recognized in principle that disablement may take many forms and have many causes, and inequities are bred of rigid categorizations. Thus, the newest comprehensive British legislation is designed to promote the welfare of 'the disabled' and 'the chronically sick', with no distinction made between their needs; an 'invalidity' pension has been introduced which acknowledges that some other state may exist between 'permanently disabled' and 'temporarily sick'. Many voluntary societies and other independent organizations have also widened their definition of their clients (though some may be restricted by their trust deeds) so that now the scope of their interests may include much more than their formal title and statement of aims might suggest.

In part, again, this movement towards looser categorizations is humanitarian, designed to provide more equitable and comprehensive services; in part, it is impelled by economic and administrative considerations. Disability is unproductive and expensive, and it is realized that the greatest amount of physical impairment is now caused by progressive or fluctuating chronic conditions – lung disease, cardiac conditions, arthritis, mental illness, an unnecessary degree of deterioration in old age – rather than by the stable conditions more usually called 'disablement' in the past. The emphasis on community rather than institutional care – again, part humanitarian and part economic – also immediately enlarges the concept of the potential client for services.

This widening of the definitions of who the disabled are can obviously be seen as a response to the reality of life as people experience it: manifestly, there are other roles being played than that traditionally ascribed to the 'disabled person'. But, in turn, the widening of definitions *creates* new roles, and raises questions about the physically impaired person's place in society. The dimensions of the role of an individual disabled by chronic or fluctuating illness, in particular, is one which society is still seeking to define with clarity (and also one which medical sociology has neglected).

Administrative definitions and the measurement of disability

The pattern of development which has been sketched is likely to present its special problems. As concern grows and services widen, more and more institutional systems become involved. Areas of national and local government previously outside this particular structure are drawn into it, special programmes proliferate, and new disability-specific groupings (for instance, voluntary societies) form themselves. At one and the same time there are pressures towards integration, and towards specialization and differentiation. Thus, while a movement towards loosening of categorizations is taking place, paradoxically, administrative definitions become more and more important. Meanwhile, legislation may also retain out-of-date and restrictive residues of this long social history, which may be ill-matched to the newer ideologies of need.

At one extreme of the system are those definitions which are necessarily rigid and dichotomous, since they distinguish groups who may or may not be entitled to nationally administered financial or other concrete benefits: sick or well, disabled with regard to employment or not, above or below retirement age, industrially injured or not. These divisions may be arbitrary, but they might be expected to be clear and comprehensible: in fact, however, even such basic definitions are often anomalous. The simplest one of all, the designation of a man as fit or unfit for work by means of a 'certificate of incapacity' may serve as an example. Obviously, this does not represent the certifying doctor's objective judgement on whether the patient is 'sick' or 'well', even though it is commonly called a 'sick certificate' and the patient is likely to describe himself (whether or not he feels ill) as 'on the sick list'; in the case of chronic illness and disability the terms sick and well have little meaning in any case. The certificate merely testifies that, in the doctor's opinion, the patient is unfit to do a particular job – the job he has, or the job that might be open to him, or the hypothetical job that he (or perhaps the Department of Employment) thinks best fits his 'normal' capacity. Thus, though the *effects* of a certificate of incapacity are clear and dichotomous in terms of whether or not he receives money support, and whether or not he has certain obligations, the categorization itself is unclear and obviously open to negotiation.

National insurance recompense for injury is another example where the categorizations might be expected to be clear. The basic historical anomaly remains, however, that where a man is injured during his working life or while serving in the armed forces, his income for the rest of his life may vary by a factor of three, depending on whether or not he is judged to have been 'on duty' at the time of his accident. Recompense depends not only on the cause of injury but also upon its effects: the principle of compensation, deeply imbedded in the welfare system, necessitates some quantitative measure of degree of disability. The rather crude measures adopted in the past are unlikely to be equitable, and are increasingly being criticized.[2,3]

The extension of services to wider groups of disabled people, and the identification of more and more 'needs' which society wishes to fill, means in fact that more and more administrative definitions become necessary. Particularly where any sort of money benefit is involved, unequivocal categories are essential. One problem which ensues is that systems of help for the disabled cannot exist in isolation from other systems which society operates: the definitions made of 'the disabled' are affected by, and in turn affect, the definitions of other groups such as 'the unemployed' or 'the poor'. A second problem concerns the essentially relative nature of impairment. If disparity in the treatment of different categories of impaired people is to be overcome, then it is necessary to find some equitable method of comparing and assessing degrees and types of handicap.

This has led to many attempts to develop functional assessments of disability which do not depend solely on the individual's loss of earning capacity.[4] Some have depended on the measurement of motor capacity, and others on assessing physical dependence or capacity for self-care and the ability to perform everyday tasks. All these have obvious limitations: measures of motor capacity exclude many of the sense-deprived, for disability does not only mean inability to move about, and measures of dependence or the capacity to perform ordinary tasks assume that there is some standard of dependence of some description of everyday life which is universally 'normal', for all ages and both sexes, and in any environment.

One way of dealing with these problems, particularly during a transition period when definitions of disability and of need are being adjusted, is to enact permissive legislation which leaves to 'professionals' of various sorts the task of interpreting its extent and defining its beneficiaries. Definitions negotiated at this level may then, as the problems are explored and professional and public opinion solidifies, be translated subsequently into formally legislated categories. The process is, however, a piecemeal one, with different elements of the system proceeding at different paces and sometimes in different directions. During this process, the informal defining processes of administrative and welfare agencies become more and more important.

Every welfare system – from a small local charity to a complex national organization – will have its own particular history, and its own legacy of ways of defining the client and his needs. Thus weighed down, it may move only sluggishly in response to newer concepts. Alternatively, agencies with a vested interest in 'their' clients and a special expertise in particular problems may try to introduce new concepts in advance of public opinion. In either case, services rarely catch up with what is currently defined as potential need, especially at a time when concepts of need in general are widening. Clients must be chosen, and the looser the agency's formal mandate the more crucial informal, organizationally created definitions will become.

Agencies necessarily have stereotypes of 'their' clients and, as Scott[5] has shown, the nature of these stereotypes will depend not only on the agency's formal goals, and on the generality or specificity of its mandate, but also on its history and the market in which it seeks its resources. Voluntary agencies, for instance, depending for resources on public generosity, may be fettered in meeting actual current needs by the traditional definition of the proper client for charity. In his study of agencies for the blind in the United States, Scott found that there was an excess of services for children, employable adults, and the totally blind, whereas these were minorities compared to the partially blind, the elderly, and the multi-handicapped. Fund-raising campaigns were necessarily projected in terms of stereotypes concerning youth, work and hope.

Of course, agencies can only conceive of a world of clients in terms of the universe that they know. Despite the large and growing body of evidence that the scale of present welfare provision touches only a small minority of those who could be defined as disabled (in particular, the evidence of the national survey, *Handicapped and Impaired in Great Britain*[6]) agencies are, typically, organized *as though* they were catering for all need. Discussion takes place on how resources might equitably be shared amongst clients, as currently defined, rather than examining the basis on which these clients are found.

Various factors may be suggested which will influence agencies' choice and categorization of their clients. Scheff[7] has suggested that stereotypes are a device for the organizational handling of uncertainty, and Sussman, that they are a normal management technique:

> Diagnostic stereotyping by treatment and control agencies is a consequence of the continuous search for model or normal cases which provide standardised explanations for easy and effective management, independent of what is known about the particular disease or disability.[8]

Scheff has also argued that various propositions about the validity of agencies' stereotypes may be propounded: the more stereotypes that are used in an agency, the more precise they will be, and the more precise, the more valid; the more marginal the clients, the less numerous and hence less precise and valid the stereotypes will be; the less the professional is dependent upon the goodwill of the clients, the less precise and valid the stereotypes will be; and the more substantial and scientific the corpus of knowledge on which the profession draws, the less important and more valid the stereotypes will be.[9]

The focus of this study, however, is not so much on how agencies' categorizations are developed, but on whether their effects can be discerned in the help-seeking careers of their clients. Clients, too, may have their stereotypes of agencies, and agencies of each other, and these may be no less important. In particular, the activities at the boundaries of agencies will be stressed. How do the agencies find their clients? They may seek them out, as the voluntary agency does, or as the medical social worker may do if she circulates the hospital ward. In this case, the agency must have a preconceived image of its clientele, whether based on identification of a condition (all those in this city who suffer from multiple sclerosis) or on a definition of need (patients whose particular circumstances make it likely that they will need help). The client may seek out the agency, for instance, the Disablement Resettlement Officer or the local authority social work department: here, the client has already defined himself and probably seeks from what he considers to be the appropriate place some very specific service, a new job, help with rehousing, an aid to mobility. He may well, in fact, find himself engaged in negotiations about the definition of his condition, but this was not his expectation.

Usually, however, the client is referred from some other agency, carrying with him their definition of his condition and needs. Obviously, the points of transfer represent crucial positions for the client.

Medical definitions

Because of the aura of authority which is attached in society to medical specialists and to medical certificates, the clinical label is one of the most important categorizations which follows the client from one agency to the next. The medical profession are the first who name and legitimize a condition involving physical impairment. It is they who offer to the patient a diagnosis and prognosis, and their treatment and advice are crucial in structuring his view of the past, present and probable future. Ideally, in the medical model, as in the social work model, there is no categorization of the patient or his needs: each is individual. Yet in so complex a structure and with much of the work so specialized and differentiated, labels are necessary, and the organization is likely to categorize in the ways which best suit the task in hand. Thus, clinical labels become important. These labels are, at the same time, administrative categories (this disease goes to one clinic, and that to another; this normally indicates surgery, that does not; this is routinely followed up after six months, that is not) and descriptive categories, carrying with them connotations of 'normal' prognoses (this condition is usually curable, that is 'serious' and has a poor prognosis; this will involve motor disability, that will not; this is likely to be handicapping for three months, that for three years).

Some of these categories are as arbitrary as those of the administrative system. Is the patient who is undergoing surgery for relief of chronic condition, or surgery which will leave a chronic impairment, a 'medical' or a 'surgical' case? Is his condition 'chronic' or 'acute'? If he has several concurrent conditions, under which speciality will he be categorized, and to which consultant will he 'belong'? The labels applied at any one moment, and especially by hospitals rather than general practitioners, are likely to be those which are administratively appropriate, and may well be very temporary or may not match the 'real' problem which the patient perceives.

In trying to trace out the influences of medical categories upon the careers of patients, it is not only categories of clinical condition which may be relevant, but also categorizations of medical 'need'. Situations may arise where it may be clear that the patient is in need of help, but where there may be doubt about the proper nature of that help. Is alcoholism a medical, a social, or a psychiatric problem? If disease is directly associated with self-neglect or a poverty-stricken environment, who should be concerned in its 'cure'? What are a doctor's proper functions in helping to recognize, legitimate, or provide for, needs for rehousing, or household help, or new jobs? These questions may have obvious answers at the health service policy-makers' level, but may still present problems at the level of the individual doctor facing his patient. The doctor's definition of what the patient's needs for help are may well influence the help he gets, no less than the clinical categorizations.

As soon as the doctor moves out of the strictly clinical sphere, however, he becomes involved with other agencies whose function it is to define need and offer help. Increasingly, as part of the movement towards the integration of health and welfare, and the loosening of definitions of what a 'problem' is all about, medicine is involved in, and asked to co-operate with, the other major systems of society; education, employment, welfare. As social organization becomes more complex and formal institutions multiply, the necessity grows for some expert to adjudicate, to measure, to sign a form; increasingly, the chosen experts are the medical profession.

There are two implications of this trend to which particular attention will be paid in analysing the careers of the patients of this study. The first concerns the nature of the categorizing systems used. It can be suggested that there may be unavoidable incompatibilities between medical defining systems, which ideally are individual, qualified and provisional, and administrative categories, which are necessarily rigid, dichotomous, and designed for large groups of people. If so, how are they accommodated? The second concerns the relative positions of medical personnel and others within the complex welfare structure. The medical profession has been used to claiming almost complete autonomy, at the level of service-delivery, over the content of its service, and if not complete autonomy then at least a very powerful voice in more general decisions about the allocation of medical resources. As Freidson[10] commented:

> When we look at occupations engaged in such a complex division of labour as is found in the field of health, we find that the only occupation which is truly autonomous is medicine itself. It has the authority to direct and evaluate the work of others without in turn being subject to formal direction and evaluation by them.

Will this be found to be true, in a British context and in a field where integration and co-operation are especially stressed? What is the practical effect upon service-provision of using the medical profession as adjudicating experts concerned in the allocation of non-clinical 'goods' – money, services, motor vehicles, houses, telephones? Where is it necessary to use them, and what are the reasons for their involvement in areas where the use of other professionals might seem rational?

Freidson went on to suggest that

> ... By and large, physicians refer to and communicate extensively with those who, within the medical division of labour, are subject to their prescription, order or direction. Indeed, physicians are likely to be very poorly informed about any of the institutional or occupational resources that lie outside their own jurisdiction.

Again, an attempt will be made to show whether this was found to be true.

Self-definitions

Amidst all this, it must not be supposed that the individual, the patient, is passive. In one sense the clinical labels and the administrative categories are facts: the medical records, the pieces of paper giving assessment of money entitlement, are true and real. But the reality of the individual's situation is a different sort of truth – an amalgam of official facts and private realities, of emotions and intentions, impressions and opinions. To him, the only reality is his own definition of the situation.

His behaviour will depend on how he defines himself. Is he well, or sick? Permanently impaired, or convalescing until he returns to normal? Others may call him disabled: what meaning does the label have for him? Compared to his neighbours, or to his younger self, is he handicapped in taking what he sees to be his normal role in society? What is his understanding of his physical condition, and what his picture of the future?

Even when 'the disabled' were only those with a restricted range of static impairments, to whom the description was commonly applied in the past, it seems obvious that to speak in terms of 'the disabled' role was to oversimplify. If it is accepted – as it is now accepted in legislation and welfare – that any physical impairment may be disabling, and the most common impairments which do result in handicap tend to be fluctuating, chronic or deteriorating in character, then in fact a very complicated pattern of 'disabled' roles is likely to exist.

The individual's self-definition will be continually changing, and the present study focuses on processes rather than states. Time is an essential component. An attempt will be made, in considering these patients' careers, not only to take account of subjective time, which may of course differ from objective time measured on the calendar, but also to see each present moment within its context of remembered past and anticipated future. For the individual, past, present and future cannot be separated, for he continually recreates the past in the light of the present, and interprets the present in the light of the imagined future. If he has rewritten his medical history in the light of subsequent events (and it will be the evidence of this study that this is a very common practice) then it is this reinterpretation, and not the 'real' events or his contemporary understanding of them, which will influence his present behaviour. Not only does his definition of *now* depend on his memory of *then* ('I was in the cardiac unit, with a great deal of attention being paid to me; I am someone who has been near death; it is necessary now for me to take great care') but the meaning he gives to *then* depends upon what has happened subsequently ('Those symptoms five years ago were not trivial ones, though I did not know it at the time; my disablement began then'). If we seek to explain the patient's definition of his condition and his behaviour, then we must ideally try to take into account not only what has 'really' happened but also the successive meanings he has given to events as they have occurred and the future which he has seen in front of him.

The particular focus of this study is on the way these fluid and continually recreated definitions influence people's views of what their problems are and how they might be solved, and thus influence their help-seeking behaviour. Their own definitions, and the way in which they present themselves to agencies, will in turn affect the definitions applied to them by agencies. The patient can present himself to the doctor, for instance, as suffering from something he feels to be serious and threatening, or from a familiar symptom which he knows responds to treatment: the choice depends not only on the severity of the symptom but also on his perception of its meaning. It may be expected that the doctor's response will depend not only on measurable clinical facts but also on the account he is given. Again, how the Department of Employment defines a client might be expected to depend to an important extent on whether he presents himself as temporarily ill, resigned to premature retirement, impaired but anxious and eager to work.

In turn, the behaviour of helping agencies will affect the development of the client's self-definition. The process seems likely to involve continuous reinforcement or resistance, adjustment and negotiation.

Disability as deviance

This approach, stressing the importance of labels and categorizations, is obviously influenced by concepts developed in the sociology of deviance, which draws attention to the societal reception of deviant acts rather than their individual aetiology:

> Deviance is not a quality of the act the person commits, but rather a consequence of the application by others of rules and sanctions to an 'offender'. The deviant is one to whom the label has successfully been applied; deviant behaviour is behaviour that people so label[11]

The literature of disability as deviance has argued that, like other stigmatized groups, the disabled tend to be evaluated as a category, rather than as individuals. The physical characteristic becomes a master trait, swamping personal differences. Indeed, two stereotypes are usually involved, both predominantly negative: one which describes the particular impairment (blind, spastic, crippled) and one which is attached to the general category of 'disabled'.

Freidson, in particular, has pointed out that since 'disabled' as an agent's category includes only those who have been so identified, and

> . . . by definition, a person said to be handicapped is so defined because he deviates from what he himself or others believed to be normal and appropriate[12]

then labelling, segregating and feed-back processes apply to the disabled as to other deviants. These processes have certainly been clearly illustrated for a range of visible, stigmatized conditions of the sort first defined, historically, as 'handicap' – disfigurements, epilepsy, sense deprivation – and there is evidence that people may develop wide ranges of concealing techniques in order to avoid the stigmatized label.[13] The process of deviance-creation by identifying agencies has been demonstrated most clearly by Scott, who showed the relevant welfare agencies for the blind as engaged in '. . . a socialization process, the purpose of which is to prepare a disabled person to play a type of deviant role' and 'make blind persons out of people who cannot see'.[14]

As some sociologists have pointed out, however, there are problems about the concept of the disabled as a stigmatized minority group.[15] The potentiality for joining the group exists in everyone, and hard distinctions between members and non-members are difficult to draw. The disabled are not a homogeneous group, but vary very widely in the characteristics such as visibility or severity on which discrimination may depend. Moreover, although negative attitudes towards the disabled have certainly been shown to be widespread over both time and place, there exists equally a strong cultural norm in our society that these attitudes are reprehensible and ought to be overcome.

Obvious dilemmas arise. Negative attitudes may be rationalized and disguised as concern. The more the group are singled out for special consideration, the more obvious the labels become. Society's anxiety to redress stigmatization by seeking out and helping the disabled, and providing those things which will enable them to perform tasks 'normally', may in fact emphasize those characteristics which make the disabled 'different'.

The overall structure of helping agencies is now based on an assumption that 'disability' is a loose category, including many degrees and types of impairment, which may or may not be visible or stigmatized. What the general category of 'disabled' means, and whether it is either treated as deviance by others or felt to be deviant by actors, remains to be shown. What specific variants of the label are found to be advantageous or a liability? What is the effect of a multiplicity of labels simultaneously applied, and what the position of a man who is in need of a label which he cannot find? These are all questions which will be asked of the career-patterns found in this survey.

It is a basic hypothesis of the study that the categories

available and the definitions negotiated between client and agency are – for good or ill – crucial to an individual's own definition of himself, and to his progress through whatever services may be available to help him. The acceptance or non-acceptance of categorizations is, however, seen as perhaps more problematic than conventional 'labelling' theory may allow: the emphasis is on the actor's own constructions, and on the processes by which he helps to delineate the categories, the ways in which he uses, amends, or suffers them in his attempt to control the social world as he sees it.

SUMMARY

Various hypotheses are suggested by this discussion: that the clinical and administrative categories applied to disabled people are often irrational and may not represent the reality of the situation as the patient sees it; that these categorizations depend upon the history and structure of the institutions concerned; that (for any given degree of functional impairment) variables of the disabling condition and personal characteristics of the sufferer are likely to affect the way in which he is defined; that attempts to apply a holistic approach to social welfare may cause confusion; and that the definition of 'need' (related as it is to the definition of 'client') may not match the needs that people perceive themselves to have. These are the major questions on which evidence will be sought.

REFERENCES

1. Tomlinson Report (Cmnd. 6415), London, H.M.S.O., 1943; Piercy Report (Cmnd. 9883), London, H.M.S.O., 1956; *Health and Welfare: The Development of Community Care* (Cmnd 1973), London, H.M.S.O., 1963; McCorquodale Report (Cmnd 2847), London, H.M.S.O., 1965; Tunbridge Report, *Rehabilitation*, London, H.M.S.O., 1972; Mair Report, Edinburgh, H.M.S.O., 1973.
2. Townsend, P., *The Disabled in Society*, Greater London Association For the Disabled, 1967.

3. Sainsbury, Sally, *Registered as Disabled*, Occasional papers on Social Administration No. 35, London, G. Bell & Sons, 1970.
4. See, e.g., Jefferys, Margot, Millard, J. B., Hyman, M. and Warren, M. D., 'A Set of Tests for Measuring Motor Impairment in Prevalence Studies', *J. Chronic Diseases*, 22.5, 1969; Harris, Amelia I., *Handicapped and Impaired in Great Britain*, London, H.M.S.O., 1971; Garrad, J. and Bennett, A. E., 'A validated interview schedule for use in population surveys of chronic disease and disability', *J. Prev. and Soc. Medicine*, 25.2, 1971; Garrad, J., 'Impairment and Disability: Their Measurement, Prevalence and Psychological Cost', in Lees, D. S. and Shaw, Stella (*eds*), *Impairment, Disability and Handicap*, London, Heinemann Educational Books, 1974; Sainsbury, Sally, *Measuring Disability*, Occasional Papers on Social Administration No. 54, London, G. Bell & Sons, 1973.
5. Scott, R. A., 'The Selection of Clients by Social Welfare Agencies: the Case of the Blind', *Social Problems*, 14, 1966.
6. Harris, Amelia I., *Handicapped and Impaired in Great Britain*, London, H.M.S.O., 1971.
7. Scheff, T. J., *Being Mentally Ill*, London, Weidenfeld & Nicolson, 1966, p. 105.
8. Sussman, M. B., 'Outcomes and Outlooks', in Sussman, M. B. (ed.) *Sociology of Disability and Rehabilitation*, Washington, D.C. American Sociological Assn., 1965, p. 233.
9. Scheff, T. J., 'Typification in the Diagnostic Practices of Rehabilitation' in Sussman, M. B. (*ed.*) *Sociology of Disability and Rehabilitation*, Washington, D.C. American Sociological Assn., 1965, p. 143.
10. Freidson, E., 'Dominant Professions, Bureaucracy and Client Services' in Rosengren, W. R. and Lefton, M. (*eds*), *Organisations and Clients*, Columbus, Ohio, Merrill Pub. Co., 1970, p. 71.
11. Becker, S., *Outsiders, Studies in the Sociology of Deviance*, New York, Free Press, 1963, p. 9.
12. Freidson, E., 'Disability as Social Deviance' in Sussman, M. B. (*ed.*) *Sociology of Disability and Rehabilitation*, Washington, D.C. American Sociological Assn., 1965, p. 72.
13. See, e.g., Hunt, P. (*ed.*) *Stigma: the Experience of Disability*, London, Chapman, 1966; Davis, F., 'Deviance Disavowal: the Management of Strained Interaction by the Visibly Handicapped' in Becker, H. S. (*ed.*) *The Other Side: Perspectives on Deviance*, New York, Free Press, 1964; Goffman, E., *Stigma: Notes on the Management of Spoiled Identity*, Harmondsworth, Penguin Books, 1968.

14. Scott, R. A., 'Comments about Interpersonal Processes of Rehabilitation' in Sussman, M. B. (*ed.*) *Sociology of Disability and Rehabilitation*, Washington, D.C. American Sociological Assn. 1965, p. 135.
15. See, e.g., Safilios-Rothschild, Constantina, *The Sociology and Social Psychology of Disability and Rehabilitation*, New York, Random House, 1970.

2
THE PATTERN OF SERVICES

The historical and organizational background which has been sketched can be given some reality by a consideration of the pattern of services actually available in the City of the study. This particular pattern, with all its background of social history, of organizational pressures, of competing ideologies, is the setting within which the 194 subjects of the survey had to find their place. It was in these areas of life, and to these agencies, that they had to relate themselves and their needs.

In the City, in 1972–73, fifty-nine different agencies were found whose function it was, entirely or in part, to help in the community with problems caused by sickness or disability. 'Agencies' are here defined as separate organizations, or branches of organizations, having distinct functions, and located at different offices. The list is very long and the general impression is of a system potentially ready to solve almost any problem. A diagram can be drawn (Figure 2.1) to show what goods and services were available, and which agency was responsible for supplying them. This particular picture of a system is of course specific to one City at one moment of time, and will differ in detail from that which might be found elsewhere. Many of its components are national rather than local, however, and differences in detail hardly matter: there is no reason to suppose that it is any more or less complex than that which would be found in other places, or untypical of the British system in general.

The system is obviously complex, though this is a simplified model. Only services designed for the physically ill or disabled person of 'working' ages are included: to add services for children, or the old, or the mentally ill or handicapped, would introduce new agencies and complicate the diagram considerably. Some of the agencies named represent systems in themselves; 'the hospital', for instance, does not distinguish between all the people in that building who might offer pathways to help: consultants, doctors, nurses, ancillary workers, even receptionists and clerks.

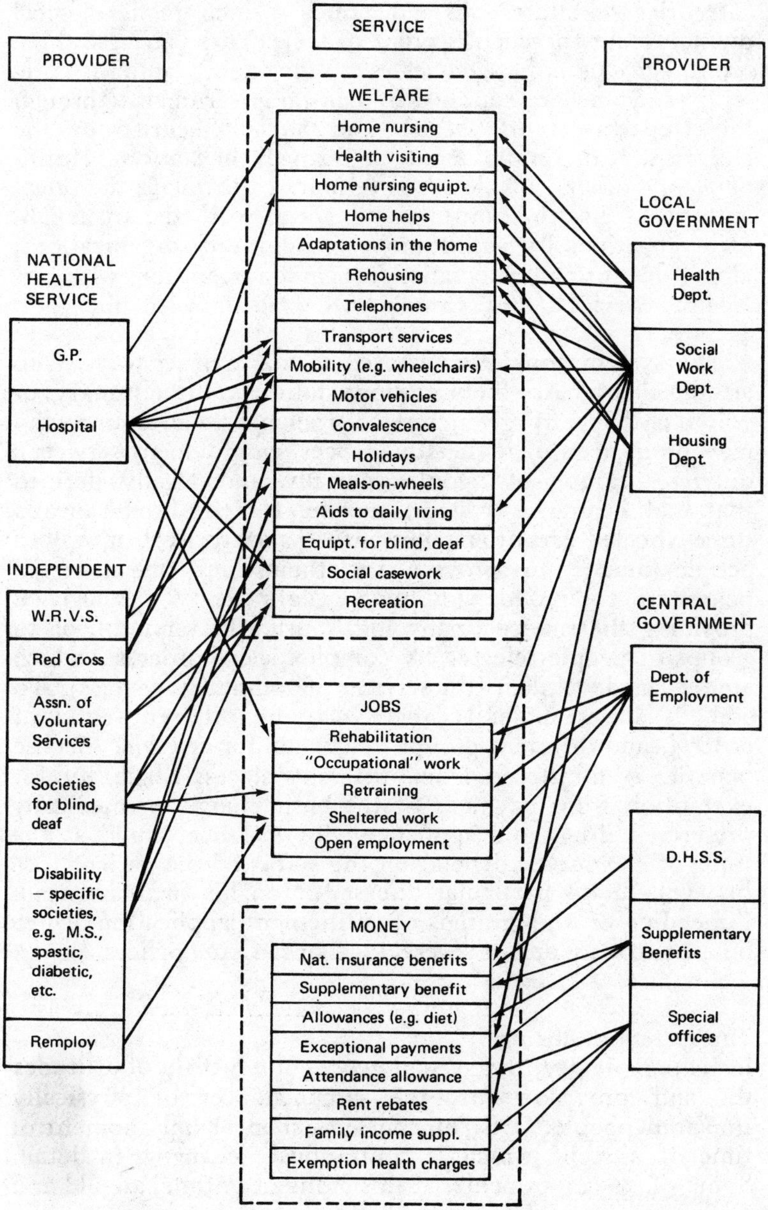

Figure 2.1 Services for the physically impaired available in the City, and who provided them.

In the diagram, the services have been grouped in three categories – welfare, jobs and money – since this is a logical division from the client's point of view. There are also three broad groups of agencies supplying and administering services. Some are supplied by central government (through the Department of Health and Social Security or the Department of Employment, or through the National Health Service), others by local government (through the local authority's health, housing, and social work departments), and yet others by autonomous or voluntary organizations, alone, in formal association, or in co-operation with the Health Service (Red Cross, W.R.V.S) or with the local authority.

The system could be analysed in many other ways. Who are the clients? Are the provisions statutory, discretionary, or voluntary? Is any given service available to everyone who may be in need of it (health services, employment services); only to groups of people specially and legally defined (national insurance system, services for the blind, invalid three-wheeled cars or car allowances); statutorily, but only to people unable to provide for themselves (means-tested benefits); to groups of people defined by the agency providing the service (many local authority services); or to groups of people selected by complex social processes which are not made explicit (the services of voluntary agencies)? To add to the complexity there may be different sorts of criteria, and different groups of clients, for any *one* specific benefit, administered from different places. Eligibility for exemption from payment of the basic charge for medically prescribed drugs and appliances, for instance, could at the time of the survey depend on the status of the patient (e.g. his age), or his particular disease, or on his financial need. Depending on the grounds of entitlement, application had to be made to any one of several local or national offices.

The system as history

In its complexity, the system echoes the history of attitudes to, and provision for, the circumstances of physically impaired people. It is, of course, a map at one moment of time of a scene which is continuously changing in detail. Some of its components, at this moment in time, are old and some are new. The City's 'Blind Asylum' was founded in 1843, and when in 1973 the Workshop for the Blind was at last able to move, with great relief, to modern industrial buildings, the 'listed' Georgian building, the fate of which caused some local controversy, had been its home for 130 years. At the other extreme, the local authority social work department,* as the agency for supplying many practical services to disabled people, came into being only at the Social Work (Scotland) Act of 1968, and many of the relevant duties were legally created only at the extension of the Chronically Sick and Disabled Persons Act to Scotland in 1973.

Thus, all the stages of society's thinking about the 'needs' of disabled people are represented. The history of charitable concern is summarized in the roll-call of voluntary societies, now all loosely grouped around the Association of Social Services, an organization which began its life as the Association for Improving the Conditions of the Poor. The original title epitomizes older attitudes to charity, as the earliest history of the Asylum for the Blind illustrates contemporary ideas about the welfare of the handicapped. It is recorded, for instance, that in 1843:

> During the summer the inmates had to meet at 6 a.m. Family worship was held each morning at 6.30 and every evening at 6 o'clock when work stopped. In addition, a portion of every Saturday after 3 o'clock and every morning was appropriated to the reading and explaining of the Scriptures.

The institution's changing function is mirrored in its present-day title – the Royal Workshop for the Blind – though even this is now out of date, since it is used as a sheltered workplace for other disabled people as well as the blind. The Town and County Association for Teaching the Blind at their Homes, founded in 1879, has not changed its name although its functions now include welfare as well as teaching. The other pioneering local society, the Benevolent Society for the Deaf and Dumb (1895) retains a strong religious affiliation but is now simply the Society for the Deaf.

These older societies retained, in this City, the curious status of 'statutory-voluntary', that is, they were paid by

*The equivalent, in Scotland, of English social service departments.

local government to act as their agency for duties laid down by national legislation. This use of independent and charitable bodies as an agency of government, though it permeates the whole of the British welfare system, is particularly common in the field of sickness and disability. The arguments used to justify such arrangements include the specialized expertise of the voluntary bodies, the particular qualities of the 'volunteer spirit', and the flexibility, responsiveness and freedom of action which might be held to characterize voluntary rather than official services. There are, of course, many instances of imaginative, pioneering service provided by voluntary agencies, of the sort the state could not or would not undertake; on the other hand, 'agency agreements' concern services which the state has agreed it ought to provide, and it is argued that in these cases the arrangement may have disadvantages. Services may be supplied unevenly, the local authority may neglect its responsibilities, and the ratepayer and taxpayer may in effect be subsidized by the charitable giver. An example of the diversity that can hide under 'agency agreements', and evidence of the anomalies that can arise, is the fact that at the time of the survey the local authority was paying the societies £6 p.a. for the welfare of each deaf and dumb person, and £20 for each blind person. No official recommendations about capitation fees, or centrally held statistics about them, existed. In other parts of Scotland where agency arrangements persisted, fees appeared to range from £14 to £20 (deaf) and £14 to £22.50 (blind).

Next in time among local voluntary societies came those especially concerned with the war-disabled, such as the Limbless Ex-Servicemen's Association, in 1945, or Remploy Ltd, in 1951: both rather later than their national parent bodies founded in 1920 and 1945 respectively. Remploy remains another example of a statutory-voluntary agency, now providing sheltered work for all sorts of disabled people.

Then disability-specific voluntary societies began to proliferate, beginning with those with a particular interest in crippling diseases of children (The Spastic Association in 1953, The Infantile Paralysis Fellowship in 1956). As other disabling diseases came to the fore, and interest extended to adults, new societies appeared (among many others, the Migraine Trust, the Spina-Bifida Association, the Multiple Sclerosis Society) or older ones changed their names (the Tuberculosis Care Committee, founded in the City in 1955, became the Tuberculosis and Chest Diseases Committee in 1960). Most recently of all, local branches began to form of societies acting as welfare pressure-groups, concerned with advice rather than care, rights rather than charity (the Disablement Income Group, 1972).

Most 'welfare' services provided by statutory rather than voluntary agencies are shown on the diagram to be administered by the social work department of the local authority. Prior to the Social Work (Scotland) Act of 1968 these services, if they existed, were perhaps the responsibility of the local health department, or welfare department, or other agencies; their administrative centralization demonstrates the comparatively recent attempts at integration. The range of services provided, many of them under the Chronically Sick and Disabled Persons Act, also demonstrates the enlargement of concepts of 'need' from the bare necessities of life to such relatively sophisticated services as the provision of telephones or of social casework, the extension of the potential client for 'welfare' from the 'incompetent poor' to a much wider group of people in need of specialized help, and the current concern with supporting people in their own homes as an alternative to institutionalization.

The systems of income support and of employment help – both very comprehensive in principle, and potentially seeming to cater for almost every 'need' – represent intermediate stages in society's thinking about 'welfare' and about 'the disabled'. Both are being continually revised in detail (indeed, during the period of the survey the Department of Employment began an active consideration of its whole system of help for the physically impaired) but the basic principles on which both systems were erected fall somewhere between the 'charitable help for the needy' approach and current holistic thinking about the problems of disability. The system of social security in particular mirrors, in the details of its current structure, the history of the ebb and flow of changing, and sometimes opposing, concepts of welfare. Financial support for the sick and disabled was extended in 1948, as of right, only to those within the national insurance system, and basically the deep gulf between statutory benefits, linked to national insurance, and discretionary help for the needy still remains, symbolized by the separation of the offices administering them. Now, however, the insurance principle exists side by side with newer provisions based on quite different principles, and perhaps administered at different places, as well as with elements which are obvious descendants of the still older Poor Law.

It is obvious that health affects income, and adequacy of income affects other needs. It would seem logical, therefore, that agencies of financial help should be clearly linked to agencies of health and social welfare. Their separation is a clear reflection of the ambiguities of the social philosophy on which the system is based. Goods and services may be supplied to those who 'need' them, but the allocation is firmly in the hands of the expert agencies who 'give', and the recipient gets only what it is thought good for him to have. Money, to spend as one wishes, is a different matter. This, of course, is a principle enshrined in the history of welfare but now to some extent outmoded: instead of being 'prescribed' an invalid car, a disabled person may be given a 'mobility allowance' which he may spend in any way he chooses. Society now recognizes, in principle, that very legitimate money needs may arise from physical disability, and benefits have been instituted to fill a very small and selected proportion of them. Yet, as the discussion of money problems in Chapter 5 may show, these fit uneasily into the general pattern of welfare.

Similarly, there are few links between health and welfare on the one hand, and employment services on the other. For historical reasons, the only direct link is for the blind, who have special Resettlement Officers at the Department of Employment. For other disabled people, an elaborate structure of employment help does exist. The Department of Employment's ordinary placing services will, of course, be used by many people not defined as disabled, or who refuse so to define themselves, though their ill-health or disability may in fact be very relevant to their job problems. There is also a special service organized by Disablement Resettlement Officers for those whose physical impairment presents them with job problems. The client may be referred to the D.R.O. from the hospital, or he may be transferred from the 'able-bodied' section of the employment office, particularly after a long period on sickness or unemployment benefit and especially where he has been certified as fit only for light work.

The structure of employment or occupational services, again, symbolizes the divisions still existing in society between the 'economically valuable' and 'the rest'. It would be logical to provide for an easy progression, for those able to achieve it, from an occupational workshop where disabled people might do very light work, through sheltered workshops providing special conditions but requiring a full day's work, to rehabilitation and retraining centres and finally to normal, or only slightly adjusted, work in open industry. Administratively, however, this progression is interrupted by discontinuities. 'Occupation' is a welfare service provided by the local authority or a health service provided in industrial therapy units attached to hospitals. Sheltered employment is supplied by independent bodies (Remploy or the Blind Workshop), and it is not until competitive, truly 'gainful' employment is in question that rehabilitation or placing services are administered by the Department of Employment.

The structure in practice

It may be expected that the cross-cutting categories of agencies, of clients, and of criteria of eligibility for services will prove to be of more than academic interest, when the actual delivery of services is examined. The resources used for all the forms of support and rehabilitation of the sick and disabled come ultimately from the same source – the public purse – but different principles may well be applied to their expenditure by the taxpayer, the ratepayer, and the charitable man. The work of individuals in different helping occupations may ostensibly be directed to one end, and indeed may seem very similar (medical social workers, health visitors, local authority social workers, professionals employed by voluntary agencies, voluntary workers) but the organizational setting of that work will affect the selection of clients and the way in which the work is done. The extent to which the system is understood by the clients will affect their use of it.

The patients who were the subjects of the survey will become better known in the central chapters of the book. In order to provide a preliminary glimpse of the effect of this confused system upon people's lives, however, two of them will be briefly introduced:

> There was, for instance, Mrs Crombie, blind, diabetic, suffering from a heart condition, and living alone in a wholly unsuitable environment, who eventually had a procession of eleven people who were trying to solve her

problems. One was a medical social worker from the hospital, and another a professional social worker from the local association of voluntary social services: two people whose function might be expected to be the same but whose employing organizations were very different. She was also in contact with the Department of Health and Social Security, an agency of central government which might be expected to be bureaucratically organized, and with the housing department, an agency of local government subject to all the normal local pressures. She was being visited by a professional worker for the blind, representing a long-established charitable society now used by local government as their agent for the performance of duties for the welfare of blind people statutorily laid upon them by Acts of Parliament. She was also being visited by a voluntary worker from a newer society for the welfare of people with a particular disability, and by a young volunteer from a church group. She had, of course, a general medical practitioner responsible for her health, who might or might not consider that her environment and her social needs came within his sphere of interest, and she was attending regularly at the hospital where she was in the care of other doctors. Her daily care was in the hands of two people employed by different organizations: a home help responsible to the social work department of local government, and a district nurse whose administrative position, at that time, was in the process of being moved from the health department of local government to the National Health Service.

Other sorts of confusion could be illustrated by the example of Mr and Mrs Ritchie, she in a wheelchair following a stroke and he progressively disabled over many years by chronic illness. They too were involved with departments of central government (for money allowances) and local government (for housing and home help). They needed, and were entitled to, various aids in their home: the hospital, G.P., district nurse, health visitor, and local authority social worker had all been involved in these. They needed, and were entitled to, a telephone: the officials involved had great difficulty in deciding whether the rental should be paid for out of the taxpayer's pocket or the ratepayer's. While Mr Ritchie was defined as able to work, legitimation for his absences while sick and support while he was not earning were the business of his doctor and the Department of Health and Social Security. When he became defined as needing special employment help, he was the responsibility of a special office of the Department of Employment. If he were defined as capable only of work in a specially sheltered environment, that work would be provided by an independent (but central-government supported) organization acting as the agent of the local authority, and if he were defined as incapable of economically worth-while labour but in need of occupation, then this would be the responsibility of a department of local government. At one time it had been suggested that Mr Ritchie might usefully have a disabled person's vehicle: he was entitled to this only while he was working and in fact gave up his job – in part because he could not get to work – before the formalities were completed. In the provision of this particular welfare aid, consultants at the hospital and an office within the National Health Service were involved.

Referral pathways from 'health' to 'welfare'

For welfare needs arising because of illness or disability, the pathway of referral should begin, if the patient is in hospital, by doctors or nurses (or the patient himself or his family) bringing them to the attention of the medical social worker. In the community, welfare needs may be identified by the general practitioner, the district nurse who provides home nursing services, or the health visitor whose particular functions include advice and assistance for the old, children, and the handicapped. The channel of referral for most services then runs through the social work department.

In the sample of survey patients, however, there were examples of consultants, hospital doctors, and ward sisters directly contacting, by telephone or letter, the housing department, the home help service, and the Supplementary Benefits Commission, and of consultants and doctors personally contacting employers and the medical officers of large firms or industries. These services were very much appreciated by the patients and tended to be effective: it is, however, questionable whether writing letters about benefits, or trying to organize home helps, is the most efficient use of the time of these highly skilled people. The medical social worker is the only member of the hospital staff whose training includes a study of care and support systems in the community. The main reason why all the referrals for help for the people of this sample did not come through the M.S.W. is, however, simple: if they had, the number of hospital social workers would have had to be doubled or trebled. A secondary reason was an apparent lack of appreciation of the M.S.W.'s function on the part of some hospital doctors, and a lack of organized links in some wards.

The situation in the community was very similar. General practitioners sometimes concerned themselves with their patients' jobs, contacted the hospital about equipment, and in one case went in person to see the housing department. Again, these interventions were effective and the patients were grateful. However, it was found that a very great deal of need – in all areas of life, and in some cases amounting to acute and desperate hardship – remained, which general practitioners had not known about or had not defined as being within their sphere of competence. Again, organizational links – whether or not a practice had health visitor attachment – might be expected to form an important variable.

Some of the conflicts and ambiguities in the doctor's role, at a time of change, are exemplified by the range of attitudes and practices displayed in connection with those patients' social problems. At one extreme, doctors expressed pride at offering (though necessarily to only a minority) personal and comprehensive service to their patients; they saw themselves as counsellors, concerned with both psycho-social needs and the practical problems of daily life. This emphasis on personal service appeared in some cases to be based on a dislike, especially among older doctors, for 'bureaucratic red tape'; more than one practitioner expressed the opinion that 'the only way to get anything done is to do it yourself'. Other doctors, however, deliberately restricted themselves to service 'on demand' for strictly medical attention, and believed that it was not their function, nor within their competence, to assess mental, social or financial stresses within a family. The majority of doctors, however, appeared to occupy an uneasy middle position. On the one hand they recognized how often social problems lay behind the medical problems presented to them, and they were willing and anxious to offer personal support. On the other hand, they did not see themselves as part of a larger network of services.

Few general practitioners appeared to find the currently fashionable concept of themselves as 'the leader of a team' a practicable one, at least if the team were to extend beyond ancilliary health workers. The wish of the Standing Medical Advisory Committee[1] that the general practitioner should be the co-ordinator of 'the available resources for recovery or adjustment to handicap' was accepted in principle but found difficult in practice, largely because practitioners were so ill-informed about the resources that were available. In the whole sample, only two patients were referred to social workers by their general practitioner, and one by a health visitor. Little effective difference was found between types of practice: the large group practice might make more use of the health visitor when problems were perceived, but the single-handed practice or small partnership might be more likely to perceive the problems in the first place. If the area of concern is extended from practical welfare to the fields of money and employment, the complexity of the system which confronts the general practitioner is, of course, daunting: he cannot be expected to be an authority in these fields himself, and he has no easy links into the system.

This lack of easy contact between community doctors and agencies of welfare has, of course, been found in many other studies. In one study of 100 elderly patients,[2] 45 of them were receiving a statutory welfare service, but feed-back to the general practitioner was so poor that in 31 cases he was not aware of the fact. Jefferys' classic study of social welfare services in Buckinghamshire in the 1960s came to very similar conclusions about general practitioners:

> On the whole, doctors did not seek help from the domiciliary social welfare services in dealing with social difficulties, sometimes because they were aware of the shortage of facilities, sometimes because they were not fully aware of available services, and sometimes because they doubted the competence of the available staff . . . it appeared to be essential that new attitudes to other social welfare services should be acquired during medical training.[3]

'Wrong' pathways of referral were also commonly used by other health workers. There were few referrals from medical social workers to social workers in the community, and indeed the social work department tended to be bypassed by many other helping agencies whose personnel did not appear to understand the 'new' (since 1968) structure of responsibility. This was especially true of most voluntary organizations. Less understandably, the structure of community help was also misunderstood by a few health visitors and district nurses, who gave patients 'wrong' information about other agencies.

It may be asked – does this matter? If people find the services they require, then whether 'correct' or 'incorrect' pathways are used may have little practical relevance: indeed, informal pathways may be more efficient than formal ones.

In fact, however, the consequences can be important. Firstly, informal pathways may be difficult to find, so that people may never get the services they need. Formal pathways are likely to be more visible and easier to comprehend. Thus, where a formal pathway was well-established and simple, many people would be found to be using it – the direct approach to the housing department for rehousing on health grounds, with the passport of a general practitioner's certificate, for instance. Secondly, some of the irregular pathways observed were manifestly wasteful and inefficient:

> A consultant, making a domiciliary visit, advised bedboards. The patient telephoned his doctor, who sent a district nurse, who applied to the hospital stores. The hospital contacted a local authority social worker, who is reported to have said, several days later when she brought the boards, 'Didn't you know you should have got in touch with us in the first place?' Again, after a ward sister had promised a patient that she would 'see about' getting her a home help, the patient found it astonishing that, one after another, her general practitioner, a health visitor and the home help organizer from the local authority all came to visit her and discuss with her how much help she needed. A complicated communication and referral system was also illustrated by the young woman who said, 'The nurse [a health visitor attending because of young children] came to see my mother while I was in hospital, to tell her to tell me when she visited to tell the specialist when I saw him that he [the consultant] could put in his word to the housing, too, and maybe it would be quicker'.

Thirdly, informal referral systems breed jealousies and discontents. Occasionally, patients were found who *expected* their general practitioners to offer services far removed from a doctor's central concerns, because they had heard of other people who had received them.

Finally, the 'incorrect' pathways cannot bear the traffic of too many referrals. The hospital doctor certainly cannot spend his time personally negotiating with the D.H.S.S. on behalf of every patient in financial need. People have to be chosen for such special service, and the grounds of choice may be eccentric, related to the agent's own perceptions of the function of his organization, or his own concepts of what constitutes need. The social worker is especially likely to do all that he can, in the area of special referrals about money benefits, for families where children are at risk; hospital personnel are more likely to bring the patient to the attention of welfare agencies if he cannot be discharged from hospital until some arrangement is made for his after-care. The categorizations of formal defining systems are already confused, and to add the eccentricities of individual defining systems makes confusion worse.

The clients' views

It is not perhaps surprising that in fact the people in this survey were found, in very many instances, to be misunderstanding the system. Very few patients could distinguish between the 'social security', the social work department, and an amorphous body called 'the city', by which they usually meant the housing department. The differences between the various offices where one might apply for money – the Department of Employment, the Department of Health and Social Security, the Supplementary Benefits Commission and, exceptionally, the local authority social work department – were rarely appreciated. The local association of voluntary social services, with its staff of professional social workers, was invariably confused with the local authority social work department. The distinction between health visitors, community social workers, and hospital social workers was not usually understood. Addresses are important: in the City the common practice appeared to be to call agencies by the names of buildings or streets, without any clear knowledge of the identities of the agencies situated there or the connection between them.

Historical names tended to linger, and this caused some confusion where functions had in fact changed. The medical social worker was still, to most patients (and to a few doctors), the 'almoner'. The Supplementary Benefits Commission was still the 'assistance'. One elderly man spoke of the 'Guardians', forty-four years after their abolition.

Several services and benefits were frequently put into 'wrong' categories. Despite a vigorous governmental publicity campaign, for instance, rent rebates under the Housing Finance Act, 1972, were seen as a completely local matter, or even as a 'charity'. There was considerable confusion, not only among the clients but also among some doctors and other health and welfare workers, about responsibility for the supply of certain appliances – wheelchairs, home nursing aids, vehicles. These confusions might obviously affect the efficiency of service-provision, but perhaps more importantly they also influenced people's willingness even to ask for what they might need.

The great majority of people misunderstood the social work department's function. Whereas the social workers saw themselves as helping agents, the potential clients saw them as arbitrating and inspecting officials almost exclusively concerned with financial aid, decreeing whether this electricity bill might be dealt with, or allocating charges for this house adaptation. Where patients had been in previous contact with social workers, the problem had usually been connected with law-enforcement agencies (probation, child delinquency, non-payment of bills) and the negative associations lingered. As Freidson[4] has pointed out, 'new' occupations such as that of social workers originated in the perception of people in policy-making positions of 'the needs of the layman for whom they had obtained, or were trying to gain, responsibility'. The social worker began as an agent for other organizations, not for the client, and to rely upon others for a clientele necessarily means divided loyalties:

> The critical problem of the dependent profession occurs when it seeks to become independent – to attract its own clientele. Its problem is even more severe when it tries to attract clients in the early, everyday stage of seeking help, and when it tries to practise preventively.

This precisely describes the dilemma of social workers in relation to their relatively new duties towards the chronically sick and disabled. Even when, at all levels of their own and collaborating organizations, their functions become clear (which was found to be by no means the case as yet) it may be long before their services are neither seen as 'charity', nor confused with 'the security' by their clients.

The patients' attitudes to 'security' (by which they usually meant all benefits and services *not* directly associated with national insurance) were complex, and will be considered in detail in the context of money problems. At one extreme, some younger people adopted a militant attitude towards the Supplementary Benefits Commission, demanding benefits as of right; at the other, many older people appeared to have a resigned but comfortable relationship with discretionary benefits. For the most part, however, and particularly amongst those with no recent experience of needing help, to accept 'the security' was seen as passing a watershed.

Some of the administrators who were interviewed in connection with this study suggested that this sturdy pride was a local, or at least a particularly Scottish, characteristic: 'People round here won't accept a cup of tea if they think it's charity', 'Of course, traditionally, we're a proud lot, and independent with it'. It may, however, be pointed out that the comments of City people about 'welfare' and 'charity' can be paralleled from many other studies in other places.[5] 'People are too proud to accept help, and proper pride must be respected' may be a seductively dangerous excuse for failures in service-provision, whether at governmental or local level.

Benefits which were 'rights' appeared to come into quite a different category in the minds of the City's people, though what were or were not seen as 'rights' might vary between groups, change with changing circumstances, and bear little relationship to administrative fact. All money benefits perceived as having a national insurance basis were 'rights' which people were fierce in defending. Housing and home helps also came into this category, as 'rights' of citizens and ratepayers, and the process of obtaining them was seen as a negotiation between the individual and the City. The connection between 'our money' and the services provided was felt to be close.

Medical services were also very definitely seen as a 'right', though of a different sort. The people of the survey gave the impression very strongly that the right of all to medical attention, based solely on need – a right as fundamental as that to education, or to protection by the rule of law, or to a supply of wholesome water, or any other basic 'necessity' of modern organized society – had become taken for granted in the years since the setting up of the National Health Service in 1948. Gratitude was in order to the individuals involved, and for the most part patients were very loud in their praise of doctors, hospital nurses, community nurses, and consultants for what they saw as personal kindnesses. (It must be added that the City is one where the general reputation of the medical services is high.) Aspects of health administration not so directly seen as a personal service were more likely to be criticized (for instance, the organization of the ambulance service to clinics) and since expectations were high, any perceived failure in service was a matter for great indignation.

One effect of this attitude towards health services was that willingness to apply for any specific requirement depended very much upon whether it was seen as coming within the category of 'health' or of 'welfare'. There was no hesitation in demanding those things thought to be clearly supplied by the N.H.S., such as nursing aids (in fact provided through the local authority), just as there was no hesitation in demanding a prescription for drugs, or a consultation with their doctor. Attitudes were ambivalent to services seen as coming into intermediate categories; people might happily accept wheelchairs, if they appeared to come from the hospital, or incontinence aids, if they were brought by the district nurse, but were reluctant to apply themselves for these things to any agency seen as 'welfare'.

Attitudes to expense – on the part of both the providers and receivers – reinforced the deep split which appeared still to lie between 'health' and 'welfare'. While the N.H.S. must order its own priorities, nevertheless it is part of the medical model that cost ought not to stand in the way if 'need' is established. Problems of the distribution of resources are separated from the individual case (and the load of heavy decision-making taken off the doctor's shoulders) by policy decisions made at a higher level: home dialysis machines, or intensive care units, will be supplied at a previously determined level, and the citeria of need then drawn up to use the resources supplied. The amount of money involved is not at the forefront of the individual consultant's mind when he prescribes a certain treatment, and in any case the ultimate source of the money is far removed from the local situation.

Though the survey patients were grateful for the health services they received, they never mentioned the cost. They might have opinions about health service priorities (which suggests that they did acknowledge that resources were not unlimited) but for the most part health services were a 'right' and cost was immaterial. Services supplied by 'welfare' were, however, quite different. Here the money did not come out of government's bottomless pocket, but out of local funds from local ratepayers. The cost became relevant.

A family who were equipped with a home dialysis unit provided a clear example of these attitudes. They accepted the unit as they would any other medical appliance and never mentioned its cost: they knew to the last penny, however, how much the necessary house alterations had cost. In other cases, it was reported that social workers had in fact often stressed the cost of some adaptation or piece of equipment to the client: a practice it would be difficult to imagine as being common among doctors.

Social workers are, of course, forced to be conscious of cost. The sources of money they use are much closer to them, and the responsibilities are less likely to be lifted from their shoulders by the existence of ostensibly clear-cut clinical criteria. And they have been used, in the past, to disbursing relatively small sums of money. An additional complication is that many of these local authority services are means-tested, with the client expected to pay at least a share if he can. This, again, makes people cost-conscious where local authority services are concerned, as they are not where health services are concerned. Several people in the survey, for instance, received free wheelchairs from the hospital, but were charged by the local authority for the ramp to their door which made the use of wheelchairs possible. The justification for these charges may rest on a moral feeling: politicians and (to a lesser extent) administrators may suggest that 'people only appreciate what they have to pay for', 'only the *really* poor should get things free'. Thus, many authorities (including the City authority at the time of this survey, though procedures were subsequently changed) justify having a minimum charge for, for instance, home helps which could not be disallowed under any circumstances: the position arose in many cases that people were paying pennies for their home helps, which were then reimbursed by the Supplementary Benefits Commission, often with delay and difficulty. Because of this, although the sums involved were often tiny, the procedure gave rise to quite disproportionate resentments and hostilities.

Within the system of welfare the problem of defining 'need' is most acute for those services now centred around the local authority social work department. These practical services will be discussed in more detail in Chapter 4. Many of them are new, and potential demand has barely been estimated. Since legislators, social work administrators, social workers themselves, referring agents, and the clients, may all see eligibility differently, it is not surprising that these services were found by tortuous ways if found at all.

SUMMARY

The complex system of agencies – some interlocking, some isolated – found in this City echoes the history of attitudes to, and provision for, disabled people. The overall picture of the system seemed to match well the description by Scott:[6]

> Social welfare problems are, therefore, set within and responsive to, a variety of organisational and community pressures which are highly determinative of programme policy and implementation . . . The causes of the specific problems, and therefore the needs of a handicapped person, are not the same factors which determine what kinds of welfare services are offered to them. Clients' needs and the kinds of available welfare services run in two separate orbits, which may coincide only at certain points.

Referral networks were found to be influenced not only by ignorance, but also by some confusion about the 'proper' functions of various groups of professionals. The patients' own perceptions of the system were an important factor: in general, people were eager to accept those goods and services they could see as coming into the category of 'health' but were uneasy about those coming into the category of 'welfare'.

REFERENCES

1. Ministry of Health Circular, 1963.
2. Gilholme, K. R. and Newell, D. J., 'Community Services for the Elderly', *Problems and Progress in Medical Care, 7th Series*, London, Oxford U.P. for the Nuffield Provincial Hospitals Trust, 1972.
3. Jefferys, Margot, *An Anatomy of Social Welfare Services*, London, Michael Joseph, 1965, p. 130.

4. Freidson, E., *Patients' Views of Medical Practice*, New York, Russell Sage Foundation, 1961, p. 221.
5. See, e.g. Outram, Jane, 'The Right to Help?' *Case Conference*, 16.3, 1969; Gould, T. and Kenyon, J., *Stories from the Dole Queue*, London, Temple Smith, 1972.
6. Scott, R. A., 'The Selection of Clients by Social Welfare Agencies: the Case of the Blind', *Social Problems*, 14, 1965.

3
THE SAMPLE

Within this framework of services, the lives of the 194 physically impaired people of the sample were structured.

Two complex variables were used to explore the central hypothesis of the study: *careers* (what happens to people who become physically impaired? who needs help in what area of life? who gets it, from whom?) and *definitions* (what labels are applied to people who become physically impaired? what categories are available for them in the welfare and employment systems? how do these fit with the categories employed in medicine? who becomes defined as disabled, by whom, and what does 'disabled' mean to the patient himself?).

The analysis of careers in this chapter surveys the sample as a whole. The complexity of the data, in a relatively small sample of people, makes questionable any reliance upon quantitative analysis. It is certainly not suggested that counting the proportions of different groups of people – who felt themselves to be disabled, and who did not? who became unemployed? who was in financial need? – has any explanatory power. Explanations of events and demonstrations of patterns in the lives of these people must rely much more upon the detailed (though of course disguised) case-histories of succeeding chapters. Thus, the general analysis is offered merely as a starting point, as a way of demonstrating some facts which require explanation. Noting the relative proportions of people whose careers followed this or that pattern will often produce obvious commonsense facts – that people living alone are likely to have practical problems of daily living, for instance, or that men who have hard manual jobs are likely to find it more difficult than sedentary workers to earn a living if they become physically impaired. On the other hand, less obvious and more interesting facts do emerge.

The pathways open to these people can be crudely summarized in the flow diagram opposite.

All the 194 people come by definition into the category of 'some permanent impairment', no matter how slight. They

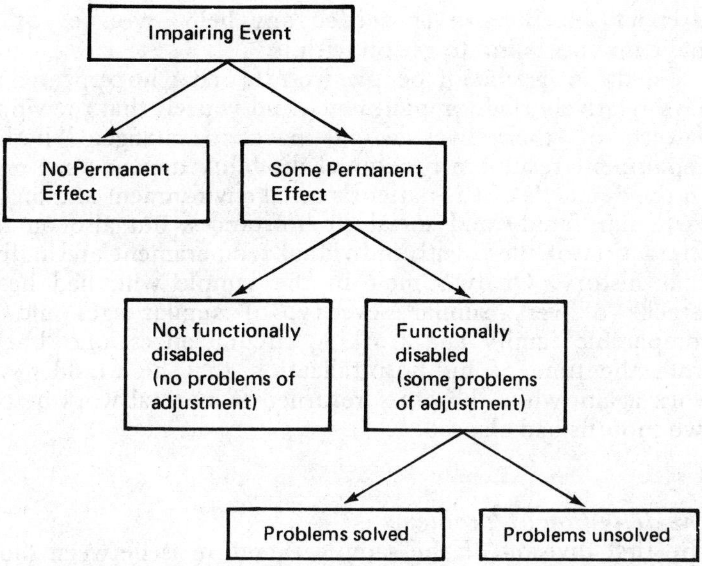

are not necessarily 'disabled', however. Functional disablement is defined by the necessity to make some adjustments in any aspect of daily life – adjustments to the household activities, the social life, the ways of getting about, the occupation, the family relationships, previously considered normal for the individual involved. The shorthand term used in this study for such adjustments is 'problems', and throughout it is the patient's own perception of his problems that is used.

A simple preliminary point which can be made is that the sample demonstrated very clearly that (keeping degree of impairment constant) disability is a social rather than a clinical fact. How disabling any given impairment may be depends on the individual's normal circumstances: a laboratory technician found a relatively slight loss of co-ordination extremely disabling, while a council labourer hardly thought the loss of sight in one eye worthy of mention. Several people in the sample appeared to an observer to be distressingly disabled, but refused adamantly to admit that the label applied to them in any way or that they might come into any category eligible for help. Typically, a woman severly crippled with arthritis denied vehemently that she was disabled, saying: 'I find different ways of doing things, I've been widowed for a long time now so I've *had* to look after myself. I've never needed any help – you've got to make up your mind to get on with it.'

On the other hand, people were found who appeared to have relatively slight impairments, and yet felt that the whole pattern of their lives would have to change. Whether impairment results in functional disability depends not only on the demands of the patient's usual environment and on his particular family and social circumstances, but also on the interaction of these with individual temperament and individual history. Of two men in the sample who had heart attacks of very similar severity, of similar ages and in comparable family and working circumstances, one 'knew' from the time of his hospitalization that he would never work again, while the other returned to normal work before two months had elapsed.

The definition of 'problems'

The first division of the sample therefore is between those who are impaired but not disabled, and those who are impaired *and* disabled, to whatever extent, and however temporarily.

To be dis-'abled' in any area of life is to be presented with problems. A pilot study for this survey, in which 47 people were interviewed two or three times during the 6 months following a hospitalization, was used to investigate the broad categories of problem which the subjects perceived themselves as having. These were found to fall into four groups: *practical problems*, including difficulties of personal care, activities of daily living, housing, getting about; *job problems*, associated with getting or keeping suitable work, or adapting a job to impaired capacities; *money problems*; and *social problems* of family relationships, occupation and recreation.

All these are obviously interrelated; job problems may well lead to financial difficulties, and social problems might be caused by practical considerations. Given unlimited money, many problems may not arise, or at least may be more easily solved. Given a close and supportive social network, practical difficulties are less likely. The different sorts of problem do not *necessarily* arise together, however, and analytical separation seems useful because it may appear that the areas of life in which problems are experienced both affect and are in turn affected by the way in which an individual defines himself and his condition.

In deciding whether or not an individual had any specific problem, the question of the definition of 'need' was obviously raised. These were the needs which the patients themselves perceived, not those defined by agencies, or by standards set by society at large. An attempt was made to include only those needs associated with the physical impairment, but in practice the distinction seemed hardly necessary; if not directly caused by, then any problem is certainly exacerbated by, physical impairment, and it was rarely possible to discern any problem to which the disablement was completely irrelevant.

A deliberate distinction was, however, made between needs which a man perceives himself to have, and needs which society presumes he ought to have. The historical aim of formal rehabilitation systems was shown in Chapter 1 to be the return of as many disabled people as possible to gainful employment. Yet not all the unemployed who are disabled or chronically ill feel themselves to be in need of a job. The pressures of an upbringing in the shade of the Protestant ethic might incline some towards the conventional view (as well as the more direct pressures applied to them by agencies) but many – especially older men – were perfectly content to retire, and such men could not be defined as having job problems. A corollary might well be, however, that they did have money problems. Again, other things might be more important to them than their working lives. Where both of a couple were in poor health, the precarious balance of their domestic arrangements possibly depended upon both devoting themselves full-time to the household and to each other. Another practical example might be the case of a man who, with a complicated list of symptoms, but no firm diagnosis, was discovered leading a semi-invalid life, waited on by a kindly home help, and devoting to five motherless children all the energy left over from cherishing his symptoms and dreaming of the lucrative business he might set himself up in, had he any money. His life was very full, and he certainly did not define himself as in need of a job.

Similarly, the two interviewers involved, whose standards might be different from those of their respondents, made particular efforts not to define as in need of practical help those men – there were several of them – found living alone, recovering from broken limbs or coronary thromboses, surrounded by the utmost domestic squalor and discomfort, but clinging militantly to their independence and viewing with genuine horror any suggestion that a home help might tidy them up.

The form in which needs were expressed depended, of course, on knowledge of what might be available. A crippled woman might say, for instance, not 'I need a stocking-puller-upper', but 'I get along fine at dressing myself, only I have to get my girl to put my stockings on.' Men might not specifically define themselves as being in need of formal advice and assistance over their jobs, but they would very readily express their anxieties, rehearse what they were going to say to the foreman, and speculate on the adaptations they were going to have to make. Thus, it seemed possible to attempt to describe 'problems' as seen by the patients. (A more detailed discussion of the information-gathering and data-analysing procedure employed will be found in the Appendix.)

Problems solved and unsolved

The problems thus defined might, of course, be trivial or temporary, and easily solved, or they might be intractable, seeming to present permanent difficulties. Thus, the next division is between those whose problems remain, and those who have solved them – by whatever means, whether it be the formal help of agencies, the informal help of family and friends, or even simply by the passage of time. Of those whose problems are solved, one may ask 'by what means?', and of those whose problems remain, 'why are the problems intractable? did agencies try to help, and if so why did they not succeed? An attempt is made to answer these questions in the detailed chapters which follow. First, however, a very general analysis is offered.

The proportions of the sample who perceived themselves as having problems in the different areas of life, and the proportions of those whose problems were solved, at *any* time during the year after they had left hospital, are shown in Table 3:1.*

*Throughout this study, the sample, for quantitative purposes, is defined as the main sample of 194 people. Wherever proportions of people are being counted, the pilot sample of 47 people, since they were studied for only six months, are not included. Case-history material used in illustration may occasionally, however, refer to patients in the pilot sample.

Table 3:1 People who perceived problems of adjustment (any time during the survey year)

Nature of problem	% of the whole sample (194 people) who had: No problems	Problems which were: solved	unsolved
Any	26	34	40
Personal care	70	26	4
Daily living	86	6	8
Housing	86	4	10
Jobs	52	30	18
Money	80	8	12
Social	68	13	19

The simple fact emerges that only about a quarter of the sample never at any time during that year perceived any problems. Despite the elaborate structure of services described in Chapter 2, over half of those who had problems found them unsolved a whole year afterwards. Jobs emerged as the area most likely to present difficulties, though quite a high proportion of these were eventually solved. The problem most likely to be solved was that of personal care: this is, of course, the most likely to be a temporary problem, since many people might require care for a convalescent period but not permanently. It also represents the fact that this problem could hardly be left unsolved – it might well be that someone *had* to care for the patient – and does not mean that considerable hardship was not endured meanwhile either by the patient or by the person caring for him.

Who were the people who had problems? Table 3:2 shows the result of analysing by age, sex, marital status, household and socio-economic class based on occupation. It might be expected that, since youth is obviously favourable to *recovery*, advancing age would be strongly associated with unfavourable careers. It has often been suggested that rehabilitation services focus disproportionately upon the relatively young, and that vocational help and physical rehabilitative help, in particular, may be denied to the middle-aged. In fact, the difference between age-groups in this sample was found to be small. It was true that a greater proportion of people below the age of 30 found solutions for their problems, although this may reflect no more than the 'recovery' component. Certainly, young people were found for whom it appeared that every possible service was swinging efficiently into operation – for instance, a young paraplegic, or a man in his twenties who required renal dialysis. On the other hand, there were young people who seemed to have been neglected from childhood onwards, with no attempts to help them create a reasonably satisfactory way of life. It was also true that the occurrence of problems was high for the over-sixties, but – in part, of course, because their expectations were lower – a relatively high proportion felt that satisfactory solutions were eventually found. It is evident that the relationship between age and different sorts of problems of adjustment cannot be a simple one.

It was only to be expected that people living with their spouses should have the fewest problems, and those living alone the most. There is some likelihood of a couple being able to offer each other practical help and social support, and people living alone are particularly likely to be in financial need. The difference between married and single people, and 'others' (widowed, separated, divorced) was striking.

It is not suggested that the crude division of the sample into four socio-economic classes, based on occupations (or occupations of husbands, in the case of housewives, or late husbands, in the case of widows) is a very meaningful categorization of the relationship of the individual to the economic structure of society. However, this classification does show clearly the obvious relationship: intractable problems are much less likely if the patient has a professional or managerial job, than if he has a semi- or unskilled manual job. However, the material resources and greater power to control events which can be expected to be associated with a professional or managerial job do not protect altogether from the problems of disability: over one-eighth of the people in social classes I and II were unable to find solutions for their problems. The difference between the professional and the other non-manual classes was not in the *occurrence* of problems, but in the ability to solve them: the same proportion of problems arose, but fewer were solved. The main difference between non-manual and skilled manual classes, however, was in the occurrence of problems in the first place: many more skilled manual workers did perceive difficulties (especially in the area of work) but a slightly higher proportion of those with problems managed to solve

Table 3:2 Characteristics of those people with and without problems (at any time during the survey year)

	% of people who had			
		Problems which were		
	No problems	solved	unsolved	(number)
Sex				
Male	26	31	43	(116)
Female	27	37	36	(78)
Age				
<30	29	52	19	(21)
30–39	32	18	50	(28)
40–49	31	36	33	(45)
50–59	27	30	43	(63)
60–64	13	38	49	(37)
Marital Status				
Married	30	36	34	(135)
Single	27	35	38	(26)
Other	12	21	67	(33)
Household				
With spouse or cohabitee	30	36	34	(135)
With kin	20	36	44	(25)
Other	17	21	62	(34)
Social Class				
Prof. and managerial	49	35	16	(37)
Other non-manual	48	21	31	(29)
Skilled manual	13	48	39	(62)
Semi- and unskilled manual	17	24	59	(66)

them. The difference between the skilled and the semi- and unskilled manual worker lay in the ability to find solutions: in the lowest class, nearly 60 per cent of the patients had problems which were unsolved at the end of the year. Thus, four patterns arose:

	Lower likelihood	*Higher likelihood*
of problems	Professional & managerial Other non-manual	Skilled manual Semi- & unskilled manual
of solutions	Other non-manual Semi- & unskilled manual	Professional & managerial Skilled manual

These broad descriptions, like the analyses in terms of age, sex and household, are simply starting-points. Explanations will be sought in subsequent chapters.

Clinical conditions and disability

So far only the personal characteristics of the patients have been considered as variables. The type and severity of their clinical condition is obviously another important way in which people may differ. The sample included many different sorts of disease, resulting in different degrees and types of impairment. Which of them proved to be most likely to result in problems of rehabilitation?

In some ways this is a particularly useful sample of people to ask such a question about, for it includes – as samples of people chosen from diagnostic categories, or already labelled 'disabled', may not – all the difficult-to-diagnose conditions, or diseases not usually thought of as disabling, which may be important. Yet it is not a question which is entirely easy to answer, since considering the different effects of different types of impairment necessarily involves attaching a diagnostic label to the patient. A broken bone or a heart attack, in a previously healthy man, may be easy to categorize, but few of the sample proved to have such clear-cut conditions.

Even if – for the moment – the patient's own perceptions are ignored, and conditions as medically diagnosed are considered, and even if the categories are simplified into major systems (disease of the cardiovascular system, diseases and injuries of the bones, joints and muscles, diseases of the digestive system, etc.) many of the sample had diagnosed conditions of more than one system. If a blind diabetic has a heart disease, to what extent is she disabled by each of the conditions? An epileptic falls: is he to be categorized by his disease or his broken bones? Will any disease not have an entirely different meaning if it is complicated by other pre-existing conditions? These are questions that must be asked of any study that uses disease categories to describe people, remembering that a *majority* of people, it appears, have multiple rather than simple conditions.

Nevertheless, the sample as a whole gave a strong impression that there *were* certain conditions which were more likely to lead to problems. An analysis will first be made to see whether this was in fact so.

The six major categories found in the sample at the beginning of the survey year, each with at least twenty (and up to 68) people having a diagnosed disease of that system (alone or in combination with other diseases) were diseases of the cardiovascular system, the digestive system, the nervous system and sense organs, the respiratory system, diseases and malfunctionings of the endocrine system, and diseases or injuries of bones, joints and muscles. There were, of course, other conditions applying to smaller numbers of people. A seventh category is that which has been called 'no diagnosis'. This may to some extent overlap with the others: it may be obvious that a patient's symptoms lie, for instance, in the digestive system, but it may not have been possible to diagnose more precisely. Into this category come not only those people whose conditions are obscure and difficult, but also those whose symptoms may be suspected of being psychosomatic, and those where doctors 'wait and see' before making a definite diagnosis. Also, the few cases where a diagnosis was made but none was, for whatever reason, conveyed to the patient are included: as far as he is concerned, he has no diagnosis. This is, therefore, not as clear-cut a category as the other six, but it nevertheless represents a group of people who, in simple terms, did not know what was wrong with them, and whose careers might present special features.

There was indeed a considerable difference between the careers observed in these seven broad categories. Table 3:3

Table 3:3 Disease categories and problems (at any time during the survey year)

	% of people with disease in this category who had			
		Problems which were		
Diseases of:	No problems	solved	unsolved	(number)*
Digestive system	40	28	32	(47)
Bones, joints, etc.	23	32	45	(64)
Respiratory system	21	25	54	(28)
Cardiovascular system	18	39	43	(68)
Endocrine system	16	21	63	(20)
Nervous system	12	26	62	(43)
'No diagnosis'	0	26	74	(22)

*Total more than 194 because a patient may have a disease of more than one system.

shows that nearly 90 per cent of those whose diagnosis included disease of the nervous system, and over 80 per cent of those whose diagnosis included endocrine or cardiovascular diseases, had problems of adjustment or rehabilitation during the year. The least disabling major group was diseases of the digestive system. Not one of the people in the category of 'no diagnosis' was without problems.

Which of these were temporary problems, solved during the year? The proportion of 'solved' to 'unsolved' problems was small for those with 'no diagnosis' or with endocrine or nervous system disorders, and diseases of the respiratory system were also likely to lead to long-lasting problems. This could, of course, be simply a function of the seriousness of the condition. If all those people with diseases of the nervous system were more seriously impaired than those whose diagnosis included cardiovascular or digestive conditions, then it would not be surprising if their problems were greater. (It would not seem likely, however, that undiagnosed conditions could be expected to be exceptionally serious ones.)

In order to test this, the various disease groups have been analysed according to the degree of physical handicap remaining at the end of the year. The rather broad categories used are those of the National Survey,[1] which are based on the practical difference which the impairment makes to the everyday life of the sufferer. Those who had returned to their previous working and family roles are categorized as 'not handicapped'. Those who had to make some adjustment in their lives, but had no difficulty in performing ordinary everyday tasks for themselves and did not require any personal care from other people, are categorized as 'impaired' in the National Survey. The next category of seriousness, including those people who had some difficulty in getting about or in the activities of daily living, is 'appreciably handicapped'. Finally, the 'severely' and 'very severely' handicapped are those who require personal assistance with everyday activities, the chairfast and bedfast.

The proportions of people in each of the major disease categories who had each of these four degrees of impairment are shown in Table 3:4. It can be seen that *in this sample*, diseases of the nervous system were found to be the most likely to be seriously disabling. Because of the way in which the sample was selected (from a restricted number of wards in one hospital) no general conclusions can necessarily be drawn, though it has been found before that the most

Table 3:4 Disease category and degree of handicap*

Diseases of:	% of people with this disease who were 'Not handicapped'	'Impaired'	'Appreciably handicapped'	'Severely handicapped'
Digestive system	53	32	5	10
Bones, joints, etc.	25	39	23	13
Respiratory system	11	57	21	11
Cardiovascular system	22	45	21	12
Endocrine system	26	37	21	16
Nervous system	19	32	23	26
'No diagnosis'	21	42	37	0

*The categories used are those of Harris (1971), described in the text, page 48.

seriously disabled are those with diseases of the nervous system. The table shows, however, that other groups of diseases including those of the cardiovascular and respiratory systems were as likely to result in *some* degree of handicap.

In order to test whether these different patterns of severity were an important part of the relationship between disease groups and likelihood of problems, each of the categories of severity was analysed separately. Of course, for all diseases, the least severely handicapped were less likely to have problems of adjustment, and the severely handicapped were unlikely to be without problems. If those in the middle categories of severity are compared, however, excluding the extremes, considerable variation between diseases still appears.

Table 3:5 shows that, even in the middle degrees of severity, diseases of the nervous system and the 'no definite diagnosis' group were the most disadvantageous.

The careers of the sample were also examined to see whether the categories of 'chronic' or 'acute', or 'medical' or 'surgical', seemed to define different groups. In fact, these

Table 3:5 Disease categories and problems (with the 'not handicapped' and the 'severely handicapped' excluded)

	% of people with this disease who had		
		Problems which were	
Diseases of:	No problems	**solved**	**unsolved**
Digestive system	24	24	52
Bones, joints, etc.	10	35	55
Respiratory system	18	27	55
Cardiovascular system	8	42	50
Endocrine system	9	27	64
Nervous system	4	17	79
'No diagnosis'	0	18	82

divisions were found to have little meaning. Some conditions could be clearly labelled in these ways, but for the most part these are but temporary labels applied at a given moment for a given purpose. The acute episode from which the patient is suffering may well arise from a chronic illness; much surgery is for the alleviation of long-term conditions. Thus, in this sample (who, it must be remembered, had all been hospitalized) most people came into both 'chronic' and 'acute' categories.

The number of diagnoses given to the patient did, however, prove to be an important indicator of problems of adjustment. Only the diagnoses formally entered on the patient's hospital record are being considered here, and the

Table 3:6 Number of diagnoses and problems

	% of people with this number of diagnoses who had			
		Problems which were		
No. of diagnoses	No problems	**solved**	**unsolved**	(number)
1	33	35	32	(90)
2	19	31	50	(68)
3+	7	31	62	(36)

number could be enlarged by adding other conditions – whether medically diagnosed or self-diagnosed – which had not been noted down at this point. Even so, Table 3:6 shows that the greater the number of formal diagnoses the more likely the patient was to experience difficulties. This was not solely due to the fact that those with several distinct diseases were likely to be more seriously handicapped, for again, if degree of impairment is kept constant, exactly the same pattern appears.

Time patterns

So far, the patients' careers have been considered in rather static, and so unreal, terms. One conspicuous result of the method employed, frequent interviews over the year, was to show that an immense complexity of patterns can be hidden in 'before and after' analyses. If the intention is to try to explain why things happened as they did, these patterns must be explored, for two people may reach the same place by very different routes. Consideration of careers over time may help to show where the important turning-points in these routes may be.

Time is, of course, continuous, and to choose any single point is to falsify to some extent. As a starting-point, however, the careers of the patients at arbitrary points after hospitalization – at one month, and at three, six, nine and twelve months – may be considered. Simple counting of the numbers of people who had unsolved problems at the different stages indicates that many problems are solved between one and three months, but subsequently the proportion of people with problems *rises* in every area of life, though some of these new problems are likely to be solved again by the end of the year. This very noticeable trend obviously points to periods of time which require examination: it may, however, conceal differences between typical careers in the areas of working life and of social life, or problems of personal care and problems of money, and so each type of problem should be examined separately.

The patterns which emerge are shown in Figure 3:1. Obviously, problems of personal care loom very large in the early months after an illness episode. A high proportion of these disappear, as the patient improves or, in cases where permanent care is necessary, as arrangements are made. It is, however, remarkable to note that so high a proportion of

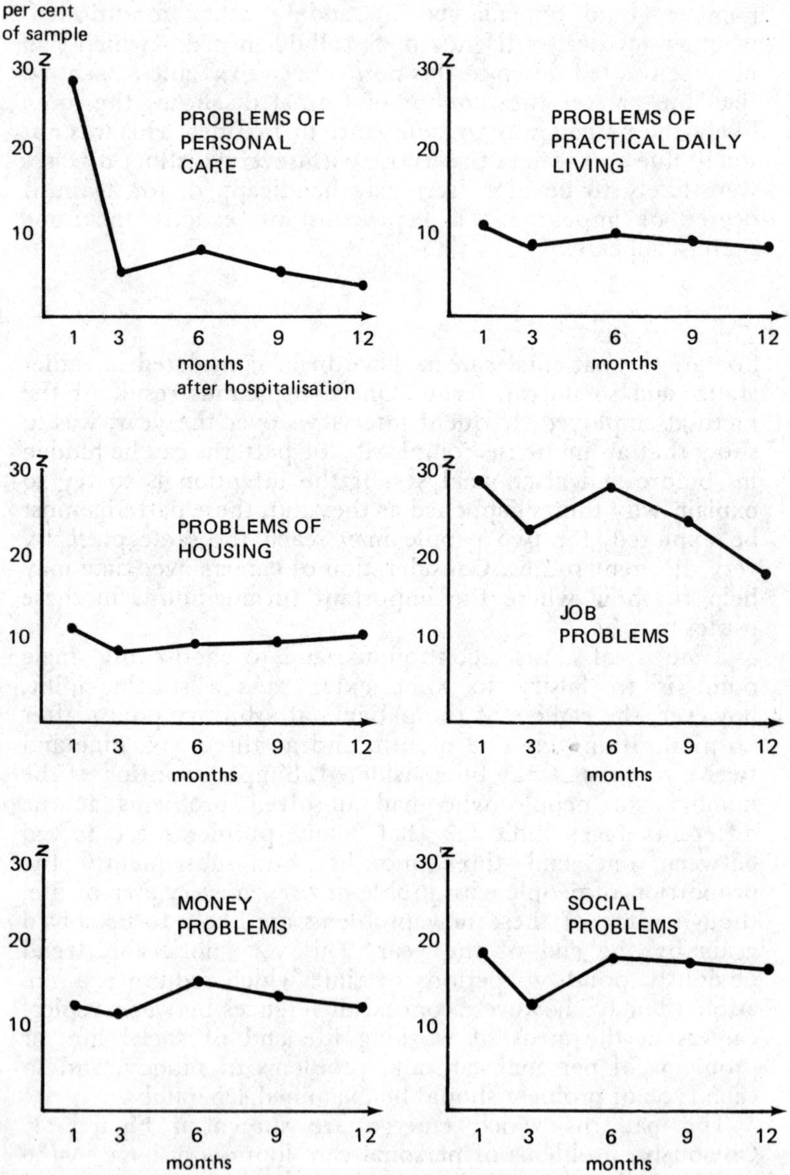

Figure 3.1 Time patterns of the existence of unsolved problems.

these patients – 27 per cent – were presented with problems after their discharge from hospital; 'problem' in this context is defined as needing more care than the normal arrangements of that family could provide, and thus in over a quarter of the families this situation meant either that the patient was inadequately cared for or that someone (usually, of course, a family member) had to disrupt his own life in order to act as nurse or housekeeper. The *rise* in the number of people with problems of care after three months might be expected to represent the failure of temporary arrangements. Few people still had problems a year later, but it must be noted that these are patients who, for a whole year, had had difficulty in looking after themselves, or whose care represented considerable hardship to someone else.

About one-tenth of the sample expressed a need for help in the areas of housing and daily living, needing for instance practical aids, adaptation to their house, the assistance of home helps, aids to mobility, or ground-floor housing. Some received these things, but as time went on others developed new needs, so that in fact the total extent of 'need' was hardly reduced over the year.

'Jobs' emerge as the area of life in which most problems were perceived. Almost 30 per cent of the sample felt, after their discharge from hospital, that they had some difficulties. Some of these were soon solved, especially for the less severely impaired, as their health improved or they managed to make satisfactory adjustments. The rise in the number of people with problems at six months after their illness episode was particularly marked, however. Though unemployment is not the only possible job problem, the highest proportion of unemployed (over 20 per cent of those previously in the labour market) occurred at the nine-months stage. Obviously there are important questions to be asked about the causes of these findings.

The proportion of people with money problems might have been expected to drop steadily as the less severely impaired went back to work and recovered their earning capacity. In fact, however, the number who did so were cancelled out by the number who newly acquired problems, so that the proportion of people in financial need barely changed over the whole year. Again, causes must be sought (perhaps within the system of national insurance) for the apparent intractability of money problems. In part, of course, they must echo the pattern of job problems.

The category of 'social' problems included those which, although they may have been caused by or connected with practical problems, were not themselves of a practical nature. It is possible to have an adequate income, and not define oneself as having a job problem (perhaps because any work is impossible) and yet to be desperately lonely and isolated. Family difficulties, amounting in some cases to the break-up of marriages, are not only experienced by those in financial need. Disabled men or women may be unable to provide themselves with occupation, or unable to get out because they have no transport, even though supplied with the basic necessities which would be adequate for a non-disabled person. It was perhaps most disturbing of all to note that, in this sample, these social problems were the ones still applying to the greatest proportion of people – nearly 20 per cent – a year after their illness or accident. An initial drop (associated with recovery) was followed by a rise between three and six months after hospitalization, as the acute stage of many illnesses passed and a significant proportion of people, trying to come to terms with a permanent impairment, became depressed and isolated.

SUMMARY

The person most likely to be functionally disabled by his impairment was one who was widowed, divorced or separated, living alone or with kinsfolk, with a manual job, with a disease of the nervous or endocrine system or with no firm diagnosis. Age was not very important. Considering only those who *were* disabled, problems were most likely to be solved if the individual was young, single, and in a professional or a skilled manual job. Even if degree of impairment is kept constant, those with multiple diagnoses, or with ill-defined conditions, were conspicuously likely to have unfavourable careers. In every area of life, but particularly where job, money, and social problems were concerned, the proportion of people with difficulties *rose* between three and six months after they had been discharged from hospital.

These are some of the facts which require examination and, if possible, explanation.

REFERENCE

1. Harris, Amelia I. *Handicapped and Impaired in Great Britain (Part 1)*, H.M.S.O., 1971, p. 17.

4
PROBLEMS OF PERSONAL CARE AND PRACTICAL DAILY LIVING

The first problem that is likely to arise for the patient who has a serious or potentially disabling accident or illness is that of personal care after he has left the hospital. Depending on the degree and nature of his impairment, he may need care permanently, or only for a convalescent period. No problems will arise if the patient's normal family structure can accommodate the situation without strain – if, for instance, there is a wife, or mother, or retired husband at home, or there is a close family group nearby who see it as part of their normal function to share the care of anyone who is ill. If, however, there is no such normal 'carer', or the situation disrupts the ordinary family organization, or the patient is so severely handicapped that his care is beyond the capacity of his family, then a problem exists within the definition used throughout the study: some adjustment is required and some form of help may be appropriate. Thirty per cent of the whole sample believed that they had problems of care within this definition at some time during the year following their discharge from hospital.

Personal care might be expected to present problems for the widowed, the elderly, and those living alone. But within the working-age population to which this sample is restricted, the most remarkable impression is of the great variety of problems of immediate care which arise, and the wide spectrum of sorts of people involved. Problems were found to arise for the young as well as the old: for the young mother unable to look after her children as well as for the widow in her sixties living alone. They were as likely to be found among professional people – among the young wives of mobile professional men, with no supportive family nearby, for instance – as amongst those whose economic resources were small, though the ease with which solutions were found might obviously vary between groups.

In the sample as a whole, the only personal characteristics that distinguished those whose care presented problems (besides, of course, the severity and nature of their illness or disability) were sex and household composition. Conspicuously, there were more problems amongst women (51 per cent of all women) than among men (16 per cent of all men). Men would, of course, be more likely to have a non-working spouse at home. Oddly, the definitions of 'need' in this respect as used by ward sisters and others in the hospital appeared to assume that women were *less* likely than men to have problems about their after-care: according to the patients' accounts, men were more frequently asked about their arrangements than were women. There was, however, evidence that ward sisters were conscientiously considering the after-care problems of those who lived alone, as a matter of routine. Sixty-eight per cent of people living alone perceived themselves as having a problem of personal care, compared with 24 per cent of those living with a spouse and 36 per cent of those living with kin.

Families and neighbours

By their nature, most of these problems of care were in fact 'solved'. How were they solved: who provided this care? Overwhelmingly, in this city, it proved to be daughters, or to a lesser extent sisters, mothers, other kinsfolk and neighbours. There were nine patients who could not have been at home if neighbours had not cared for them; most of these were people living alone, though some were married women.

> Mrs Macandrew explained the reciprocal nature of this neighbourly system: 'Last year I looked after [neighbour] when *she* was ill, so I don't mind her coming in now.' Later in the year she seemed to think she had run out of credit, and was reluctant to accumulate too large a 'debt': 'It's gone on far too long now, and I don't want to be beholden: I'll just have to try and manage more myself.'

Neighbours were essential only if there were no female relatives available, however. In Sainsbury's study of disabled people in London and S.E. Essex, it was found that 'the absence of help from relatives outside the home was striking',[1] but family structures appeared to be closer and stronger in the City of this study. Of 57 people whose care presented problems to their normal household, 15 were cared for by daughters who either came to stay, had a parent to stay in their own home, or (living nearby) made long daily visits. Nine people were cared for principally by mothers (not normally resident in the same household), eight by sisters, and many by a combination of neighbours and various kinsfolk. Several of the mothers and two or three of the sisters gave up their jobs temporarily in order to come and help.

It appeared to be taken for granted by all concerned that if female relatives were available, no problem could exist. There were many cases of patients refusing to consider any form of outside help, such as a period at the convalescent hospital or an application for a home help, because 'of course, my daughter/sister/mother will manage'. Caring relatives also took this duty for granted, and none ever expressed any resentment, though sometimes it represented considerable hardship.

Some of the most obvious failures in ensuring necessary care arose because this assumption, that daughters, sisters and mothers will automatically provide it, was shared by the professionals whose job it was to recognize 'need'. If a daughter or sister was visiting the patient in hospital it was assumed that no problem existed, though in fact there might be special difficulties or the family might be too over-burdened to provide adequate care.

Mrs Burnett, diabetic and nearly 60, separated from her husband and living with her daughter, provided a typical example. Since this was a large family (she had 28 grandchildren, all in this city) who visited her in hospital regularly and vociferously, it was assumed that the patient's after-care presented no problems. At her first hospitalization, for a myocardial infarction, it was never elicited from Mrs Burnett that she had in fact been housebound in her daughter's top-floor flat for some six years, quite unable to manage the stairs because of breathlessness, overweight and the condition of her feet and legs. The neglected state of her diabetes might have offered some clue to the fact that the whole family, though very close, were in general non-copers, burdened with very many health and other problems, and without the resources to provide adequate care for an invalid. When social workers at the hospital were asked why they thought this case had never been followed up, they thought regretfully that she had probably never been brought to their attention because 'it was thought that the family was coping'. At this point the opportunity to instigate some caring services was lost, and the problems intensified.

In many cases where caring arrangements broke down or were unsatisfactory, patients readily admitted that they themselves were responsible, and that hospital personnel could not be blamed for neglecting their problem. In part this was because of the shared assumption that families could cope, and in part because the patients had underestimated the amount of care that they would need, or had been so anxious to get home that they had deliberately minimized their difficulties. This was particularly true of women, and to some degree explained why more women than men in fact found themselves to have problems of care. It seemed that, in the hospital situation, 'discharge' was such a momentous and longed-for event that they found it difficult to see beyond the actual moment of leaving the ward. There were some complaints that discharge had been too sudden, so that they had not been given time to consider and discuss with their relations what the best plan might be. The impression was gained, however, that the more important stumbling-block in the way of making plans for the future was a psychological one. While ill, the patients had necessarily relaxed into dependency and had avoided thinking about the future; they now needed time to adjust to the 'real' world, where decisions had to be made. Their own definitions of their condition were fluid for some time after discharge, and tended at first towards over-optimism.

A perhaps typical example was Mrs Stewart, living alone, self-effacing and anxious not to be troublesome, who seemed to have assumed until the day before her discharge that leaving hospital and being 'better', and thus able to resume her independent life, were synonymous. On being asked by the ward sister who was going to look after her, she had given a sister's name in a sort of unthinking consternation. Her sister was sent for and did indeed look after her conscientiously for the whole of the survey period, but it was not a happy arrangement. The sister was a brisk and domineering personality, not wholly sympathetic to the 'weakness' of disability, and the subject was only too aware of 'being a nuisance'. It seemed here that if there had been some prior discussion and planning, and if the sister had been asked to help rather than being presented with the situation so abruptly, the whole situation might have been happier.

It was also assumed, by hospital personnel and by the patients themselves, that problems of care were less likely for people living with their spouses. Though this was broadly true, there were nevertheless quite serious problems in certain cases. In particular, it seemed that the difficulties of young wives and mothers were perhaps overlooked. They possibly needed more care than a home help could provide, and in any case there were few examples in this age group where anyone had suggested a home help; general practitioners, for example, seemed a little less sympathetic in general than they might have been to elderly women. The only solution if no parents were available, and especially if there were young children, was for the husband to take time off work. How drastic a step this might be would depend, of course, on the nature of that work: in some cases, leave might be granted without trouble, but in more, the result was at least financial hardship and at worst the loss of the job. This applied equally, of course, to working wives and daughters; though the consequences in their cases might not be so serious, they were still sufficiently disrupting to cause great distress. The great cause of resentment, on the part of people who had to be absent from work to look after relatives, was not only that no national insurance benefits could be paid, but even more that insurance stamps could not be waived: if the insured person wished to protect his future benefits, then he must buy the stamps himself. Several people, faced with a life-and-death situation where a wife or mother could not be left, were incredulous and resentful at what seemed to them to be bureaucratic and unsympathetic treatment of their problem.

The 20-year old daughter of Mrs Baxter, for instance, had been told by their general practitioner that her mother must on no account be left alone, and the doctor had helped her to get unpaid leave of absence from her job. As months went by, however, and the prospect of being dismissed seemed to her to become likely, she began to worry because she was using up all her savings. The doctor advised her to see the 'social security', where there would surely be some help available. Her reception there angered her very much: 'All they said was, we'll make a form out to get you off our backs, but you won't get anything. They said don't you know your father [working away from home] should pay you £7.70 a week? I said try and make him!'

It seemed to people that they were caught in a double bind. On the one hand it was a strongly-held cultural norm that families should be responsible for the care of incapacitated members – the patients themselves expected it, and it appeared that medical agencies expected it too. They felt that to 'fail' in this elementary duty would have been severely stigmatized. Yet other agencies of society – those concerned with income and employment – not only did not recognize this duty, but appeared to see it as an indulgence to be condemned. Strategems might be employed to escape this dilemma – a man might 'go sick' too, or might find shift work that could provide an exhausting but adequate compromise. In the case of Miss Baxter above, her general practitioner explicitly recognized the dilemma and abetted a manipulation of the situation: since the young woman was in fact attending him for a minor chronic complaint he made the suggestion, unasked, that he should supply her with 'certificates of incapacity' for a month or two, until the emergency was over.

Caring agents in the community

In difficult situations such as those which have been described, the formal help which might be available includes the nursing services of district nurses, the domestic work of home helps, and the advice and organizing assistance of health visitors and social workers. Patients may seek these services themselves, if they know what help is available and where to find it: since the 'need' arises on medical grounds, however, there is some responsibility upon hospital personnel and general practitioners to identify it, and a tendency on the part of the patients to rely upon their doing so.

As the diagram of services (Figure 2.1, p. 19) showed, almost every one of this group of helping agents is administratively separate. Medical social workers were, at this time, under the administration of the hospital, and community social workers were employed by the local authority. District nurses were, formally, an independent organization, but administered by the local authority health department and largely under the day-to-day direction of general practitioners. The home help service had recently become part of the local authority social work department, but was still regarded by many people as an independent local authority service.

The work of these caring agents in the community was, in general, very much appreciated, but it is hardly surprising that referral systems were found to be less than wholly efficient.

There were many cases where ward staff and medical social workers had been wholly successful in arranging for the patients' care:

> Mrs Howie, a widow in her 60s, living alone in a split-level flat, was immobilized after an arthroplasty followed by a fractured femur. A sister came to stay with her for the most difficult post-hospital period, but the M.S.W. helped to rearrange her house, organized the provision of a telephone extension in the bedroom, personally went to the D.H.S.S. over financial support, arranged for a home help, and persuaded both the general practitioner and the hospital to submit applications for rehousing on a ground floor.

Where failures in providing care in the community occurred, they could be attributed in part to features of the administrative structure, and in part to a lack of agreement among hospital personnel as to how far their legitimate interest in the subsequent care of patients extended, or what distinguished a medical from a social need. The major reason why all relevant patients could not possibly be followed up has already been noted: there were simply too few medical social workers, and their choice of clients depended not only, or even principally, upon their own specialized training in the recognition of social problems, but also upon the differing attitudes of individual medical and nursing staff, and upon historical accidents of administrative structure.

In the four wards from which the sample patients came, there were two which had 'regular cover', that is, a particular social worker was attached to them and routinely glanced through every case. The other two wards had not, and referrals depended on the recognition by ward staff that social work help was needed: the workers described their dependence on 'being stopped on the stairs' or 'just being seen around'. Simple shortage of staff precluded regular cover of all wards, though social workers obviously preferred the more clearly recognized status it offered. They hoped that the 1974 reorganization might lead to improvements in staffing, and meanwhile thought it preferable to continue giving what they saw as a 'proper' service to some wards, rather than attempt to spread too few workers too thinly.

Which wards were chosen for regular cover depended on combinations of historical events – whether a given worker stayed in her post or left, for instance, or whether the ward had, either now or in the past, a senior consultant who was particularly conscious of social problems.

In fact, for the particular groups of people in the sample, there was found to be little difference between wards in the level of service given or the numbers of cases of need which were missed. This was probably because other ward variables cross-cut the administrative division, the most important one being the attitude of the medical personnel: in one of the wards without a regular social worker, the senior consultant was very conscious of the problems their disability might cause for people, and anxious to use social agencies where appropriate. In general, the social workers believed that the use made of their services 'all depended on the atmosphere in the ward' and described how practices varied: in some wards their attention would be drawn to the same patient by 'three or four different people, from the consultant downwards'; in others only the ward receptionist seemed to be interested. Another variable was the division between medical and surgical wards, and the social workers believed that 'medical' patients were more likely to have their social needs considered than surgical patients. Length of stay might be a factor here, for several of the saddest cases of people going without help were patients who were in hospital for a comparatively short time. This was not always true, however, and if length of stay is kept constant, then no difference appeared, in this sample, between medical and surgical wards.

Nursing care

Thirty-seven people received nursing services in their homes, and they saw it as an excellent service. In one case the district nurse, together with a home help, was managing the total care of a bedfast and wholly disabled person living alone, and many people described how nurses were 'popping in', 'keeping an eye' on them, and offering help and advice beyond the boundaries of a nursing function. Only three patients ever expressed unfavourable opinions of the community nursing services: one was a patient who was categorized by her general practitioner as exceptionally difficult and demanding, and in the two other cases there was some long-standing conflict over what was seen as criticism of the management of children.

It was, however, difficult to perceive any rational distribution of this much valued resource, the district nurse. Incapacity, or need for nursing care, or lack of material resources, or absence of family 'carers', certainly did not distinguish those (the majority) who needed care and received it, from those (a minority, but not an inconsiderable number) who appeared to be in equal need yet received no nursing service. No quantitative statements can be made about the extent of unfilled need for professional nursing, for this would involve clinical judgement, but amongst those who themselves expressed such a need there was, for instance, Mrs Dey, already suffering from arthritis and on crutches, who sustained multiple fractures and injuries in a road accident, and who was left at home for six days after her discharge from hospital, completely without help until a neighbour telephoned her doctor.

Failures such as this appeared to be largely due to poor communication between the hospital and the G.P.: he had not yet been informed that the patient had been discharged, or had not yet visited the patient or realized that nursing care was required. This could hardly apply to patients requiring permanent or very long-term nursing care, of course, and all those very severely disabled people who needed permanent professional nursing at home were receiving it.

Many of them were in fact receiving services which might have been defined as social rather than medical, and beyond a nurse's function. The criteria for the allocation of district nursing services are formally medical, and the distribution is in doctors' hands. Yet (as Sainsbury also found) of the thirty-seven people who had assistance from nurses, at least a third – and these the most demanding in time – were receiving help that had little to do with medical treatment. The nurse was going on errands, contacting agencies on the patient's behalf, bathing or washing the patient or giving other sorts of personal care.

Domestic services

A similar extension of functions was observed in the other domiciliary source of help, the home-help service. Home helps are intended to offer domestic help rather than personal care. Yet, again, in many cases they were providing the personal services of washing and dressing patients and acting as a link between them and other agencies.

Formally, there was an unfilled gap between nursing services directly associated with medical treatment and domestic services not intended for personal care. That the gap was more formal than actual, however, was due to the fact that home helps, like district nurses, were willing to give a comprehensive 'caring' service. Of the small number (eleven) of people who required long-term care, but were without a normal 'carer' at home, all but one received very adequate home-help service.

> In the case of Mr and Mrs Ritchie, for instance, the home help was their lifeline, doing the shopping, collecting pensions, and pushing Mrs Ritchie to the hospital in her wheelchair to visit her husband. Mr Ritchie said, 'She's a jewel, she does everything, when the wife's been in the hospital she's gone out there and got her things and taken them home to wash – this is all in her own time, mind!'

There were other cases where husbands or sons of home helps were performing small voluntary services for a handicapped person – cutting a lawn, doing handyman jobs in the house – which the clients perceived as being offered in a wholly acceptable manner.

The rate of provision of this service, like most local authority services, is known to vary widely. The range of expenditure found in a sample of authorities in England and Wales in 1973 was £32–122 per thousand population, with an average of £73.[2] The City's expenditure was well above this average, and recruitment was not a problem. Because this was an old-established and highly thought of service, all of the sample patients knew about it and many were willing to apply for it. General practitioners, nurses and health visitors suggested it, or patients asked their doctors, or – since they understood quite clearly that it was a local authority service – made enquiries at the city offices.

There were numbers of people, however, who might have been eligible for home help service who would not apply for it. In part, this was because of housewives' great dislike of defining themselves as 'unable to cope'. In the case of severe disablement there would, of course, be no alternative, but in the more numerous intermediate cases where housework was simply very difficult, somehow the assistance of family and friends did not put them into the category of 'disabled housewife', whereas professional help did.

> Mrs Ogilvie, for instance, was suffering from a back injury and thrombosis and was completely unable to care for herself for some months. 'We dinna' like strangers in the house – I've got a family – the family can cope. I'm independent – I like to be able to manage', seeming to imply that the capabilities of her family and herself were indivisible: to say that she could not manage was a slur on her family, and to suggest that they could not cope was a criticism of her. In fact, the situation seemed a little hard on her school-age children and her shift-worker husband, and financial problems arose because of his absences from work.

Very few men who might have been eligible for a home help refused to apply for one. There were one or two independent eccentrics, but for the most part men alone (or with the sole care of children) were readily referred to the home help service and happily accepted help with household tasks.

Housewives have, of course, the advantage of being able to define their own job. A bedfast woman, directing the household operations actually performed by her family, can still feel that she is 'the housewife', and if on the other hand she is only able to do her tasks with difficulty she may set her own standards and her own hours. Unless wholly helpless, she is not forced to accept someone else's definition of her capabilities. She is thus in a position where she has much greater control than an employed person over the way in which she is permitted to define herself. On the other hand, her eligibility for the help that she may need depends upon her willingness to define herself as incapable. The conflict could be seen to affect not only the use of home helps, but also the acceptance of other practical services.

In part, however, under-use of the home help service was also due to some mismatch between the service as it was, and the service as it was thought to be by the prospective clients and their advisers. It was seen as a very clear-cut service, with rigid criteria of eligibility, and a restricted specification of duties. Many patients explained how home helps were available only to certain groups, or only for a prescribed number of hours, or only for certain duties. 'The system' was that if you came into one category, you were entitled to two hours a week, or into another, four. These ideas were shared by some referring agents – a general practitioner was reported to have said, for instance, that home helps were only for the old and for maternity cases, and a health visitor insisted that they were never allowed to do washing – and seemed in fact to be fostered at the lower levels of the administration of the service, according to the accounts of people who had made enquiries. This was, of course, an excellent protective device for restricting demand.

The senior administrators of the service presented it as supremely flexible, with an informal allocation procedure: 'Each person is different and so we assess the individual need – no, there's no system'. Duties were also flexible, and the proper status of a home help was far above that of a domestic servant. Another administrator said, 'The primary function is care, not cleaning. They put the client's needs before the house, and they do a tremendous amount beyond what they're supposed to do.' (The word 'supposed' would appear to indicate two distinct levels of formal ideology existing side by side within the agency.) 'Good home helps do everything,' he went on. 'They generally love helping. It's a preventive service, too – if there's a home help in the house you don't need a social worker.'

Those people who did depend on their home helps knew that this eulogy was not undeserved, but it seemed obviously to be presented as a plea for higher status. A formal gap existed between nursing and domestic services, and one way to fill it was by an enlargement of the home help service into a caring profession. At a date subsequent to this survey, a training programme in the best ways to help people with various types of disability was instigated, and was said to be popular among the home helps. On the other hand, the solution sometimes suggested, that the service should be upgraded by instituting a hierarchy of different sorts of home help, was not favoured by these administrators: they felt that formalization would affect their recruitment adversely and destroy the flexibility of the service.

The gap was not only one of functions, but also a practical one of hours of service. The four or five people or couples who were so ill or disabled as to be wholly and permanently dependent on professional care were poised in a knife-edge position: emergencies at times when the home help was not there, or unavoidable absences of nurses or home helps because of illness, found them dangerously vulnerable. There were only two instances in the sample year of real emergencies of this sort actually happening, but several people appeared to find the possibility an ever-present threat haunting them continuously. If they were defined as wholly helpless then residential care would be the only solution. They resisted the definition as long as they could, however, because 'being put away' was seen by most of them as the final degradation, and welfare agencies were also reluctant to impose the definition because of their orientation towards 'keeping people in the community'.

No matter how great the effort made to help these most disabled people, no solution could really be satisfactory within the available resources: they required a specially sheltered environment or a network of immediately-available 'carers'.

Severly disabled people living with families were found to be more likely than people living alone to have neighbours who were in fact providing this emergency service, but even in these cases the situation was felt to be precarious and a gap in services was felt to exist. In a small contemporary survey of the needs of disabled people in a different Scottish county, one of the services most frequently suggested was a 'sitter' service to supplement nurses and home helps.[3]

PROBLEMS OF HOUSING AND PRACTICAL DAILY LIVING

The range of concrete aids, as distinct from services, available to help with the daily living problems of sick and disabled people is very large. The hospital supplies, for instance, crutches, walking aids and wheelchairs, surgical boots and orthopaedic appliances. Home nursing aids such as bed cages or commodes were, at the time of the survey, held by the local authority health department and supplied through district nurses. 'Aids and equipment for the home' – lifting equipment, extension W.C. seats, bathing and walking aids – were the responsibility of the social work department. Aids which required structural alterations to a house, such as handrails, special doors, or ramps for wheelchairs were also the responsibility of the social work department, but arranged through the local authority architect's department. Rehousing, either in specially adapted or in more suitable ordinary housing, was the responsibility of the local authority housing department. Certain elaborate or expensive 'aids', such as motor vehicles or complex electronic control equipment for the very severely disabled, remained within the hospital's jurisdiction. Under the Chronically Sick and Disabled Persons Act the list of practical aids which the local authority, through the social work department, was empowered to provide was extended to include 'arranging for the carrying out of any works of adaptation in his home or the provision of any additional facilities designed to secure his greater safety, comfort or convenience' – a hopefully ambitious but vague prescription. Special mention was made of the provision of telephones, equipment associated with their use, and wireless and television. For all the things which have been mentioned, purely commercial suppliers on the one hand, and charitable organizations on the other, existed side by side with the health and welfare services, offering the same goods.

Aids and adaptations in the home

Potentially, it would seem that the system of provision is very comprehensive. In fact, rather few of the patients in the sample were found to have had any attempts made to solve their problems of daily living. Twenty-eight people had long-term problems of the sort which could have been solved by the provision of aids and adaptations in the home. (The temporary provision of such things as nursing aids or crutches is excluded here.) These included more women (20) than men (8), and the majority were suffering from accidents or diseases of bones, joints and muscles, either alone or in combination with other diseases. Of these 28 people, only 11 wholly solved their problems during the survey year, though *some* aid or adaptation (it might not have been adequate or might not have been the right one) was supplied in 15 cases. The aids or adaptations obtained were wheelchairs or other aids to mobility (9 cases), the provision of banisters or bathroom rails (5), alterations to W.C.s (4), outside ramps (2), telephone extensions (2), gadgets for housewives (3), and single instances of specialized aids such as a ripple mattress, a 'talking book', an altered doorway, an outside pully for washing.

Though the number of people involved here is of course comparatively tiny, this level of provision may be compared with that found in the National Survey,[4] where the only adaptations found to have been provided for any substantial number of people were the replacement of coal fires (12 per cent of the sample), banisters and bathroom rails (9 per cent), and altered W.C.s (3 per cent).* Most importantly, the National Survey found that 77 per cent of the 'handicapped and impaired' had no aids or adaptations whatsoever. The low level of provision in the present sample is therefore not surprising.

The National Survey also found that those people who were registered with the local authority as 'handicapped' were considerably more likely than others to have had some substantial aid or adaptation. This was also true in this sample, for the simple reason that a consequence of an adaptation being made was that the client's name was added to the register.

The present survey also echoed the National Survey in finding that very many people – most of them housewives – were struggling with problems of daily life that might have been solved by quite simple aids or rearrangements. There were eleven people with motor disabilities, usually suffering from rheumatoid arthritis, who had no special equipment and were struggling to do small daily tasks in a completely unadapted environment.

In fact, many housewives gave the impression of a positive and stubborn satisfaction in overcoming the environment rather than admitting that it needed adaptation. Most of these women had long-term crippling diseases, often very painful, but not defined by them as 'illnesses'; they readily called themselves 'arthritics' or even 'cripples' (half humorously) but would never admit that they were *disabled* – they continued to keep their houses and prepare meals for their families, so their functions remained unaltered. To admit that their kitchens should be 'special' would label them, in their own eyes, as disabled.

Mrs Lilian Farquhar may speak for all this group: 'I often wonder what it must be like to wake up knowing you're going to have day without pain. People going about don't know they're born. But I manage. I've served my apprenticeship to pain. There's worse off than me – I can still move about a bit. I'm lucky, really –

*It must be noted that the National Survey included, as the present study does not, all the elderly 'handicapped and impaired'.

comfortably off, and a nice house and all. When my father died I was eight and Mother was left with seven of us, so things were never soft, we weren't allowed to be ill. You get used to putting up with things and I manage very well, I decorated this room last year though I couldn't do it now. We just have to take what comes. I just wait to see what comes next. I don't need any help, and whatever happens I won't take to my bed. I've got my work to do.' This might be interpreted as a stoical 'account', a brave face presented to adversity. It must, however, also be interpreted in the light of the observed behaviour: that Mrs Farquhar had made no concessions to her disability in her household arrangements; she had not removed the numerous ornaments requiring laborious dusting, her hall had a flooring which somehow was polished, she was only able to use the top burners of her cooker, her electrical appliances remained permanently plugged in since she could not manage floor-level switches.

With regard to the more general provision, not only in cases of motor disability, of what the Chronically Sick and Disabled Persons Act called 'additional facilities' for 'greater safety, comfort and convenience', the level of supply (and indeed of demand) was low. There was general ignorance among the clients about what might be provided. There had been publicity about the Act's recommendations with regard to telephones and television sets, and among the minority who knew anything about the Act at all, it was these provisions that they had heard of. It was never considered that it might be possible under the Act, or indeed under the earlier Social Work (Scotland) Act, to have showers installed instead of useless baths, or to have coal fires replaced, or to obtain assistance for the alteration of outdated power systems which would not carry labour-saving electrical equipment. These things were not generally known to be done, so few people defined themselves as having any 'need' for them. The provision of adaptations was generally confined to certain well-defined, unequivocally 'medical', and relatively cheap things such as rails, ramps and adapted W.C.s. These were the things which doctors and community nurses were most likely to suggest to their patients, and the things which the patients were most likely to define as needs.

Problems of housing

Adaptations may not be sufficient, and a new house altogether may well be the most urgent 'need' of a chronically sick or disabled person. Twenty-eight people – 14 per cent of the sample – expressed this need. This was perceived need, not need as judged by some objective standard, for there were others living in what appeared to be wholly unsuitable housing, who nevertheless did not wish to move. Since the service of the local authority in providing houses or rehousing on grounds of health seemed to be very well known to all the people of the sample, and readily used by them, in every case except two the patient had in fact applied for or been referred for housing.

Eight of these people were actually housebound because of their housing: they could not manage the stairs, or the district was too hilly for a wheelchair or for a patient with chronic respiratory disease and unless they were rehoused on a ground floor they were imprisoned. Fifteen of the rehousing applications were from married couples, five from men alone and six from women alone. Eleven of the applications were from one-person households, nine from two-person households and six from larger households. Fifteen were from council tenants (13 per cent of all council tenants), nine from private tenants (30 per cent of all private tenants) and two from owner-occupiers. All lived in the City rather than in the surrounding towns or rural areas; although a few country-dwellers did have dwellings which might have been thought to lack amenities, none of them had any desire to move.

Of these twenty-eight people with a housing need, eight had solved their problem by the end of the survey year. Amongst the remainder, there were several urgent cases, a few of which may serve to illustrate the range of problems.

> Mrs McHardy, living alone in an upstairs council flat on the outskirts of the City, had always to stay away from work if she was unable to manage the stairs or when the weather was bad. The district was rather difficult of access, and she said that she would have made more effort to join clubs or otherwise break out of her extreme isolation if she had been nearer in to town.

> Mr Finnie, 60 and separated from his wife, suffered from a complex of chronic diseases and was unable to work. He lived in one cold, dark and dingy tenement room which, for the whole of the survey year, he was unable to leave.

> Mrs Forsyth, who lived with her husband in a cramped two-roomed tenement flat, whithout a bathroom and with a shared toilet, had

little strictly 'medical' need for rehousing, but had been referred on psychiatric grounds. For the whole of the survey year, while her depression grew worse and her family troubles multiplied, she was convinced that this place was the cause of all her problems and 'getting out of here' the only solution.

Against these failures of the system, however, must be set the majority who had no problems, and the satisfied and grateful occupants of new, purpose-built bungalows for the old or disabled, rehoused from their old dwellings before the survey began. That the City's record in housing is above average may be judged from the fact that the average length of time on the housing list of the 20 people still waiting at the end of the survey year was not quite two years. This may be compared with the findings of the National Survey[5] that, nation-wide, 12 per cent of disabled local authority tenants and 16 per cent of private tenants had been waiting for between 5 and 10 years, and 3 per cent of local authority tenants and 18 per cent of private tenants had been waiting for over 10 years to be housed or rehoused. Most of the City's tenants were reasonably satisfied with the housing system, and expected to be rehoused before very long.

However, the system as it existed formally, and the system as seen by the clients, were very different. To the tenants, the system was in theory objective and thus 'fair'. It depended on collecting 'points', which were acquired (so far as the medical components of the 'need' were concerned, although there were of course the other possible components of over-crowding, basic lack of amenities, etc.) by persuading a doctor, a hospital sister, a medical social worker, or best of all a consultant, to write successive letters to the housing department. People frequently said – 'I've got my G.P. to put in another line, to see if I can get another point', or 'You get more points if the hospital does it.' Community social workers also had points at their disposal, though these would be non-medical.

Since medical personnel would never actually refuse to 'put in a line' when requested (though they might 'forget', or warn that it was unlikely to produce any change) the burden of responsibility, and of blame for any seeming anomalies, lay – in the clients' eyes – wholly on the housing department. Since the system was so simple and straight-forward, if it did not appear to be working satisfactorily then the reasons must lie in individual inefficiency or undue influence. In particular, people compared what they had been told about the number of points that would put one at the top of the list, and muttered angrily about any discrepancies.

In fact, most of the seeming difficulties, and many of the serious cases of unfilled need, were probably due to the problems inherent in assessing need and balancing 'social' against 'medical'. The housing department, particularly its junior personnel, liked to give the impression that the system was as simple as the clients believed it to be. Obviously, however, it could not be. Responsibility for awarding points was split between the housing department and the health department, thus spreading the burden of invidious choices. The health department awarded points, up to a given maximum, on receipt of forms from doctors (letters in support were, formally, said to be irrelevant, though the patients did not know this) and sometimes after seeing the applicant. Since this was not sufficient to reach the top of the list, other non-medical points would have to be added by the housing department before rehousing was assured. Thus, each department had a measure of autonomy and could not be dictated to by the other in its own special field of expertise. At one time the maximum medical points had, according to a housing official,

> 'meant going straight to the top, the medical factor was given absolute priority. But we had to bring it to the notice of the Housing Committee that this was leaving some people, without medical points, but in the worst possible circumstances of overcrowding and no toilets and so on, in a hopeless position, so we had to change the system.

On the other hand, within their limits, the doctors were autonomous: the official went on:

> I sometimes see people now with good medical grounds, and I think you haven't got a good crack of the whip – but we can't alter the medical points, our opinion doesn't count. We've been told we're laymen.

In fact, of course, in a really urgent life-or-death case, medical need *would* be decisive. There were such cases in the sample – a young man going on to renal dialysis, for instance, who was provided with a suitable bungalow at once. The selection of such cases, and the definition of urgency of need, depended upon the medical profession. It appeared that some of the more serious cases which had not been rehoused, such as those quoted, had simply not had a doctor or consultant who knew enough about their living conditions or saw it as his responsibility to single them out for special representations.

There was another list of cases, 'urgent on medical grounds', which was held by the social work department. When, in order to allocate a new block of semi-sheltered housing, this list was compared with the housing department's, it was found that there was little coincidence between them. One disabled woman in the sample, who knew that her name was held by the social work department, had assumed that this was equivalent to being on the housing list. Others, who certainly should have been on the social work department's list (the department were particularly anxious to know of those who might be forced into institutions, if not rehoused) had no knowledge of its existence.

There were additional reasons why the simplicity of the system was bound to be deceptive. One was the fluctuating supply and demand for any specific type of dwelling. Supply would obviously depend to some extent upon building decisions made long before, which in turn might depend upon concepts of need held at that time by particular individuals or promoted by government. There was, for instance, a particular shortage of single-person dwellings, for an emphasis on the possibility of avoiding the institutionalization of people living alone by semi-sheltered housing was comparatively recent and only now being translated into bricks and mortar. Even now official definitions of need seemed over-simple: a current circular from the Scottish Development Department requesting from local housing authorities a return on provisions and plans for 'the disabled' defined them solely and specifically as 'Persons who are dependent for their mobility on the use of a wheelchair.'

Supply and demand might make the strict application of a points system impossible. Another complication arose when needs had to be distinguished as medical or social. Points on social or lack-of-amenities grounds were awarded after inspection by officials of the housing department, and social workers' reports (whether hospital or community), though added to the file, had no direct effect on the assessment, though they could of course set an application in motion. One particular set of problems arose where the most 'needy', in material terms, of the clients were concerned, which was a point of conflict with some social workers: it was a strict rule that applicants were taken off the rehousing list altogether for six months if (being already council tenants) they were in rent arrears or the house was judged to be dirty and ill-kept. Thus, some people appeared to be in a double bind: those who might in fact most need rehousing, because their living conditions were particularly poor, or who were too over-burdened to cope with their environment, were seen as least likely to 'deserve' the service:

> Such a case was that of Mrs Burnett, the house-bound widow living with her daughter, also in poor health, in a top-floor flat, where the housing department records noted censoriously that the flat's condition was 'only fair, with filthy scullery'. After several years on the housing list, and after the belated intervention by a consultant who had been shocked to learn of the circumstances, the family was eventually rehoused towards the end of the survey year. Unfortunately, Mrs Burnett died three weeks later in the ground floor flat which had been her dream for so many years.

Particularly where illness or disablement are concerned, arrears of rent or an uncared-for house might be simultaneously the symptoms of a need for rehousing and the barrier against obtaining it. Even this rule about rent arrears and ill-kept houses, very central to the formal ideology of the housing department about 'good' tenants, was not as rigid as it was believed to be. Flexibility was obviously indicated in cases where a smaller house was required than the one which the tenant found too big to manage, and there might well be unpopular houses in particular districts available, so little prized that they were felt to be 'extra' to the system. Whether refusing to accept one of these houses was interpreted as 'refusal without reasonable cause', another cause for being taken off the housing list for six months, appeared to depend upon the housing department's assessment of the family: in some cases the offer was made tentatively, and no stigma attached to a refusal, while in others the tenants were told there would be penalties for not accepting.

Other problems might arise because of a conflict about how a medical problem was to be defined. Did Mrs Forsyth, suffering from severe depression and growing daily more suicidal in her cramped and dingy rooms, have a medical or a social problem? In the housing department's view, her social need was not acute, since she was not living in an overcrowded or seriously dilapidated property. In doctors' eyes, her medical need was urgent, but there were indications of conflict here between the health department and the housing department. A health department officer described years' old battles over the definition of need in such cases, saying:

> 'People are still unwilling to recognise that psychotic conditions are illnesses no less than a gastric ulcer or a broken leg. This survival continues – this refusal to accept that psychological diseases are real diseases and can kill. There's still almost a hostility, and the neurotic and psychotic worry me.'

On the other hand, a housing official said:

> 'We in our ignorance think this "depression" thing can be overdone. It's amazing how frequently our least-deserving tenants manage to get a diagnosis. We have to be fair to the good tenants, after all.'

Given that the housing department – very reasonably – saw their major function as the equitable and efficient distribution of a resource, with any welfare function very secondary, it was only to be expected that cases which were 'difficult' should seem sometimes to be treated unsympathetically. They were, indeed, sometimes faced with insuperable problems:

> One patient who was very indignant about the length of time she had been on the housing list illustrates this: she lived with her daughter's family and there were 'medical points' for her (heart disease and epilepsy) and for one grandchild. The flat was on the ground floor, and Mrs Mutch's only real objection to it was an intense dislike of the district. The household was certainly badly overcrowded, and one child was sleeping in the same bed as the epileptic grandmother. On the other hand, the overcrowding seemed likely to recur wherever the family lived: there was a large extended family and it was often not quite clear which members of it were in fact living there. The housing department's neat formulae for assessing overcrowding were inapplicable, in a subculture where there was a strong tradition that members temporarily homeless, or in difficulties of any sort, or changing jobs or marriage partners, should be offered hospitality as a matter of course. With a long history of financial trouble and rent arrears, the family would have

been unlikely to be able to afford a bigger house. Mrs Mutch expressed a wish for somewhere on her own – 'one of those nice little bungalows' – but she could not have lived alone, and she provided (despite frequent epileptic fits) the baby-sitting service which enabled her daughter to have a job.

The housing department could not be expected to have any solution for problems such as these, which it defined entirely as 'social'.

THE PROBLEMS OF DEFINING 'NEED'

The use made of the welfare services connected with problems of health which has been described was obviously not very extensive or efficient, except perhaps in the area of housing. 'Needs' had, formally, been defined and provision made to fill them, but in fact need remained unfilled.

Simple ignorance of the system was one reason for the low level of demand, rather than lack of self-perceived needs. In fact, at least four systems existed side by side: a 'hospital' system, supplying things (largely without payment) under the N.H.S.; a 'private' system where people could buy or hire what they required; a 'welfare' system of things provided by the local authority, in some cases free but in others on a means-tested payment basis; and a 'charitable' system of things provided free for the needy.

But usage was not so clear-cut. People who could afford to buy many aids for themselves would nevertheless accept such things as crutches from the hospital without question. The availability of certain equipment on loan from the Red Cross appeared to be better known to the more affluent than to the less. There was continual bewilderment and resentment because people did not understand what equipment, under what circumstances, might be given to them free and what might be charged for: they tended therefore to make their own categorizations on empirical grounds – 'If the nurse brings it, it's free; if a social worker brings it, it has to be paid for, unless you're on supplementary benefit.' It would, however, be over-simple to attribute confusions only to inefficiency in service-provision. The under-use of some services, and the unclear lines of referral to others, could both alike be clearly connected to two fundamental problems: firstly, the difficulties inherent in 'integration', especially where the services to be integrated had grown up in different historical periods, with different organizational ideologies underpinning them; and secondly, the problems of loosening and widening definitions of need.

The relevant provisions for practical care, now under the administration of the social work department of the local authority, rested upon two pieces of legislation: the Social Work (Scotland) Act 1968, which transferred certain duties from other departments to the social work department, and the Chronically Sick and Disabled Persons Act, which was extended to Scotland not long before this survey began. This Act was a private member's bill which, although supported by the government of the day, did not have the financial provisions of a government bill. Additional expenditure on services for the chronically sick and disabled had to be provided (apart from some which could be related to a rate-support grant) from local, not central, funds. Thus, the services had been, from their inception, very vulnerable to all the current and perhaps contradictory societal pressures: generosity towards the unfortunate versus the puritan ethic of self-help, civic pride in comprehensive service versus care with ratepayer's money, concern for the aged or for children versus concern for the disabled. It had already become evident that implementation of the Act was very variable in England and Wales, and this had caused considerable pressures to build up.

Authorities in Scotland, acquiring these duties rather later, had some English experience before them, but little assistance with the problems.

The Act imposed two duties upon the local authority, relevant to this study: one was to provide specific services (but the level of provision and criteria of need were left unspecified), and the other to seek out and compile a register of potential clients – the 'chronically sick and disabled' – who were left without further definition. The second was perhaps more difficult than the first.

Since 1948, local authorities had been required (under the National Assistance Act) to keep registers of the blind, deaf, dumb, and 'other persons who are substantially and permanently handicapped'. The nature of such registers, and indeed their actual existence, remained problematic. When kept by health departments, they were often more accurately described as lists of people with specific diseases, in clinical categories, than registers of all 'the handicapped'. When, with the reorganization of social services, they passed into the care of social work departments, their nature and purpose were called into question and in many places the keeping of them lapsed until the Chronically Sick and Disabled Persons Act renewed the question of the assessment of needs and numbers. There was, however, some resistance by social work departments, since categorization by condition rather than need, on the medical model, was in many ways antagonistic to the newer social work ideology. Murray and Orwell[2] commented:

> ... Two Directors [of social work] in our sample kept no register as such, and one made the omission as a matter of conscious policy. He believes that clients should be classified according to their needs for services and that a register of names *per se* serves no useful purpose. A number of others, while maintaining a register, express a dislike of categorising people according to impairment.

A study in Scotland found similar doubts and ambivalences among social work departments. [6] In the City of this survey, a register did exist at the time, but its form was under revision and it was not in fact used for any practical purpose. Social work administrators were exercised by the very obvious problems: how to define disablement? how to identify without stigmatizing? how to distinguish (if a distinction is necessary) between impairment and old age? how to keep such a register up-to-date? whether the register should be one of need, or of potential need, or of people within certain categories with no reference to their needs? what level of identification would prove effective as a lever to demand more resources, and what level might be counter-productive because overwhelming?

As for the relevant patients in the survey, almost all were unaware of the existence of a register, or whether or not their names were on it.

Some of the difficulties inherent in the first task of social work departments – deciding what services shall be initiated or maintained, at what level, for which clients – can be illustrated by considering some of the specific services mentioned in the Act. The laudable desire of legislators to 'improve the quality of life' for chronically sick and disabled people opens up the possibility of providing quite new goods and services, different in principle from the emergency-help or medical-necessity categories used in the past. Yet problems are immediately raised: the problem of equity (do we supply these things to the aged, as well as to the disabled?), the problem of unknown levels of demand (what if we open floodgates and drown our organizational structure and our resources?), and the problem of setting criteria for eligibility. In his study of Scottish local authorities, Smith[6] found many tragi-comic examples of the administrative contortions such dilemmas can create.

> The Director of Creeltown Department observed: The crux is this. I find a disabled person of 45. I give him a phone, T.V., holidays, new bathroom. Next door is an old-age pensioner, just as incapacitated. Do I give him the same? And then what do I do about all the other O.A.P.s, the thousands of them? In some heart-searching about the nature of organisational and professional goals, the same Director pondered: 'Why did we get landed with all that lot? It's impossible to implement and our hands are full – it all gets political in the end. What most of the disabled need is money and not social work.' In certain of the instances which Departments cited, experience had proved a hard, if useful, master. In one department, for instance, the former Health and Welfare authority had initiated a small garden maintenance scheme to assist 'substantially and permanently handicapped persons'. Rapidly, it seemed, demand snowballed for the service amongst the aged, who appeared not unhappy to be defined as disabled, in order to avail themselves of the service. The scheme now principally serves the aged, around 2000 gardens are being tended, and the new social work department foots an annual bill of around £25,000.

> In Dunshire Department, a disabled man and his wife, who went to live 'half-way up a mountain' requested a telephone so that local authority and other services could be contacted 'in case of an emergency. The Committee and Department were said to have considered questions such as 'should a disabled man have as much right as anyone to go and live in a remote area, if this puts a strain on local social services?' and 'if a disabled man does something which is clearly unreasonable, can he then expect to land other people with his predicament?'

These problems are not, of course, specific to the field of services to the disabled, but apply to all discretionary welfare services. In a study of local authority services for the elderly,[7] it was found that many authorities were adamant that even if they were able to undertake surveys of 'need' they would not do so, lest they should uncover problems with which they could not deal:

> In one area, the Council of Social Service has carried out a survey, and suggested a need for a laundry service. The medical officer asked home nurses about the number of cases they had who would require this, and on the basis of what they told him, decided, 'there was nothing doing, because if you open this door you will run into trouble'.

Contrived ignorance may be a necessary organizational device.

In the end it is local councillors who will decide what local money is spent upon. Inevitably, some alternatives will be seen as more easily comprehensible, or more prestigious, or more in tune with current local pressures, than others. Some social work directors have expressed the view that visible bricks and mortar may be preferred to domiciliary services.

Special issues may also arise if the goods and services suggested are things which many non-disabled members of the community would also like. The issue of free telephones for the disabled who 'need' them – an issue which was found to be exercising local administrators to a quite disporportionate extent – illustrates very well some of the problems involved.

In this case these problems seemed so insoluble that fixed criteria (which do not exist for any other provision of the Chronically Sick and Disabled Persons Act) had to be suggested, in guide notes issued by the Association of Municipal Corporations and the County Councils Association in England and Wales, and the Social Work Services Group in Scotland. These suggested that telephones should be supplied to people who were *either* medically defined as being in danger if left alone *or,* if the telephone was needed to 'avoid isolation', living alone and unable to leave the house. The emphasis was on medical criteria, and on the life-saving possibilities of a telephone. The usual interpretation of these criteria was that to need a telephone in order to call the doctor was legitimate, but to want it in order to gossip was not. This created its own difficulties since the value of a telephone as a lifeline can be questioned – some local authorities pointed out that an alarm bell or warden system may be very much more efficient for the purpose.

There were several people in the sample who met the local authority criteria for a 'need' for a telephone, and many more who might have been considered to meet the looser criteria of the Act itself. At one extreme was blind Mrs Crombie who, on the occasion when her electricity supply fused, had to find her way down to the street and ask passers-by to get her a policeman. The local chemist and grocer were helpfully prepared to deliver for her, but she had to rely on her home help or on casual callers to take her orders, and since she had no way of communicating, simple tasks like arranging for the repair of her gramophone seemed insuperable to her. In her case a telephone would not only have been a lifeline but would also have saved considerable time and trouble for those trying to care for her. At the other extreme, there were many couples in poor health who were both *sometimes* housebound, or people living alone to whom a telephone would have been a most valuable service, though not a necessity on medical grounds. However, no agency ever suggested the possibility of a telephone, nor did any patient in the sample ask for one: it is, of course, relevant to note that only 36 per cent of the households in Scotland (and only 28 per cent of the handicapped and impaired, according to the National Survey) owned telephones, so that it would represent something quite outside the normal life-style of many people.

One couple in the sample, both disabled and housebound, did find themselves unable to pay the rental of the telephone already installed. In this case the social work department, preferring to rely upon the definitions of 'need' of the National Assistance Act rather than the Chronically Sick and Disabled Persons Act, went to considerable trouble to help the clients to obtain the rental from the Supplementary Benefits Commission.

The provision of television sets presented even greater difficulties, since no 'medical' or life-saving use could be envisaged. Murray and Orwell[2] noted: 'It is clear that no other section of the Act is regarded with such mixed feelings by directors, by some with open hostility.'

There were two or three people in the survey sample who were housebound and either had no television or could not afford to pay for the licence. In the terms of the Chronically Sick and Disabled Persons Act 'need' was obvious, and they did feel their deprivation keenly. No one had suggested to them that this need could be filled, however, and indeed none of the disabled people themselves distinguished this need from a more general need for more money. Anyone whose resources were as low as this might obviously be likely to have other priorities. If any attempt *had* been made to fill this need as defined by the Act, almost insuperable problems of equity would have arisen: how to deal fairly, amongst all those living on the basic minimum allowance, with those who did manage to afford their television licences and with those who chose instead to spend a little on, say, cigarettes. The only equitable solution – an expensive one – would have been to establish criteria for a general eligibility for sets or licences. This is, of course, the solution long adopted in the case of radio sets for the blind, but the blind are a smaller and more easily defined group than 'the housebound chronically sick and disabled', and moreover a group whom society has, for a long time, regarded as having special needs.

One solution which has been very commonly adopted for this type of problem has been to set the medical profession as gate-keepers for desirable 'goods'. This is the explanation for several seeming anomalies, one of the most interesting of which was the supply, prior to the 1976 introduction of a cash mobility allowance, of free single-seater, three-wheeled vehicles to disabled people. In exceptional circumstances converted motor-cars were supplied, one of the eligible classes (for no very clear reason) being disabled ex-servicemen.

Vehicles are obviously of social rather than clinical benefit, yet the service remains within the hospital, supplied from 'limb and appliance' centres. One reason for its original place in this setting is, of course, that it has grown out of a service for crippled ex-servicemen; that it remains within the 'health' rather than the 'welfare' orbit, however, would seem to be because it is expensive, potentially highly demanded, and difficult to fit into equitable social criteria.

Many people who find it difficult to get about would like to have a vehicle, or to have their cars adapted, or to have some of the financial and practical concessions allowed to disabled drivers. There is, again, a time-lag between the attitudes represented by legislation and the current social reality: the system is erected on the principle that cars are a luxury. An expensive luxury cannot be too widely distributed; it was publically suggested for many years that the reluctance of government to replace the three-wheelers, which are disliked and held to be unsafe, wholly by converted motor-cars, was solely due to the fear of stimulating demand. Alf Morris, the 'author' of the 1970 Act, wrote:[8]

> My researches show that it costs no more to provide a disabled person with a four-wheeled vehicle than with the three-wheeler . . . Why then are Ministers apparently so wrong-headed? The reason is that there would be a sharp increase in the number of applicants.

A committee reporting in 1974 recommended that the three-wheelers should be replaced by cars, but suggested even more stringent criteria of eligibility.[9] Applications for whatever form of transport is provided are always likely to be limited by the complexity of the regulations, which results in confusion among both clients and many helping agencies, and by the use of powerful gate-keepers; doctors must adjudicate on the 'need'. Thus, the vehicles were officially regarded as an individual health appliance which could be 'prescribed' according to clinical criteria. Since these are ostensibly clear-cut and are operated by powerful professionals, it is not easy to argue about them. The criteria which applied to the survey subjects were, in fact, an intriguing mixture of economic policy (enabling disabled people to join the labour market) and social considerations ('need' to get to work was joined by a housewife's 'need' to go shopping), but since clear definitions can be made only in clinical terms, it was medical criteria which were paramount. Firstly, the patient had to have an above-knee amputation or else his ability to walk had, for other medical reasons, to be 'severely limited'. These criteria met, he or she had to be employed and need the vehicle to travel to work, or for the duties of a housewife.

It appeared to the patients that these criteria, and the way in which they were interpreted, were full of anomalies and injustices. Three people in the sample had in fact received vehicles. One was a young ex-serviceman who was severely disabled in a motor accident. Two who received Invacars were a young man who in fact had a below-knee amputation, but happened to be an employee of the hospital, and a student whose walking ability was fairly limited and who had a progressive disease.

There were three others who made application and were refused. One was a middle-aged man who had had to leave his carpark-attendant job, and since it was not clear that he would be able to work again, he was obviously outside the formal criteria of eligibility. His comment was:

> 'A man sitting at home, can't walk, can't get out, he's expected to sit, he's no use any more. If it was the wife, *she* could have one to do the shopping. But if it's his wife has to go out to work, *he* can't do the shopping. Doesn't make sense, does it?'

The second was, in fact, a housewife, a woman in her 50s, who was completely housebound by a crippling disease. For some years her husband had had to do all the shopping, and take time off work to take his wife to any essential appointments. This patient was refused her Invacar on the grounds that she was not in fact 'carrying out the duties of a housewife'. Her reaction was:

> 'I can't do the shopping because I can't walk, and I can't have a car because I don't do the shopping. You can't win, can you?'

The third case was a particularly interesting one. Mr Kerr was a young man, with a family to support, who had a severely disabling disease, and was employed in a sheltered workshop. He lived some 40 miles away and, for reasons outside anyone's control, it became extremely difficult for him to reach his work by public transport. If he had given up work, the support of the family would have cost society almost exactly the same as he earned, and would have saved the local authority (who were subsidizing his employment) a considerable amount. However, he was very anxious not to become 'useless – just a burden', and the local authority social workers, who gave the family a great deal of much appreciated support, thought it essential for the family's emotional well-being that he should keep his job and agreed that it would be unfair and undesirable to expect them to move away from their home. The obvious solution appeared to be the provision of a disabled person's vehicle, since he could certainly not afford to buy a car for himself. Despite the vigorous efforts of social workers, however, his application was refused, on the grounds that his walking ability was not sufficiently limited. The facts that he was unable to reach his work without a car, and that this was the only work he could obtain, were judged irrelevant: the clinical criteria were impossible to waive. The consultant underlined the issue involved by commenting: 'In my view this case is a social and not a medical problem.' This was incontrovertible, but the solution to the social problem remained firmly within the medical sphere.

When, in 1976, a new system of mobility help was introduced in the form of a cash allowance, potential customers were greatly increased. The 'work' and 'shopping' criteria were withdrawn, and the new allowance might be expected to be attractive to many people who had not previously wanted, or been able to drive, a three-wheeler. At the same time, however, the floodgates were closed by the imposition of stricter medical criteria: eligibility was conferred only on those 'unable or virtually unable' to walk. Practical considerations ensure that again an apparent widening and loosening of definitions results in the introduction of more restrictive categorizations.

SUMMARY

Over a quarter of the sample had problems of personal care after their hospitalization. Women were more likely to have problems than men, and (obviously) those living alone more likely than those living with families. The greatest burdens of care fell upon families, and were readily accepted, although some details of administrative systems appeared to hinder rather than help. The work of community 'carers' – nurses and home helps – was greatly appreciated, though referral and usage did not seem altogether efficient. Some conflict was evident between formal rules and organizational ideologies, and between the services as they were and as they were seen by the public; this could be attributed to historical changes in administration and to the problems of expressing the newer ideologies of welfare – prevention, looser categorization of clients, individually tailored service, 'the person, not the problem' – through the instrument of local authority structures.

That many self-perceived problems of housing and daily living went unsolved was, again, primarily due to ignorance, organizational factors, and the difficulties of defining 'need'. In particular, the loose formulation of the major relevant legislation – the Chronically Sick and Disabled Persons Act – made the services very vulnerable to different pressures.

The attempt to widen the provision of social services to larger groups of those in need because of a physical impairment appeared to be leading to many problems of defining eligibility. One solution was to use the medical profession as defining agents, with the obvious danger that the process might turn full circle. Potential clients were much happier to be defined on 'medical' rather than 'social' grounds, but this might mean the reimposition of rigid categorizations. This theme of the difference between being seen as (or seeing oneself as) 'in need' *per se*, and being seen as 'in need' because of particular characteristics, is one that is also very relevant to the money problems discussed in Chapter 5.

REFERENCES

1. Sainsbury, Sally, *Registered as Disabled*, op. cit., 1970.
2. Murray, Joanna and Orwell, S., *The Implementation of the Chronically Sick and Disabled Persons Act*, Report by Social Policy Research Ltd., for the National Fund for Research into Crippling Diseases, London, 1973.
3. Woodward, J. I., *Report to the Case Committee, County Council of Banff*, 1972.
4. Harris, Amelia I., *Handicapped and Impaired in Great Britain* (Part 1), op. cit., 1971.
5. Buckle, Judith R., *Work and Housing of Impaired Persons in Great Britain* (Part II of *Handicapped and Impaired in Great Britain*), London, H.M.S.O., 1971.
6. Smith, B., *'Physical Disability and The Social Work (Scotland) Act, 1968,'* M. Litt. Thesis, University of Aberdeen, 1972.
7. Sumner, G. and Smith, R., *Planning Local Authority Services for the Elderly*, University of Glasgow Social and Economic Studies No. 17, London, Allen and Unwin, 1969.
8. Morris, A., *No Feet to Drag*, London, Sidgwick and Jackson, 1972.
9. Sharp Committee Report, *Mobility of the Physically Disabled*, London, H.M.S.O., 1974.

5
MONEY PROBLEMS

It is well known that poverty and physical impairment are correlated. Every study of families in poverty always finds a high incidence of chronic sickness or disability, and every survey of the physically impaired notes that incomes are likely to be below average.[1] Financial difficulties may be the obvious, direct and sudden result of an impairment. On the other hand, sickness may begin a slow drift downwards, and often a vicious circle may be set up: sickness causes unemployment or under-employment, which in turn helps to cause more sickness. Poverty may also affect health in more subtle ways: it may breed apathy, or it may breed resentment and aggression, and not only welfare authorities but also the medical profession may come to be amongst the 'them' who are on the other side. The vast majority of this sample were on excellent terms with their medical practitioners, and the minority who were not were not necessarily poor. Nevertheless, there was some evidence that financial need and a poor relationship with the medical profession might go hand in hand.

It will be suggested that the attitudes of the patients to money benefits – influenced strongly, of course, by the structures and mechanisms of financial help – are a particularly important factor in determining whether or not that help is received. The categories of 'sick' or 'disabled' may overlap with the categories of 'dependent' or 'the poor', but they are in many ways fundamentally different kinds of categorization. The interaction between them produces problems for the structure, for the agencies concerned and for the potential recipient.

The definition of money problems

It soon became very obvious that the simple problem of money loomed very large for the subjects of the study. Often it was connected with employment problems, and it might be either the cause or the effect of problems of practical care, but often it was simply the major problem in its own right.

A money problem is, of course, a very relative and subjective thing. There are very few people to whom a total disablement does not present some financial difficulty: to that extent, it is a function of the degree of impairment. To most people any long-term sickness or impairment means at the least some adjustment in their financial affairs. Yet one man's adjustment may be undreamed-of wealth to another. Thus, it is difficult to set any standard except perhaps the official poverty-line calculated, at the relevant time, as the minimum considered necessary to sustain adequate life – a line which may well in fact be unreasonably low if impairment means special and essential expenses.

There is no doubt that sickness and disability almost inevitably do mean extra expense. If a disabled person lives alone, help may have to be paid for, and even the most trivial household repairs become expensive. People whose functioning is impaired cannot shop efficiently and there may be extra expenses for diets and clothing. People who are housebound, or less mobile, are likely to spend more than the average on heating. The special expenses which the subjects of this survey found to be most difficult were, in fact, heating costs, laundry, and the necessity to use taxis for those whose mobility was too impaired for public transport.

Some of these expenses are indeed recognized as 'needs' for those supported by welfare benefits, and allowances for (for instance) heating, diets and household help may be added to the benefit level. It therefore seems reasonable to consider, for each case, these recognized expenses before deciding whether or not the individual is below the poverty-line set by the welfare system.

Thus money problems, for the purpose of this analysis, were defined as problems which:

a) were perceived as such by the patient;
b) were caused by, or at least affected by, the illness or impairment;
c) were serious enough to cause hardship of the sort which society has agreed (through welfare legislation) ought to be alleviated.

Requirement (b) caused few doubts, for there was of course an overwhelming likelihood that, even if financial problems preceded the illness, they would be worsened by it. Requirement (c) meant that only people near the official poverty-line were being included (though always allowing for special expenses), since those whose resources are much greater than this are of less interest in the context of welfare services. People were included if provision existed in principle, even though some quirk of the system might exclude them in practice: those whose benefits were wage-stopped, for instance, or those who were certainly entitled to some benefit but whose application had – whether because of a mistake by the client or by the agency – been refused.

The requirement that people should define themselves as having problems, in keeping with the general orientation of this study, meant that a few patients who seemed by objective standards to be living in poverty, who might be well below the official poverty-line and entitled to many benefits they were not receiving, would nevertheless not be defined as having money problems if they themselves insisted that they had none. This small group were all elderly, all married couples, and more likely to be rural than urban dwellers. They were all people whose impairment was of a slow, chronic nature, who had never had to meet sudden crises, and who prided themselves on 'managing'. Obviously, expectations were an important factor, and the relative standards current in their particular social group. One couple, for instance, explained how they 'managed very well' on £12.05 a week* by relating their life stories, and describing the poverty of their childhood and early life, when the wife (one of 14 children herself) 'went without my dinner many a time when the bairns were young, to see they got.' The processes of defining oneself as in financial need will be one of the themes to be discussed in this chapter. For the moment, however, and for the purpose of a first analysis, attention is concentrated on those people who met the criteria which have been given.

*It must be remembered, in connection with all money sums mentioned, that the survey took place in 1972 and 1973. The following basic weekly rates of sickness or unemployment benefit (single person) may be compared, to allow for the effects of inflation:

Operating from	September	1971:	£6.00
	October	1972:	£6.75
	October	1973:	£7.75
	July	1974:	£8.60
	April	1975:	£9.80
	November	1975:	£11.10

Details of money problems

A profile of those who did, and those who did not, have money problems at any time during the survey year is given in Table 5:1, which also shows who was able to solve the problems and who was not, by the end of the year.

Table 5:1 Characteristics of those people who had money problems (at any time during the survey year)

	% of people who had			
		Problems which were		
	No problems	solved	unsolved	(number)
Sex				
Male	80	7	13	(116)
Female	79	9	12	(78)
Age				
< 40	78	8	14	(49)
40–49	86	5	9	(45)
50–59	80	10	10	(63)
60–64	75	6	19	(37)
Household				
Living with spouse	83	7	10	(135)
Other	71	9	20	(59)
Dependent Family				
Without dependent children	85	7	8	(68)
With dependent children	79	6	15	(66)
Social Class				
Non-manual	95	3	2	(66)
Skilled manual	81	9	10	(62)
Semi- and unskilled manual	63	9	28	(66)

It was not surprising that those in unskilled manual jobs, or those without a marital partner, were likely to have problems. Both these situations represent, in different ways, a lack of resources in the crisis of illness. Services are intended to provide support for the vulnerable. Some questions are immediately raised about the effectiveness of these services, however, by the proportion of people whose problems remained unsolved. It was these two vulnerable groups who were disproportionately unable to find solutions. Problems might also have been particularly anticipated among the older rather than the younger patients, but in fact the difference between age-groups was not very great.

Money problems might have been more likely among the men than among the women. Sixty-nine per cent of the sample were married and living with their spouses, and since the husband is more likely to be the main bread-winner, an impairing illness of the husband is more likely to cause financial difficulty than an illness of the wife. Yet, surprisingly, there was no difference in the proportions of women and men whose illness caused financial problems in the family. Even allowing for the fact that there was a slightly higher proportion of women than of men in older age groups and living alone, this seems to indicate that the financial effect of a wife's illness can be considerable.

Families with dependent children are, of course, more vulnerable than couples without children or with grown-up children, but on the other hand, their welfare is the object of special provision – family allowances, family income supplement, free milk and school meals – and special efforts might be made to see that children did not suffer because of a parent's impairment. It was, however, found that there was a greater likelihood of couples *with* dependent children having money problems.

Finally, in this general analysis, it may be asked: which of these patients had pre-existing long-term money problems, so that the current illness episode could not be said to be the cause of their difficulties? Eleven people were found to be in this situation, almost all of whom were either parents of dependent children or else elderly people. Three of these long-standing problems were solved during the year, and eight were not.

The nature of financial problems

In considering these families in financial difficulties, it is almost impossible to give a coherent picture of their 'incomes'. A point-of-time survey can produce tidy results: so many people, with such-and-such characteristics, are receiving invalidity benefit, or supplementary benefit, at such-and-such a rate. A longitudinal study over a year, however, reveals the chaos that lies behind any point-of-time statistic.

When an individual within the British national insurance

system becomes ill, he receives sickness benefit, which may be enhanced by an earnings-related supplement for a period of six months if his previous earnings have been high enough. If he remains incapable of work for more than six months, his benefit changes its name to 'invalidity' and is increased by a small long-term addition. If, taking into account his family circumstances and expenses such as rent, this is below the officially set poverty-line, he may apply for some additional 'supplementary benefit' to bring him up to this level. If he (or more frequently she) is outside the national insurance system, because he has never worked, or his contributions to the insurance system are inadequate, he is entitled only to supplementary benefit. People may also, of course, have other sorts of pension (war injuries, widow's) and these are ignored where the payments of insurance-based benefits are concerned, but may be taken into consideration in the calculation of discretionary supplementary benefits. They may also have continuing payment from their employer while they are sick. Since basic sickness and unemployment benefits are at the same rate, to be defined as ill while unemployed makes no difference to income, though it removes the obligation to be actively seeking work.

The system is thus firmly based on dual principles: support 'as of right', insurance-based in theory (though not in economic fact), and shared between employer, employee and the state, on the one hand, and humanitarian support through supplementary benefit of those who can prove 'need' on the other. These two categories are in fact becoming increasingly confused, for reasons which may appear later, and are complicated by historical residues (the special treatment of the industrially injured) and by a few new provisions based on quite different principles (family income supplement, constant attendance allowance). Basically, however, the system seems rational and reasonably simple.

The reality is rather different. Before attempting to give any general analysis of the incomes of those who defined themselves as having money problems, a few case histories will be offered in an attempt to illustrate the client's point of view

Richard Kinnaird was a young, single man who had a handicapping disease, but who was not so visibly disabled as to make officials feel they ought to offer him special consideration. He fitted awkwardly into administrative categories, and although he appeared to be treated with fairness by all the officials he came into contact with, he tended to be passed from one to another so that there was little continuity in his affairs. When he first became ill he was receiving sickness benefit. Then he gave in his notice to his employer, because he disliked his job and felt that he ought to make a new start. He was defined by the Department of Employment as having left his job 'without good cause', and was told that sickness benefit would stop. At this point he was still attending the hospital, and its seems likely that he could have continued to receive certificates of incapacity had he sought them or realized that this would have been advantageous. He was advised to go to the supplementary benefits office, and for two weeks received some money from them. After two weeks (though he had been told it would be twelve) this was changed to unemployment benefit paid at the Department of Employment, until later in the year when he was told he had 'run out of stamps' and was returned to the S.B.C. At various times during the year he was receiving from £6.70 to £10.60 a week, and at no time did he understand how the money was made up or why it fluctuated.

In fact, his expenses were heavy and special. The rent, rates, electricity and other standing charges associated with his accommodation were £6.00 a week. He was initially paying for medical prescriptions and for the special gluten-free bread and flour his diet required, though he later obtained exemption from prescription charges. Although his benefit did appear, some of the time, to be including a diet allowance he was never in fact able to afford the high-protein food prescribed. His money problems were one direct cause of a deterioration in health, and were the major cause of ensuing social problems: he became isolated, bored and lonely, unable to buy the materials for his handicraft hobbies, and without even a television to provide company, for he fell behind with the rental payments and when it was out of order did not dare to ask for it to be repaired.

Another example was Mrs McHardy, the crippled lady living alone already mentioned in Chapter 4 in connection with housing. She was employed in a food-manufacturing firm but when she was hospitalized for two months after an accident she omitted to send any formal notification to her employer, or to submit her widow's pension book for deduction. She appeared to think that these had been serious criminal offences, and for many months after she had left the hospital lived in terror of them being found out. She was too confused and frightened at this point even to draw her widow's pension, and assumed that she had lost her job. For some time she had no income at all, and for several further months only the small pension; she had no knowledge about entitlement to sickness benefit, or unemployment benefit, or supplementary benefit, and was using up some small savings. It is relevant that she was extremely hard of hearing.

Another single woman in her 50s, Miss Hird, lived with her aged mother in a council house. She suffered from cardiac disease and bronchitis, and for some time it had been obvious that she was not going to be able to continue her work as a shop assistant. Eventually, and following an acute episode for which she was hospitalized, she and her general practitioner agreed that she should finally stop work, the week after her 55th birthday – the date had been chosen simply as a landmark; she had then been working for 40 years. Six months later, her basic sickness benefit of £6.00 a week was automatically raised by the long-term invalidity addition of 30p. Nine weeks later she received a notification pointing out that 'invalidity allowance is not payable because the claimant was aged 55 or over on the first day of incapacity for work' and that £2.70 had been overpaid, but 'since there is no evidence of deliberate misrepresentation' the Department of Health and Social Security did not intend to claim repayment. Miss Hird was torn between anger and rueful amusement. 'If they *had* wanted it back I'd be singing on the streets for it,' she said. She was annoyed at the letter's wording: 'Claimant! I never asked for anything!' and felt strongly that 'someone' might have told her the consequences of asking her doctor to sign a certificate a week after, instead of a week before, her birthday. 'I was only working on and off for months before, anyway. What do they mean, incapacity for work? I've been incapacitated for work for years!'

Miss Hird paid 80p out of her £6.00 a week for medically prescribed drugs. Her pharmacist remarked that he did not think she should be paying, and eventually she obtained an exemption form and had the cost refunded for one week. At this point, however, a general increase in sickness benefit became payable, and she received a letter saying that she was now no longer eligible. Since income limits for means-tested benefits were raised at the same time, this seems to have been a mistake. However, after these two experiences Miss Hird refused to 'demean herself' further. She did apply for a rent rebate after a circular from her town council, but she adamantly refused to reopen the question of free prescriptions, or to apply for supplementary benefit or any of the allowances to which she was almost certainly entitled.

These few examples – selected, obviously, because they have features of interest, but by no means unusual or unrepresentative – illustrate some of the causes of money problems to be discussed: peculiarities of the system, simple muddle and mistake, ignorance and misinformation, a multiplicity of categorizations, and the attitudes of the clients themselves. They also illustrate the difficulty of describing their sources of income. Of the 40 people in the sample who had money problems, however, 14 were living (at the time) on sickness or invalidity benefit alone. The majority of these were married people. Fifteen were living on supplementary benefit alone, or on some other benefit (unemployment, sickness, retirement, widow's) with a supplementary benefit addition: a greater proportion of these were people living alone. Four people, living alone, were receiving only a retirement or widow's pension, and seven people (five of them married with dependent children) were employed at low wages.

Time-patterns

When the patterns of money problems over time were considered, it was conspicuous that financial affairs were one of the areas where problems were likely to begin some six or seven months after the illness episode. Some people, in difficulties during their illness period, managed to go back to work three or six months later and so ceased to have problems: the number who did so, however, was smaller than the number whose problems did not arise until six months after their hospitalization.

Part of the reason for this was simply the using-up of both material and social resources: people might have small savings, or they might put off paying bills for a while, but if their circumstances did not improve then inevitably the day would come when a real problem had to be acknowledged, for it was no longer possible to see how the bills were ever going to be paid. Relatives might also help out initially, but be unable to contemplate permanent assistance.

Another important reason for the delayed appearance of money problems, however, lay in the distinction which exists in the national insurance system between short-term and long-term incapacity to work. Most people who had been employed were entitled to some earnings-related supplement to their sickness benefit, and it was at six months after they had become unable to work, when this supplement ceased, that they found themselves reduced to being what they incredulously described as 'really up against it'. It seemed to them that there was little rationality in a system which assumed that the short-term sick — who might quickly retrieve their position — needed a larger income than the long-term sick, who might have permanent special expenses.

Many people were inclined at first to over-optimism about their condition. In part, because of information-management practices employed by the medical profession, and in part simply because they were unable or unwilling to see their future as permanently and irrevocably changed, they took a considerable length of time to acknowledge that their way of life was necessarily going to alter. During this time they failed to adjust their spending, or they accumulated debts, so that when their income was finally reduced to the basic minimum they were in a vulnerable position. Few people did not know about the cessation of earnings-related supplement, but it was only towards the end of the six-month period that most of them began to worry. In cases where the prognosis was genuinely uncertain, or where, for whatever reason, the patient had not been told or did not understand the probable pattern that the future would take, it was particularly likely that money problems would arise at this six-month watershed.

Mr Scott had definitely been permanently disabled through a factory accident, but since treatment was still continuing a year later, it was perhaps not possible to pronounce on the residual likely impairment. In any case, he claimed that it had never been discussed with him. For the first month he was very optimistic about being back to work 'in a month or two', but as clinic examinations and assessment boards succeeded one another he became more and more apathetic and seemed reluctant to ask for information. His income (since it included an industrial injury component) was not as small as many people's, but he had been used to high earnings. In this case the problems arising from the reduction of his income were very obviously one cause of other difficulties, notably marital quarrels.

In other cases it was the re-definition of their national insurance status, and thus of themselves and their condition, which caused people to take the management of their convalescence into their own hands, and return to work, sometimes against medical advice.

Mr Milne, for instance, was a foundry worker whose work involved standing for long periods. He seemed at first to be happy in the role of convalescent, following a badly-fractured leg and ankle, but six months afterwards he suddenly became very agitated and anxious. The precipitating factor was without doubt the sudden drop in his income. He was very unsure about his ability to do his work, but was nevertheless determined to try: it seemed to him that there were only two pathways open to him at this point, to accept that he was permanently disabled or to consider himself recovered. The sudden financial hardship made the first alternative unthinkable: he needed his wage now, before another week was out.

There was little evidence that doctors managing these patients' rehabilitation took into account the arbitrary timings of the national insurance system. A few general practitioners were quoted as having enquired about dates in relation to the patient's social security position, but many people compained about hospital doctors' choice of out-patient clinic dates, especially if they had hoped to be 'signed off' at precisely the 'right' date, and then found their clinic appointment delayed.

The solution of problems

Few of the fifteen people whose money problems seemed to them to be solved during the year owed their satisfactory income to the fact that the official system of support had swung efficiently into action. One was a woman who, after trying for some months to live on a widow's pension alone, finally received some supplementary benefit; her income was still small but it seemed adequate to her when compared with her previous state. Two others were severely disabled people who each had special agencies working on their behalf, and whose particular circumstances eventually resulted in the provision of adequate incomes: one a blind person and the other a paralysed ex-serviceman.

In the other twelve cases where problems had been solved, it was by the patient's own efforts or simply through the passage of time. Seven people's problems were solved because they were able to return to work, one man who had been apparently caught in a downward spiral of ever more unsuitable and poorly paid temporary jobs managed to break out of it and obtain secure and satisfactory work, and four families solved their problems because the wife was able to begin to work. Some of the husbands concerned did not like this solution, especially where the wife was in late middle-age and had not worked before. The most outspoken was perhaps Mr Gauld who said: 'It's a plain disgrace, the state forcing a man's wife to go out to keep him, at our time of life!'

The support of sick employees

The support of employed people who are ill is shared between the national insurance system (to which both employee and employer have contributed) and the employer directly, who may choose to continue paying his employee in part or in whole and for a shorter or longer period. It seems of interest to ask how the employees in this sample were treated, since the question may considerably affect people's definition of their own position, and it proved to be of particular interest in considering the differences between the patterns of problems experienced by men and by women. The stereotype is that, at the extremes, professional people may expect to receive their full salary for at least a considerable period, and unskilled workers may expect to receive only national insurance benefits. Though this is broadly true, it was found to be an oversimplification.

All the 'gainfully employed' in this sample are being considered here, and not only those who had financial problems. Of 129 people, 93 were men and 36 women. The men were divided into three groups of almost equal size: professional and other non-manual jobs, skilled manual jobs, and semi- or unskilled manual jobs. Almost half of the women, however, were in semi- or unskilled work – many in food processing, catering, or other service jobs – and this probably reflected accurately the pattern of female employment in the area. More than half of these women were married and not the major wage-earner of their family; for them, the flexible hours of service jobs were more important than the low wages. Of the other 19 women, 4 were in professional or managerial jobs, 10 in clerical or commercial, and 5 in skilled manual. Table 5:2 shows the sources of income of these 129 people while they were unable to work.

That most professional and managerial workers received a part or all of their salaries while sick was not surprising: those who did not were self-employed people whose income stopped if they did not work. The wide variation between other sorts of worker, however, seemed of interest, and showed little relationship to the skill or pay level of the job. Those who received full or part pay while ill included, for

Table 5:2 Sources of income of the employed while ill (numbers of people)

	Job				
	Profess. & manag.	Other non-manual	Skilled manual	Semi- & unskilled manual	Total
Basic N.I. benefits only	3	1	4	7	15
N.I. benefits incl. E.R.S.	2	5	21	16	44
N.I. benefits plus part pay	1	0	3	7	11
N.I. benefits made up to full pay	16	11	7	3	37
No benefits, but part pay	0	0	0	5	5
No N.I. benefits or pay	2	4	2	9	17

	Sex		
	Men	Women	Total
Basic N.I. benefits only	13	2	15
N.I. benefits incl. E.R.S.	40	4	44
N.I. benefits plus part pay	9	2	11
N.I. benefits made up to full pay	30	7	37
No benefits, but part pay	0	5	5
No N.I. benefits or pay	1	16	17

instance, a detective sergeant, a laboratory technician, a printer – but they also included several labourers, lift attendants, porters and road-sweepers. There seemed no logical reason why 41 per cent of the sample's employers should support their sick employees, while 59 per cent did not. Obvious variables affected the existence and level of sick pay: size of enterprise, union structure, the employee's length of service, whether in the public or private sector – the reasons why these *should* be relevant variables were not, however, clear to the employees. They saw little force in the argument that if employers are forced to pay sick employees, then there would be undesirable discrimination against those with poor health histories. Discrimination exists in any case, but it seemed from this evidence to be *less* amongst those employers with sick pay schemes. The list of these employers coincides very closely with a list of those who appeared, by their actions in the specific cases followed, to be willing to help those with health problems, to take care in matching men to jobs, and to be considerate in continuing to employ an impaired worker if it were at all possible.

The effect of this dual system of support was similar to the effect of the split welfare system of national insurance benefits/discretionary benefits: the creation of two classes of beneficiary. Since workers could see no logical reason for the division – many of the men they knew who did receive sick pay were no more skilled, or highly paid, or long-standing as employees than they were themselves – resentments tended to build up, especially among those who for some reason found themselves reduced to basic benefits. Mr Cocker, a timber worker, said: 'Getting nothing from the national health for the first three days, that's a disgrace, the genuinely sick person needs all the help he can get at such a time, especially if he gets nothing from his firm. And when I hear about such highly paid workers as in the Post Office [this was a reference to a current dispute] it annoys me – they're fully paid every week when they're off ill, I say everyone should be fully paid.' These resentments affected both their attitudes to the welfare system in general and their definitions of themselves as welfare recipients, and also their attitudes to the structure of employment. They were considerably less likely to make strenuous efforts to return to the same employment (and employers were, of course, less likely to make efforts to re-employ them). The feeling of insecurity inevitably engendered by a physical impairment was thus compounded into a more general bitterness and insecurity.

The position of women with regard to pay and benefits while ill seemed to illustrate how peripheral to the employment system they were still assumed to be, despite constituting 36 per cent of the labour force in Scotland (Census, 1971) – 21 of the 36 employed women were not fully within the national insurance system, having exercised their right to pay reduced contributions as married women or widows. Several women said that clerks at the D.H.S.S. had advised them not to pay full contributions. There may have been some tendency to try to blame others for what was now seen to be a mistake, but the numerous accounts were convincing and it is certain that the implications of not paying the 'full stamp' were never explained in any form understood by the clients. A large proportion of women, therefore, received no benefit when sick: in many cases this represented no serious hardship, since they had working husbands, but in others it did. Hardship was especially likely, at least for a time, amongst working women who had been widowed or separated from their husbands; these were possibilities they had never considered when making the original decision to pay a 'small stamp'. In most of these cases, however, and particularly if there were children involved, it seemed that they were defined by welfare authorities as people likely to need help when they had to stop work, and adequate supplementary benefit was eventually provided.

If professional and managerial workers (of whom there were only 4 women) are excluded, then in fact a higher proportion of women than of men, in the other three categories of worker, were receiving some payment from their employers while they were ill. These included several nurses and clerical workers, but they also included shop assistants, food process workers, cleaners and waitresses. It seemed that, having excluded themselves from the national insurance system, they depended more upon the generosity of employers. They were also more likely than men to be employed in jobs where there were few employees and the relationship with the employer was a personal one.

The problems of those within the national insurance system

It is the national insurance system, whether or not supplemented by employers, which is assumed to provide equitable and efficient support for employed people when they are unable to work. Public concern has primarily been directed at those disabled people outside the national insurance system, who may have no income 'as of right', and may have to rely upon supplementary benefits. In this sample, many such people did have severe money problems, and their cases will be discussed later. However, it was not only – or even primarily – among people outside the national insurance system that problems arose.

A high proportion of the people who perceived themselves as suffering financial hardship were, at least technically, in the labour market and receiving national insurance benefits. Of course, all those 129 people in the sample who were employed at the time of this illness episode were receiving sickness benefit for at least a period, and the great majority managed without serious difficulty. What circumstances characterized those who did have problems?

For those people whose wage was high enough to provide a considerable earnings-related supplement, and whose incapacity did not extend beyond the six-months period, the benefit was perceived as providing adequate support. Those who had problems were people reduced to the basic sickness benefit, either because their supplement period was exhausted, or because their earnings had been too low or too erratic to provide any. Obviously, they were not amongst those whose employers accepted any responsibility for sick workers. Some were people to whom a widely fluctuating income and a state of insecurity were an accustomed way of life; they had simply given up any attempt to plan or provide for the future. Others, however, were people whose earnings, though low, had been secure; it was with a shock of incredulity that they realized how frail the basis of their respectable security was, and how quickly they could be reduced to 'real' poverty – rent arrears, overdue fuel bills, the sale of possessions – by the accident of sudden illness.

All the self-employed workers (e.g. taxi-drivers, window cleaners) found themselves in serious difficulties, in some cases because their insurance records were confused so that entitlement to sickness benefit was contested, and in others because of the lack of entitlement to unemployment benefit.

Many of those with problems were couples where both husband and wife were impaired, so that the wife could not take a job when the husband was unable to work. Serious difficulties arose in every case where a husband 'voluntarily' left his job (in fact wishing for temporary leave of absence) in order to look after a wife who became ill, or at times when there was a family crisis over, for instance, the care of children.

Those who became unemployed after this illness episode, either because they were unable to return to their old job, or because they were dismissed during their absence, were particularly likely to have money problems: the two crises of illness and unemployment occurring *together* confused their administrative position and their own definition of themselves. Those who were already unemployed when this illness began were in a slightly more stable position, and many of them were already receiving some supplementary benefit, although the special expenses of a severe disability caused new problems in some cases.

The problems of those who were working

There were seven people in the sample who were employed for the greater part of the survey year, and who nevertheless fell into the category of people with money problems – that is, their incomes were lower than the official poverty-line, if the special expenses of disability were taken into account, and they would have received a larger income if they had been unable to work. None was over 50; four were men under 40. The *choice* of ceasing to work was not really open to them, in part because of the wage-stop regulations (whereby an unemployed man may not receive more than his 'normal' employed wage) and in part because of the significance of their jobs to them. These were all men or women with chronic diseases – early multiple sclerosis, bronchitis, severe arthritis – and they knew that to give up work was to pass a watershed, to admit that they were permanently and irrevocably disabled. The five who were men with wives and children appeared to feel very strongly that they must struggle to support their families as long as they could. While they had jobs – however arduous and unsatisfactory these jobs were – it appeared that no one, whether wives, other family, doctors, employment or social security officers, or social workers, ever seriously suggested to them that to cease working might be a feasible solution. The wives in these cases were all preparing to work themselves, 'because I'm going to be the bread-winner one day', but were hampered by young children.

The problems of these families appeared to arise because there was no proper definition of their position. To be at the same time 'disabled' and 'employed' (especially in open employment, whether or not registered as disabled on the Department of Employment's files) was a contradiction in terms; a disabled person might be due for special consideration and help, but for an employed person 'the rate for the job', equity among workers, and discipline were the themes. There were men, usually older men, who managed to find a composite disabled-worker role, who were given as much help as possible, and who did not have financial problems despite the fact that their pay was low: they had no dependent children, and their wives were probably working. The younger group, however, could less easily assume a disabled-worker role.

They tended to be unsatisfactory employees, often away from work, and there were no extra provisions in the system to enhance their basic sickness or unemployment benefits. They became 'a man who is receiving unemployment benefit (having been dismissed as an inefficient employee)', or 'a man who is receiving basic sickness benefit (because he is poorly paid and frequently off work)' rather than 'a disabled man who is struggling to retain his independence'. If the family were in touch with social workers (and few were), then social workers might indeed appear by their words and actions to be applying this last, more advantageous, definition. 'We're at our wits' end to know what to do about the X family,' said one. 'He really does try so hard to work, and it's important to him, partly because he feels his wife respects it – we've tried to get him other jobs, but there just isn't anything here – and on that pay, they can't afford to live – we're reduced to trying charities . . .' The social worker's definition, however, had no effect upon the social security position of the clients. The fact that they would have been in a better position, and would have been likely to receive more sympathetic financial help, if they had been wholly dependent on discretionary benefits, seemed to call the whole ideology of the value of work for the disabled into question.

A similar process seemed to be in operation in the case of James McPherson, though here the master-label which came to be applied was that of 'student' rather than 'unemployed man' or 'poor worker'. This young sufferer from muscular dystrophy, married and with three young children, was forced to give up a job in a busy office and decided to study for a profession in which his disability would be less of a handicap. At this point he believed he had been treated with great consideration and helpfulness not only by the medical profession and academic administrators but also by the people he dealt with in the departments of Employment and Social Security: 'Before I got the student grant, we were desperate, and eventually I went to the S.B.C. not expecting anything much. But they couldn't have been nicer or more helpful – told me about all sorts of things I could be entitled to, because of the disability, and made sure about the children's milk and so on.' He obtained generous supplementary benefit, and it seemed that he was being seen clearly as 'disabled young family man, making strenuous efforts to overcome his disability.' During the next year and a half, however, he himself began to adopt the role of student, as he became immersed in a new community. He felt that officials' attitudes towards him had changed, and in reaction he identified himself more and more with the group 'students'. During vacations he went to 'sign on' as unemployed, and said: 'They make me feel as if I'm asking for charity every time I go in. The first time, when he said what do you do and I said, "I'm a student," you could see the antagonism rising at once. He said, "Well, you'll have to take any sort of job at all if you sign on, you realize that." I can't bear going down there. My wife'll tell you, I hang about all Friday morning screwing up my courage. It's the others, as well as the man in charge. They sneer as soon as they know you're a student. The wife's parents were having us all for a week in the summer, and when I told the bloke he gave me a right going over. You could see he thought what's *he* doing having a holiday – students' life is all holiday.' He did in fact work at several jobs during vacations, but on one later occasion when he was unable to get work and had 'run out' of insurance entitlement he returned to the S.B.C. This time his reception was very different. There was documentary evidence that four months elapsed before he managed to obtain an assessment showing why his student grant precluded any entitlement (despite the special expenses of disability, and the difficulty of finding suitable vacation work) to supplementary benefit. He did not contest the ruling, but was angry about the way he felt he had been received: 'They make their own rules, and the label of student is the one that counts, once you write down "student" they have you typed at once as a scrounger.'

The problems of those on supplementary benefit

Twenty-seven people in the sample were receiving supplementary benefit at some time during the survey year, either as their sole income or as a topping-up addition to some other form of pension. This is a high proportion, which serves to underline the connection between disability and poverty.

Those receiving supplementary benefit alone, or as an addition to widows' pensions, were of course likely to be those who had never worked – those who had been disabled since childhood, or elderly widows, or single-handed mothers. The problems in these cases arose almost entirely either because of the special expenses of disability, for which extra benefits had not been claimed or not been allowed, or because of the cumulative effects of trying to live for many years on the minimum 'poverty line'. Several of these men and women were housebound, and found the cost of heating, in particular, quite out of proportion to their income.

The weekly budget of Mr Collie may illustrate the special expenses of long-term disability. In his 40s, severely disabled with a progressive disease, he lived alone in an over-large council flat. His benefit was generous compared to many others: a total, including a rent and home help allowance, and a small amount from charitable sources, of £10.80 a week. His main items of expenditure were:

Rent	£3.00	
Coal	£0.75	(fuel costs were checked as far as possible and appeared accurate)
Electricity	£1.50	
Home help	£0.30	
Share of communal cleaning (stairs and lobby)	£0.30	
Television hire	£0.50	('Every night I watch to the last dot')
Cigarettes	£1.68	('I might as well smoke myself to death: nothing else to do')
Taxi for one journey each week	£0.60	(This was the only occasion he left the house, except for out-patient visits to the hospital)
Remaining for food, clothes and household goods	£2.17	

Mr Collie's comment was: 'I just sit here, after all. But it's getting so I can't afford to live even just sitting – it's getting worse all the time. In a right mess.'

There was evidence in this survey, as in many others, that those entitled to supplementary benefit do not necessarily apply for it: eight additional people were found who were in financial difficulties and whose households were below supplementary benefit level. As Table 5:3 shows, only three people living alone or with their kin were found in this situation, all individuals who were particularly socially isolated and reluctant to have anything to do with helping agencies. Five of the households below supplementary benefit level were those of married couples.

Discretionary allowances

Supplementary benefit level is, of course, a less than firm dividing-line where disabled (or elderly) people are con-

Table 5:3 Circumstances of people at Supplementary Benefit level (numbers of people)

	Married couples		Others, M		Others, F		
	Dep. children	No dep. children	Living alone	With kin	Living alone	With kin	Total
Receiving Supplementary Benefit	3	7	4	1	11	1	27
Eligible, but not receiving	4	1	1	0	1	1	8

cerned. In theory, the line may be raised by the addition of various discretionary benefits to the basic 'needs' allowance and rent allowance. These additions are of two kinds, continuing 'adjustments for exceptional circumstances' and single payments 'for exceptional needs' (*Supplementary Benefits Handbook*, D.H.S.S., pp. 18–26). Many of these circumstances and needs are particularly relevant for disabled or chronically sick people, but it should be noted that the basic principle is the establishment of 'need' *per se*, not the categorization of groups of people whose circumstances will give rise to special needs. This principle is the reverse of that underlying the Chronically Sick and Disabled Persons Act, which says in effect 'These people are defined as likely to have needs; if they do, they must be met.' Thus, the situation arises where, in fact, the services supplied may overlap, but they are provided in different forms (one in the form of money, the other in goods or services), by different agencies (the Supplementary Benefits Commission, an agency of central government, and social work departments, agencies of local government) and on different principles.

The discretionary additions to supplementary benefit most likely to be relevant to the people of this survey include medically recommended diets, domestic assistance, 'substantial' expenditure on laundry, extra heating, the cost of renting special safety gas cookers, expense because of abnormal wear and tear on clothing resulting from a disability, telephone charges, hire-purchase instalments for 'articles of household equipment or furniture which are absolutely essential', and fares to visit relatives in hospital. Single 'exceptional needs' payments may be made for clothing and footwear, bedding and household expenses, fuel debts and rent arrears, clearance of hire-purchase debts, and removal and redecoration expenses.

Some discretionary benefits which were received, or for which the 35 people at or below supplementary benefit level were probably eligible, are shown in Table 5:4.

'Need' depends to some extent, of course, on the individual's view of what is possible. As Table 5:4 shows, people were very ready to admit a need for a diet allowance, because they saw this as part of the health service, and a doctor had formally defined the need. This was also the allowance most likely to be approved, for similar reasons: in most cases, the burden of 'discretion' had already been assumed by expert professionals. The operation of this

Table 5:4 Eligibility and receipt, selected discretionary benefits (numbers of people)

	Allowances				Single payments		
	Diet	Home help	Laundry	Heating	Clothing or H.H. goods	Rent, fuel, or H.P. debts	Expenses hospital visiting
In receipt of supplementary benefit (27 people):							
Received	9	3	0	1	5	1	4
Applied but refused	1	2	0	3	1	0	1
Probably eligible and needed but never applied	3	1	2	9	7	5	3
Eligible for supplementary benefit but never applied for it (8 people):							
Probably eligible and needed but never applied	1	0	1	2	4	3	2

A single individual may have been eligible for several different benefits.

benefit, however, like that of others which are essentially welfare benefits but which attempt to make use of ostensibly clear-cut health categorizations (exemption from prescription payments for particular diseases, or the issue of disabled vehicles) demonstrated some of the problems involved.

The range of discretionary allowances connected with needs associated with illness and disability may be viewed as a continuum. At one end are those needs, such as extra expense for laundry or bedding, for which the criteria for eligibility for help are wholly social – a demonstration of poverty by showing that the blankets are in holes, or the drawers empty of 'necessary' clothing. The need may well arise from illness, but it does not necessarily do so; potential recipients are categorized by their poverty (and with such a categorization moral judgements are inevitably, if covertly, relevant: is the poverty misfortune or mismanagement?) rather than by a clinical condition, and doctors are rarely involved. At the other end of the continuum are those allowances, such as diet allowances, offered on wholly medical criteria, where lists of eligible clinical conditions are laid down, and doctors are always involved. Between these extremes comes, for instance, fuel allowances, where the criteria are a mixture of the medical and social. These categories are all sub-sets, of course, of an initial overall category of need, that of recipients of supplementary benefit. The point of interest is that such categories *are* susceptible to ever finer and finer sub-divisions, which may not only be regarded very differently from each other by both agency and client, but may also reflect back in different ways upon the way in which the overall category is perceived.

Any reluctance to apply for a medically defined need such as a special diet, or friction in agreeing upon eligibility, arose because of the supposedly precise nature of the medical categorizations involved. For some of the patients, the rule they understood was: 'If a doctor prescribes a diet, then you are entitled to a little extra supplementary benefit.' For the adjudicating officers, however, eligibility rested on a very specific list of conditions including, for instance, diabetes and stomach or duodenal ulcer (*Supplementary Benefits Handbook*, p. 19). At the time of the survey, the 'standard reckonable expense' for these diets was 68p a week, or 'in other cases where a special diet is needed', 30p. Conflicts arose, firstly, because of the varying interpretations which were possible of the words 'prescribed' or 'needed'. Secondly, the patient's understanding of his diagnosis, and the condition his doctor was prepared to certify, were not necessarily the same thing. Particularly in the case of a self-diagnosis of ulcer, the patient might find it very hard to understand why his condition did not seem to render him eligible. Despite the residual category of 'other cases' there appeared to be a tendency on the part of some supplementary benefit officers to stick firmly to the precise list: one patient claimed that 'When I told him it was hiatus hernia, he said, oh, that's nothing, I've had that myself, it's just indigestion. You don't get a diet allowance for that.' Thirdly, the patients were at a loss to understand the principles on which the two levels of allowance were allocated, and indeed the division seemed very arbitrary. Since exact 'rules' were known to exist, and were used as justification for their decisions by officials, then 'fairness' was the quality that people required from the system. If they were allowed only the lower rate of extra benefit for a particularly expensive diet, when they knew that other people with less serious or expensive conditions had got more, their sense of justice was outraged and they tended to blame the individuals operating the system rather than the system itself. It must also be added that the rate of allowance, when considered in relation to the actual cost of some diets, was sometimes found derisory and 'insulting'.

It could be suggested that very small payments may be more productive of ill-will and resentment than no payments at all. There is, of course, a dilemma in reconciling this with the demands of 'equity', a very salient principle to the clients. Sliding-scale benefits based on the principle of making up income to a given amount can be seen to be equitable, but inevitably they result in some people being entitled to only pennies: 'They offered us 25p a week supplementary!' Mr Elmslie exclaimed: 'It's an insult – it must cost more than that in paper and clerk's time. I wouldn't demean myself accepting it.' To be told one is not eligible for help may be annoying but it is not necessarily felt as insulting: several people who appeared to be on the borderline for discretionary benefits made statements such as: 'Oh, we're not poor enough for that.' To have one's needs valued in pence, however, was felt as degrading.

Very small payments, and inertia with regard to adjustment to actual costs, are of course particularly likely in peripheral parts of the system. Much publicity is given to the basic rates of the national insurance system, but less well known payments which are not part of the major structure may lag behind, as may payments which come out of other pockets than government's. The heating allowance was one example of this, and another was the 11p a week – less than one tin of dog-food – allowed to a blind person in the sample for the upkeep of her guide dog.

Despite a cold Northern city, with a proportion of old, damp houses, comparatively few people defined themselves as having a 'need' for extra heating. To interviewers who, month after month, found housebound people huddled over minute coal fires, or the bedfast in completely unheated bedrooms, this seemed difficult to explain. In part it was due to simple lack of knowledge that any allowance might be available, and to the fact that, according to the patients, doctors or health visitors had been less likely to raise the question of heating than of diet. During the survey year, information about the possibility of heating allowances became more widespread because of some national publicity, reinforced locally by a small survey and campaign by a students' political association. The students' respondents, elderly people in one housing estate, were asked whether they had heard of the existence of 'social security heating grants'. Fifteen replied that they had, and sixty that they had not. (It was not ascertained how many were in fact supplementary benefit recipients and so eligible for allowances.[2]) This campaign obtained a heating allowance for one of the sample patients, but few others made applications.

The reluctance to define oneself as having this special need appeared to arise from several factors. One was simply low expectations. To older people, in particular, small coal fires were the normal way of heating living-rooms and heated bedrooms were an unthought-of luxury. Those who moved to purpose-built bungalows for the elderly or handicapped, without coal fires, were likely to be among the few who did consider applying for allowances to help with their greatly increased heating costs. Those who remained in older property complained of the rising costs of fuel, but did not distinguish a need for help with the costs from a more general need for more money. Another factor was the association, in the patients' minds, between 'coal' and 'charity'. 'The diet which my doctor has ordered for my ulcer' and 'bags of coal for the fire' were two very different categories of need, the first spoken of very confidently and freely, as a part of the health service, but the second only when the situation was felt to be desperate, and often accompanied by stories of the past. (It was, however, notable that actual bags of coal were found acceptable by these patients on special occasions, such as Christmas or during a fuel crisis. The differences appeared to be, firstly, that they did not have to *ask* for them and, secondly, that they were being given to large categories – the old, or the handicapped, or 'everyone in these houses' – without the necessity to prove individual need.)

The rates of allowances for fuel costs were, at the time of the survey, 30, 60 or 90p a week, and the published guidelines for eligibility (D.H.S.S. leaflet, OC2) combined medical and housing factors in an ingenious way. Either a medical condition (at least restricted mobility) *or* 'difficulty in heating' because of damp or large rooms provided entitlement at the lowest rate, and the higher rates were paid for severer medical conditions (housebound or bedfast) *or* for a combination of both medical and housing factors. These regulations were difficult for the claimants to understand, and some resentment arose because of what they saw as anomalies.

Stories about these anomalies travelled quickly, and dissuaded potential clients from applying. Another factor was distaste for the inspections necessarily involved, and the feeling that the small sums of money involved were 'not worth the bother'. Well-meant suggestions by inspecting officials tended to be rejected with some scorn.

> The account of Mrs Boyne, whose husband of 60 was housebound with bronchitis and longstanding undiagnosed neuralgic pain, was – 'There were two of them, and they stood in the room there and talked to each other about the draughts and sniffed the damp – I felt a bit bad about it, really, as if it was my fault the house's like this. I showed them the paper peeling off in the bedroom, and they said, "He doesn't sleep in this, does he," and I said, "No, he stays in the room, on the sofa." They said, "Would you like an electric fire for here," but electric, no, everyone knows you can't have electric if you're chesty. Well, it would cost too much too, wouldn't it – 30p they said, well, that won't buy much electricity. And he couldn't, with his chest – you'd think they'd have known that.'

Diet and heating allowances have been discussed in detail, as examples showing the factors involved. Other discretionary allowances may be mentioned briefly. Very few people defined themselves as needing help with laundry, although a laundry service or an allowance for commercial laundering would have been of considerable help to handicapped people living alone, or to those looking after the bedfast or incontinent. For similar reasons, only one telephone rental was asked for -- very few people at supplementary benefit level of income had ever had telephones, or considered them as a possibility – and several people had their electricity temporarily cut off, or lost hire-purchase household goods, without considering any application for an exceptional payment. Three families in difficulties over rent arrears and electricity bills were advised by the housing department to go for help to the social work department, but none to the S.B.C. In general, the needs most likely to be perceived by the patients, and most likely to be provided for, were those most closely connected to specific medical diagnoses, those where some formal criteria had been published, and those which would most obviously benefit only the sick or handicapped person himself, and not the other members of his family.

Family income supplement

Two special allowances will be discussed, family income supplement and constant attendance allowance, because these newer provisions provide an interesting contrast. One is provided only for those in full-time work, and the other only for those who cannot work. One is means-tested, the other not, and one is provided on a sliding scale and the other at two fixed rates. The criteria for the supplement are simply low earnings, whatever the causes, and the criteria for the attendance allowance are clinically defined disability, with no reference to individual 'need'.

In fact, neither was found to be used very efficiently. There were six families in the sample who appeared to be eligible for F.I.S., paid to families with dependent children where earnings fall below a given level. One obtained it towards the end of the survey year, and another ceased to be eligible when the father obtained a better job. The other four never applied. It was notable that two of the six bread-winners were registered disabled workers, and the other four filled the criteria for registration but were not registered.

The existence of, and the general principles of, the family income supplement were relatively well known to the survey subjects, and there was no evidence that it was thought of as a stigmatizing benefit. It was spoken of, rather, in the same breath as family allowances, with emphasis on the size of family, rather than inadequacy of earnings, as the qualifying characteristic. It was certainly not spoken of in the same way as supplementary benefit, as something one might 'ask for', but rather as an allowance one might 'have a right to': 'Yes, my sister gets the family supplement, but she has the four children – our wage's just too much to qualify, I think, with us, having only two'. Why, then, did six people not define themselves as eligible?

It appeared to be because of a residual problem concerning means-tested benefits, even in cases where the primary problem of stigma is felt to be less relevant: the fact that the beneficiary who is easiest to define is someone whose affairs are stable, whose income is regular and easy to assess, whereas those who most need the benefit may well be families whose incomes are erratic and whose financial affairs most likely to be in permanent confusion. The concept of 'the' family income, an expression used throughout the official literature, presented these families with problems. Except where large families were concerned, or single-handed mothers, few secure, long-term, full-time employees had wages below family income supplement level. In this sample of physically impaired people, those who were eligible were more likely to be people who found work difficult, who changed jobs frequently, who were often sick or unemployed, and whose hours of work were irregular. Wives might well be earning small casual amounts, and no proper account of these had been kept: they might also be worried (in most cases needlessly) about their income tax position with regard to casual earnings. Not only was it difficult for the families to find examples which they regarded as typical for the 'five consecutive pay-slips' required for their application, but they were also worried because they knew that no statement about their 'family income' would remain accurate for long: they saw themselves as becoming embroiled in an endless series of adjustments and complications.

Mr Stuart, a young man in the early stages of multiple sclerosis, with three young children, expressed these difficulties clearly: 'No, we did get the forms, but we gave up. You see, as far as I can see, if I'm in a good period and doing some overtime then we're above the limit, and the wife does this few hours' cleaning. But then I'll be off and on the sickness, and if I'm really bad the wife has to stay at home too. We're just going from hand to mouth – we don't have an "income" – I can't really say what it is, or what it's going to be next week. There isn't room on the forms to explain, we just gave up.'

Constant attendance allowance

The other special benefit based on principles quite new to the British welfare system is the constant attendance allowance, paid without a means-test, at a higher or a lower rate, to the severely handicapped who require personal care from someone living with them. There were at least six people in the sample who appeared to be eligible for this allowance, but only one had applied for it. The operation of this benefit, widely acclaimed as a step towards a 'disability income' for all impaired people, has caused some controversy and disappointment ever since its inception about a year before the survey began. The intention was to avoid the disadvantages of 'discretionary' benefits by setting precise criteria, removing decisions from local offices to a national agency, and separating the administration of the allowance completely from the existing social security: thus, it was hoped, stigma would be avoided and equity achieved. The reasons why at least five people in this sample declined to apply for it, or appeared to be in an inequitably anomalous position, therefore seem to be of interest.

Despite extensive publicity, lack of information was again a major cause of non-application. As a non-means-tested allowance, it was possibly applicable to many people who had no previous contact with 'welfare', and they were simply not likely to define any 'allowance' as being relevant to them.

One woman, who had cared devotedly for a completely disabled brother for some years, had assumed that the purpose of the allowance was solely to pay for an employed attendant: 'Yes, I had been told by my doctor that there was a government allowance for attendance,' she wrote. 'But I did not apply for it. Living so much off the beaten track as we do, it would have been very difficult to find the right sort of help.'

It was ironic that the novelty of the principle involved was itself a barrier to its acceptance. Several people simply refused to believe that the allowance could possibly be universal: 'Everyone knows that if you get anything extra they take it off your pension, so it's no good applying' was a typical comment from a daughter looking after her mother, who was severely arthritic and unable to walk or rise from a chair without help. One couple who were mistakenly told by a health visitor that the allowance was means-tested and advised to go to the S.B.C. were immediately adamant that nothing would persuade them to apply. Despite the intervention, eventually, of the interviewer to assure them that the S.B.C. were not involved, the couple never made an application. Their original information appeared to them to match well with their impression of welfare benefits; the necessity for proof of financial need, judgment by local officials, and treatment as a suppliant, were what they expected. No assurances could convince them that the distribution of constant attendance allowance could be different.

The one case where an application had been made but refused, and several others where the patients had been advised (probably correctly) that an application would not be successful, demonstrated some of the difficulties of the attempt to use clinical categorizations of social need. It had been realized that to rely upon lists of 'eligible conditions' would produce many anomalies, and an attempt had been made to define disability in real and functional terms. The result was, however, that the criteria laid down were imprecise and open – in the eyes of the patients and sometimes of their doctors – to varying interpretations. The handicapped person had to require 'prolonged and repeated attention', or 'continual supervision in order to avoid substantial danger' – but how were these to be defined? What of a couple who were both disabled? Mr and Mrs Ritchie might both have been eligible for the allowance, but the problem lay in deciding who was looking after whom. And what of people who *ought* to have had continuous supervision, but were in fact sometimes left alone because attendance could not be afforded or organized? Another patient was caring devotedly by day for his wife, who suffered from presenile dementia. At night, she was given sleeping pills before he left for his night-shift job. He would have liked to apply for an allowance, but was worried about disclosing this situation.

These two allowances epitomize some of the dilemmas of providing for the financial needs of chronically ill or disabled people. Eligibility may (as in the cases of F.I.S., supplementary benefit, and many discretionary allowances) be based upon the poverty which is the *effect* of disability. If, in order to tackle the problem of stigma, the allowance is conceived of as a regular pension-like payment, then it is easily applied only to those whose affairs are static and tidy. In the case of the young disabled workers with families for whom F.I.S. would be appropriate, this is most unlikely. A sliding scale of payments means that calculations of entitlement are complicated, and many people near the borderline will – rightly or wrongly – assume that only a small amount will be involved, not worth the trouble. On the other hand, if eligibility is based on the *cause* of need, the clinical condition, then problems arise about the social definition of 'disabled'. Because the category is inherently vague and potentially large, precise criteria have to be used which many people will find disappointingly severe and exclusive. Flat-rate payments mean that the decision to give or withhold, tantamount to a definition of disabled or not disabled, in need or not in need, will always seem unjust to some people.

Moreover, no benefit is perceived by the potential recipients in isolation: their own individual experience is a patchwork of pieces of the system which they fit together into a pattern as best they can. Their perception of one part of the system of money help is influenced by what they know or have experienced of other parts.

THE PATIENTS' ATTITUDES AND THEIR INTERACTION WITH AGENCIES

The previous sections of this chapter have shown that the financial problems of the survey patients arose from many different circumstances. In some cases, hardship arose from muddle and the complexity of the system: many examples of this have been given. That problems *remained*, however, a year later, was in most cases due to the system of financial help not being used. In almost every instance, additional benefits ought to have been available, but were never obtained.

A low level of receipt of, or application for, many benefits has, of course, often been documented before.[3]

In the current survey, an attempt was made, in every case

where benefits were not being received, to find out why. The evidence which has been given suggests that, although ignorance and misinformation were important causes, people's perception of the nature of the welfare system and definition of their own place in it were also crucial.

Advice and referral

The ignorance of the patients, which has been extensively illustrated, was in many cases matched by the ignorance, or dislike of becoming involved in money matters, of those whose advice they sought. Some of the instances of reported misinformation may have been due to misunderstanding by the patient, and others may have been simple slips for which the complexity of the regulations could be blamed.

From whom were they to seek advice? There is no direct evidence about the level of knowledge of social security matters of doctors and other health workers, but it appeared to be low. Even where benefits directly associated with health were concerned, few doctors were able to give precise information about the constant attendance allowance, for instance, or seemed to know all the details of the regulations for exemption from prescription payments. Many general practitioners had indeed advised people living on supplementary benefit, particularly older people living alone, that they should not pay for their prescriptions, or had pointed out to sufferers from certain diseases (notably diabetes) that they could obtain exemption. On the other hand, many younger people, or married couples, who should have been exempted from payment on low-income grounds were still paying for prescriptions. It seemed that their doctors either did not realize what the income levels for exemption were nor how likely patients living on sickness and invalidity benefits were to be below them, or else did not see it as their function to enquire whether people could afford to obtain the drugs they were prescribing.

Similarly, the fact that there were four people in the sample entitled to exemption on the grounds of their particular disease, but still paying for prescriptions, would seem to indicate some ignorance on the doctors' part about the finer details of the regulations.

It must be added that the patients did not see concern or advice on money matters as their doctor's function either, even where the connection with health was plain. No one ever reported having told their doctor that prescription charges were a burden to them, even in those few cases where the cost meant that the drugs were never in fact obtained; no one ever said that they had discussed with their doctor the impossibility of affording the diet recommended. It is only possible to speculate on the reasons for this. The people concerned were likely to be those used to low incomes, and there was no indication in their interaction with the interviewers that they felt their money problems to be a subject they preferred to avoid, or felt awkward or stigmatized in discussing. There was some evidence, however, that they tended to regard their doctors as people who could not possibly understand how 'people like us really live'. Mr Campbell, who had problems about arranging for hospitalization, had never discussed them with his consultant: 'These big doctors – you can't expect them to understand – they don't have to bother with shift pay and benefits and stuff. No, you can't expect them to take this sort of thing into account.' Many patients put on a show for their doctors: on more than one occasion an interviewer was greeted with: 'Oh, thank goodness, it's only you! I thought it was the doctor and I haven't cleaned the room yet!'

Apart from health workers, the patients were in touch with few other people who might advise them about social security problems. A handful of people agreed that they had heard of Citizens' Advice Bureaux, Claimants' Unions, or Community Advice Centres, but only one person (a taxi-driver) had ever actually approached one of these organizations. Medical social workers did quite often give advice at the time of hospitalization, but this would obviously be likely to refer to situations which were only temporary. Some of the people who were the long-term clients of social workers were in a better position, but these were few; the greater number of contacts in the sample with the social work department were simple, single requests or enquiries about a specific service.

In any case, in the relatively few examples of extended social-worker contact, it did not always appear that their social security problems had been efficiently dealt with, for several of these people were entitled to benefits that they were not receiving. In two or three cases it was the subject of money which, according to the client, had soured the relationship with the social worker.

Mr Lyall, for instance, wholly disabled and bedfast, and with a wife who was also partially paralysed, was very dependent upon welfare help. Occasionally the couple expressed themselves as grateful for a social worker's support, but their problems sprang largely from the inadequacy of their income and at regular intervals some financial question led to friction. 'She goes stiff if you mention money – it's like a dirty word,' Mr Lyall said.

Similarly, Mr Miller, a young family man with a progressive disabling disease, went to seek the advice of a social worker about his problems, which he was defining in entirely practical terms. In particular, he wanted a confused social security position clarified. He returned a little bewildered: 'I don't really know what was going on. I just wanted these forms filled in. She kept on talking about the disease – what I felt about it – what the wife felt about it. Coming to terms with it. All I want to come to terms with is these forms!'

Examples of a conflict of definitions such as this between client and social worker, where the client is seeing his problem in purely practical (and often financial) terms, but perceives the social worker as giving the encounter some other meaning, are closely paralleled in other studies.[4]

The relationship between social workers and officials of the D.H.S.S., at local levels, is commonly acknowledged by both to be not without problems. Their different positions in the system make this almost inevitable. One is staffed by civil servants, applying intricate formal regulations and entrusted in part with guarding the public purse, the other by professionals whose training emphasizes flexibility and the welfare of the individual. Social workers see themselves as caring for the 'whole person'; by statute, they are responsible (in the case of the disabled) for some of his practical needs, but they are also interested in helping with his family and socio-psychological problems. Officials of the D.H.S.S. are concerned strictly with practical need, but necessarily find themselves involved in making enquiries about family situations and relationships. Both may be asking the same questions, yet may see themselves as performing rather different tasks. They may be expected to have very different systems of categorization of their clients. Since it is the evidence of this survey that many people, especially those in infrequent contact with welfare agencies, could not distinguish between them and often did not know whom they were talking to, the potentiality for conflict and confusion is obvious.

Social workers are very conscious of the difficulties of their position where the disbursing of money is concerned. A great deal of their time may be spent in trying to disentangle the social security problems of clients, and some workers feel that this is not their proper function. There are some situations where immediate and exceptional cash payments are the obvious and only solution, yet workers are unhappy in this role also. A social work administrator interviewed for this study said: 'We can keep on doing the fire-brigading, but operating this way we'll never change things, never do more than just keep pace with situations. We pick up the pieces with emergency cash – and so often we find it shouldn't be necessary, the people are living below the official poverty-line. We shouldn't be doing this – we should be getting on with the environmental and personal problems.'

Stevenson,[5] in her report as Social Work Advisor to the Supplementary Benefits Commission, found that social workers were often reluctant to approach the S.B.C. for discretionary grants, and resented having to 'make a case out' to officials whom they did not regard as professionals. On the other hand, the S.B.C. sometimes lacked confidence in the social workers' objectivity. In her perceptive analysis of the interaction between the two agencies, this author points out that while any duplication of functions in giving financial help produces obvious problems, the complete separation of casework and financial power is not satisfactory either, since it can result in stereotypes of the social worker as giver, and the S.B.C. as withholder, which may affect the way in which services are perceived and used by the clients.

An additional complication was added, in the cases under consideration, by the fact that some patients reported having been referred to charitable agencies both by the social work department and by the supplementary benefits office. In two cases gifts in cash or kind had in fact been obtained as emergency relief from voluntary agencies. While the intention may well have been to underline the distinction between statutory provision and charity, and thus remove any stigma from the official agencies, the effect was almost the reverse. To be referred to what was unequivocally a charity was seen as a deliberate degradation, especially if it meant calling in person at different offices and repeating one's story of misfortune, and the association only tainted the official agencies in the client's eyes.

> The daughter of Mrs Murdoch, who was nursing her bedfast and incontinent mother (both were living on supplementary benefit) tried to obtain a grant for extra sheets: she was sent from the supplementary benefits office to the social work department, and thence to the R.W.V.S., and found the experience degrading and humiliating: 'Begging, that's what it was! We've never had to beg before.'

Attitudes to supplementary benefit

In an attempt to reduce the stigma of charitable 'relief', the trend throughout recent welfare history has been to move first one group of recipients and then another from the 'discretionary' sector to 'benefits as of right'.

However, the more comprehensive the system of 'rights' becomes, the wider the gulf that exists between it and discretionary benefits – a gulf symbolized by the physical separation of the offices administering national insurance benefits on the one hand, and supplementary benefits on the other. Despite attempts to bridge this gap (and despite the fact that the distinction is now largely illusory, since insurance contributions rarely in fact pay for the benefits to which they are hypothetically allocated) the survey subjects were very conscious of its existence. Indeed, measures designed to bridge the gap in one way may only open out new divisions in others: as Stevenson pointed out, the issue of order-books to be cashed at a Post Office to some classes of supplementary benefit recipients, a beneficial measure in that it avoided the need for elderly and chronically ill people to queue for their money every week, created new distinctions because it meant that the 'caller' population of the S.B.C., largely the unemployed or people in a crisis situation, became a new lower class of client.

This was one reason why various groups of people in the survey expressed such very different views about the S.B.C. Some older people appeared to have a comfortable and secure-feeling relationship with the offices of 'social security'. They were uncomplaining clients, whose circumstances did not change, and they had never been made to feel that they were accepting charity. The routine nature of their interaction with officials allowed them to look upon their benefits as a pension, and they talked about their incomes as though they were wholly within the national insurance, non-discretionary, sector instead of being wholly or partly in the supplementary benefit sector.

Mr and Mrs Rennie may be instanced as typical: he suffered from severe epilepsy and they had been living on invalidity benefit with a supplementary benefit addition for some five years. They deliberately kept all their transactions with the D.H.S.S. as impersonal as possible, writing letters or filling in forms with great care, but avoiding personal contact. They described the forms as 'as bad as the forms you used to fill in for Income Tax, some of them' which seemed to indicate that they regarded them not as a humiliating intrusion into their private affairs, but simply as part of the routine of government's financial give and take. They accepted the drawbacks of what they saw as, and treated as, a bureaucratic system with amused resignation, and liked to talk of its peculiarities ('Governments always give with one hand and take away with the other, don't they!' 'Five pence, the increase was, it's an insult to give it to you, but it's the system, I suppose they have to keep the pennies right') and of their ideas for its improvement. Only once did Mr Rennie go to the S.B.C. in person (in connection with a rent rebate query) and he reported with some surprise: 'I've no complaints – they were nice as can be – very considerate and polite.' He was, however, full of horror about the other clients he saw there, and the experience only confirmed his belief that he and his wife were somehow different, and 'entitled to' their benefit rather than suppliants for extra.

On the other hand, those people whose circumstances were not routine, who approached the S.B.C. in emergencies, as a last resort and perhaps for the first time, saw the encounter quite differently. This was particularly likely if they were not clearly and obviously disabled, or not approaching retirement age.

Mr McKenzie, for instance, the young man who left his job 'voluntarily' to care for his family, was very bitter and resentful about his first contact with 'the welfare'. 'What a rigmarole it was to get any benefit', his wife said, 'we had as many forms to fill in and he felt degraded having to go and ask, he's aye worked and never asked before.'

It must be emphasized that much of the distaste for any association with 'the security' arose from myth or misunderstanding, rather than from contemporary experience. The regulations concerning the 'tariff income' from capital, to be set against calculation of supplementary benefit, were one fruitful source of myth. Almost every patient to whom the question might be relevant had a different account, repeated with great conviction, of the rules about capital or possessions. Various sums were offered as the limit of savings which precluded any right to benefit – including the sum of £325, in fact the level at which any reduction of benefit *began*. It was widely and inaccurately held that personal possessions would be inspected and valued, and that 'you would have to sell anything you owned, you know, before you got security – you couldn't keep your own house, for instance.'

People who did apply for supplementary benefit soon learned that these things were not true, but the legends left an after-image. The necessary visits of D.H.S.S. officers were anticipated with some defensiveness and fear, and though sometimes the patients reported afterwards, with some surprise, that 'they were really nice and helpful', they were also very quick to take offence. In dealing with people who were already in an equivocal and touchy state about the decision to ask for help, the ambiguities of a combined role of helper and inspector were probably difficult to reconcile.

Memories of some long-past experiences (and whether they were 'true' memories or accretions around a painful episode of social failure is not necessarily relevant) were related again and again.

> Mr and Mrs McRobbie referred to the supplementary benefits commission as 'the U.A.B – them that can make up your money or give you a little extra,' and explained, 'We'll never have, we just make do. Folks that's workit all their life dinna' get it – there's a lot of favouritism in the social services – people that's in need dinna get, like us. I can't afford stockings, and we get our clothes from the Thrift Shop, there's no holidays for us. I'm not going to the U.A.B., though – we tried, years ago that was, and they refused us. Them that works in the U.A.B., they say they'll help you, but when you actually go they won't give anything, you'd think they were giving out of their own pockets. Maybe I'll phone and get someone to come down here, you can do that now, but I'm not going up there to be abused.' In fact, Mrs McRobbie never did phone.

Another woman explained her reluctance to ask for help by a confused story of conflict and humiliation involving an 'inspector', which she eventually admitted had occurred twenty-three years before. Relationships with agencies cast reflections not only from one to the other, but from the past to the present.

Welfare and 'rights'

The difference between the unacceptable and the acceptable was not simply between contributory and non-contributory benefits, since as this and other surveys have shown, people were not always sure which category any specific payment came into.[6] Nor was it simply a difference between 'universalist' and 'selectivist' principles, for a great number of the relevant benefits were in a hybrid category in any case.

If benefits were to be acceptable, the clients had to be able to *look upon them* as 'rights'. There were various characteristics by which 'rights' could be recognized.

For instance, their administration should be courteous and impartial:

> Mr Mearns, whose confused affairs represented a considerable amount of work for the D.H.S.S., felt very strongly about this: 'The way I see it is, the social security system the way they run it is an insult to the individual, the person. It's neither one thing nor the other. It's meant to be your right but they don't treat you as if it was. For instance, they won't tell you their names, so you can write them or ask for them on the phone. You never know who you're dealing with. They told me: 'We're not allowed to give our names because we're Civil Servants!' I ask you! Who are civil servants – to my mind nurses are civil servants. They *serve*. These people at the security deny the name. It's an ignominy, dealing with anonymous people. They know *our* name.' At a later date, after some difficulty about adjustments of benefit, Mr Mearns complained: 'Why won't they accept letters, like any other business does? I can write to the electricity, or the H.P. firm, I daresay I could write to my bank manager if I had one! But they told me, "Letters are irrelevant," they said only the form is taken notice of. That's how this bother arose – there isn't *room* on the form to explain anyway.'

Entitlement should be clear. If people were sure that they 'ought' to receive something, they might apply for it, but they were reluctant if there seemed to be any chance of refusal. They would much rather reconcile themselves to going without, than expose themselves to possible rejection.

> Mrs Marr who, like her husband, was about 60 and incapacitated by chronic illness, refused to consider even a simple enquiry about exemption from prescription charges – 'I don't know what to do – I'd hate to go and ask a stranger about it, and I don't know whether we're entitled for the bronchitis or whether they'd say we couldn't afford it. Anyway, now we've got the son and his wife living here we shouldn't be entitled, would we? We wouldn't like to ask in case we got refused. That would make you feel bad, to get refused, as if you'd been asking for something.'

'Rights' should also be 'fair' and justly distributed. A relatively high proportion of the sample (some 25 people in all) are recorded as having, at some time, offered unsolicited comments to interviewers on the frequency with which 'welfare' was abused. It was notable that these were much more likely to be people who had *themselves* had some contact with the supplementary benefits commission, or dispute about benefits. They were also more likely to be men than women, and older rather than younger people.[7]

It was difficult to estimate how important these widely expressed attitudes were. In part, they simply demonstrated a generation gap: people who had brought up their own families on a few pounds a week many years before finding it difficult to adjust to new money values. In part, they seemed to be a device, on the part of those who felt they might be stigmatized for dependency, to define a lower group from whom they could be distinguished. They themselves were the 'respectable' poor. The hypothetical existence of a large body of 'scroungers', 'lay-abouts', 'people that milk the system', appeared to have less effect upon behaviour than might be expected, largely because for people *whom they knew*, the survey subjects were usually ready to find some more acceptable category: 'Of course, his health's always been poor,' 'They're getting on now,' 'She does her best for the children.' Nevertheless, these widely held beliefs did influence people's perception of the 'fairness' of the system, and if they affected behaviour at all it was in the direction of 'I can't be bothered, it is all unfair anyway' rather than 'I am one of those who deserve to use the system, therefore I will do so.'

The subjects thought that in a 'fair' system, eligible

categories should preferably be defined by the 'factual' characteristics which were the causes of poverty – sickness, inability to work, age – rather than by poverty itself, which seemed to the patients a relative concept. Many of the poorer survey subjects discussed this with some sophistication. 'How hard up you are depends on what you've been used to. Youngsters get used to too much these days – they're the ones who are going to be poor one day.' 'I'd suppose you'd say we haven't much. But it depends on who's doing the judging, doesn't it? I suppose we'd all be poor to a millionaire.' 'We don't see ourselves as *poverty-stricken*. It's the old folks I'm sorry for – year after year – not going to get any better. But only last year we were earning good money – a hundred pounds and more I'd have in that cupboard, many a time, I don't know where it went to – now we've got this trouble with him not being able to work, we're entitled to help. Taxes all those years – it's to look after people who have special troubles, when it's no fault of their own, isn't it?'

The major distinguishing characteristic of 'rights', however, was that contributions and receipts should be clearly linked. It was not national insurance contributions only that were relevant (though this, being the clearest link, was to be preferred): people were, or had been, ratepayers and therefore they had a clear right to special housing if they needed it on the grounds of their special characteristics, or to home helps if they came into the proper categories, or to other services clearly seen as being part of 'the City's' administration. Many people called the national insurance contribution the 'health stamp', and believed firmly that it provided all the revenue for the health service; having paid it, they had a right to treatment. If their insurance record did not, in fact, entitle them to benefits or pensions, then they either fell back upon having been taxpayers, or expressed clearly a sense of the essential interdependence of citizens in a complex society: 'Them that works pays for them that can't, it's only right.'

SUMMARY

About 20 per cent of the whole sample found that they had money problems during the year after their hospitalization. Over half of these problems remained unsolved. Problems arose because of the special expenses of impairment, because of the complexity and confusion of the system of help, and because of the ignorance, misinformation, or attitudes of the patients. Many problems arose about six months *after* the illness or accident, rather than immediately.

In this sample of 194 people, 8 were found who were living below supplementary benefit level, and many more – at least 20 – who appeared to be eligible for discretionary additions to their basic income which they were not receiving. Discretionary benefits were more likely to be received if they represented a medically rather than a socially defined need and were exclusively for the sick or disabled person himself rather than his family.

It is suggested that the attitudes of the clients to the welfare system are a particularly important factor, influenced by their perception of the mechanisms of help. Analysis of the patients' comments on their help-seeking experiences and their reported reasons for not applying for benefits suggests that they had a sophisticated – if varied – view of the system as a whole. The predominating concept in their minds was 'fairness'. Disliking 'charity', they found benefits acceptable only if they could look upon them as rights. The characteristics of rights, in their eyes, were that they should be allotted to clearly defined categories (on the basis, for instance, of age, family size, nature of disability, rather than poverty, which was not felt to be a sufficiently clear category), that benefits should be clearly linked to contributions (whether through national insurance or in some more general way), and that they should be seen to be distributed in an equitable and business-like way.

The people most likely to have problems seemed to be those who found themselves in equivocal positions (severely disabled *and* working, 'voluntarily' unemployed, only partially within the national insurance system), or those who could not reconcile their definition of their needs with their definition of their rights.

REFERENCES

1. See, e.g. Harris, Amelia I, Smith, C. R. W. and Head, Elizabeth. *Income and Entitlement to Supplementary Benefit of Impaired People in Great Britain* (Part III of *Handicapped and Impaired in*

Great Britain, H.M.S.O., London, 1972; Maclean, Mavis and Jefferys, Margot, 'Disability and Deprivation' in Wedderburn, D. (ed.), *Poverty and Class Structure*, Cambridge University Press, 1974; Townsend, P., *The Disabled in Society*, Greater London Association for the Disabled, London, 1967.

2. Aberdeen University Liberal Society and Aberdeen City Young Liberals, *Old and Cold in Aberdeen*, 1973.
3. See, e.g. *Circumstances of Families*, Ministry of Social Security, London, H.M.S.O. 1967; Harris, A. I., Smith, C. R. W. and Head, E., *Income and Entitlement to Supplementary Benefit of Impaired People in Great Britain*, op. cit; Hill, M. J., Harrison, R. M., Sergent, A. V. and Talbot, V., *Men Out of Work*, Cambridge University Press, 1973.
4. Mayer, J. E. and Timms, N., *The Client Speaks*, London, Routledge and Kegan Paul, 1970; Rees, S., 'No More than Contact: the Outcome of Social Work', *B. J. Social Work*, 4.3, 1974, p. 255.
5. Stevenson, Olive, *Claimant or Client?* London, George Allen and Unwin, 1973, p. 53.
6. See, e.g. Hill *et al.*, op. cit., p. 86.
7. Pinker, R. A. and Maclean, Mavis, *Dependency and Welfare*, S.S.R.C. Report, 1974, reported similar findings.

6
JOB PROBLEMS

There is no doubt that working life is one of the most important areas where problems may arise for the physically impaired. For many people, especially those with little education, training or skill, a single serious illness or accident which leaves them a little less fit than they were before can mean a sudden change in their whole life pattern. If a man has only his strength to offer to the labour market, he may become devalued overnight. He may be able to remake his life, or he may not. On the other hand, chronic or recurrent illness can set in motion a slow downward spiral. Again, there may be points where it could be arrested, where official or family and community resources could provide a new start. Rarely, a man in this position may himself find the resources to re-plan his life, to take definite and positive steps to break out of a vicious circle. For the most part, he is likely to feel trapped in an environment too powerful for him to overcome by his own efforts.

The connection between sickness and disability on the one hand, and unemployment, under-employment and downward mobility on the other, has been well documented, especially with regard to unemployment. Every survey of the unemployed shows that health problems are prominent,[1] and every study of the impaired shows that a high proportion are unemployed, or lacking in training and skills, when compared to the general population. The national survey of the *Handicapped and Impaired in Great Britain,*[2] for instance, showed unequivocally how youthful disabilities interrupt or restrict education and make it more difficult for people to acquire skills and qualifications.

Two ways in which this may operate may be illustrated from the present survey:

Alexander Shearer, a young diabetic who also had a congenital abnormality, had been defined as 'dull normal', and his medical and employment records continually stressed his limited intelligence. At first acquaintance, this seemed odd, for he appeared to be a lively and articulate young man, though it was true that some aspects of his behaviour – blatant ignoring of his diet sheets, allowing his social security affairs to become unnecessarily muddled – seemed difficult to explain. Only later did the truth emerge: because he had been intermittently ill since early childhood, in the care of an over-protective mother burdened with financial and other problems, his schooling had been virtually non-existent and he was almost illiterate. This fact, and the stratagems of concealment which had become second nature to him, appeared to be responsible for the label of limited intelligence, and he was treated by all those agencies in contact with him as though he were barely employable.

In the second example, the young man concerned was particularly conscious of the way in which he had been deprived, as an adolescent, of skills and qualifications, because he had eventually managed to break away from the restricted pathway set before him:

Peter Campbell, congenitally partially paralysed, described with great feeling how his whole childhood was shadowed by his mother's gloomy view of his future: 'There was never any point planning, I'd never get a job.' When he left school, his family, teachers and youth employment officer joined forces to persuade him that he must have an 'easy' job, and he worked for some years in poorly paid jobs in shops, where he saw no future prospects, felt awkward and stigmatized, and was very unhappy. Eventually, about the time of his marriage, he decided to 'stand on his own feet' and find 'real work', and he was fortunate enough to find a firm willing to train him for skilled work compatible with his disability. Properly trained, and earning a high wage on equal terms with his workmates, he no longer considered himself to be handicapped in any way.

The association between disability and unemployment or under-employment is not, however, confined to those disabled at birth or in their youth. The National Survey also showed that older people, many of them disabled in later life, are still disproportionately unskilled.

This association has fostered the setting-up of various special provisions in the employment field. At the same time, however, the association has unfortunate effects: as the categories of 'the impaired' and 'the poor' may come to be confused, as was shown in the previous chapter, so also the category of 'the impaired' may come to overlap with that of 'the disadvantaged' – the unskilled, the unemployable, or the work-shy – in the field of employment, and this may affect not only the type of helping services offered but also the clients' perception of them. It was argued in Chapter 1 that the historical emphasis on the moral value of employment to the individual, as well as its economic value to society, ensured that some of the first services specifically for the disabled should be in the field of employment. An echo and corollary of this is the fact that the first and most unequivocal 'disabled' label that is offered to an impaired person may well be the Department of Employment's 'Registered Disabled Person'. What 'disabled' means in this context, and what its relationship is to other 'disadvantaged' labels, will be discussed in this chapter by examining the nature of the job problems experienced by the people in the sample and the mechanisms by which they were, or were not, solved.

The definition of job problems

The meaning of 'solved' in this context must first be examined. In the literature of social policy and administration, the term commonly used for the solving of problems connected with working life is 'rehabilitation'. Rehabilitation has, of course, a wider meaning; it is used, particularly in a medical context, to mean the restoration of the best possible degree of functioning within the limits of an impairment. Total functioning in social life is, however, not easy to measure, while the simple indicator of whether a man, is or is not, earning his living, besides being appropriate in an economically oriented society, is also easy to apply.

Therefore, many studies of rehabilitation have always used simple employment or unemployment as their indicator of success or failure in any given programme of training or treatment. This may be an appropriate measuring-tool in specific cases: in general, however, to view rehabilitation as synonymous with gainful employment bears little relationship to the reality of people's lives. There were men in the sample struggling arduously and painfully, but nevertheless successfully, to do jobs which were really beyond their reduced physical capacity; on the other hand there were men bored and resentful because the only jobs they could get were, they thought, below their capabilities.

In keeping with the principle observed throughout this study, that it is the patient's own perception which is, for him, the reality, the definition of job problems has been based on the question – 'Is this situation satisfactory to the individual concerned, taking into account whatever irreparable degree of physical impairment remains?' Thus, a man who is continuing to do the same job as before may have a problem, if he finds it very difficult or feels that his impairment is prejudicing the future as he had seen it. So has a man who is poorly employed because, for instance, he is in need of help towards better mobility. A man who is unemployed has a problem if he wishes to work, and a man who is incapable of work has a problem if he is bored and lonely and anxious for at least some useful occupation. On the other hand, a man who is technically unemployed does not necessarily have a job problem, if in fact he has no wish to work.

The position of women may be even more equivocal. In this sample, with its high proportion of people over 40, the majority of women were married and so might have the formal alternative to employment of 'household duties'. Fifty-nine per cent of the married women or widows in the sample were genuinely in the labour market at the beginning of the survey year. Many women do not appear in unemployment statistics, however, though desperately seeking work, because they are not fully within the national insurance system. On the other hand, many are for a time formally defined as unemployed when in fact they have voluntarily left the labour market. Thus, for women, even more than for men, the true extent of job problems and the official label of unemployment may be far apart.

The extent and nature of job problems

A general analysis will first be offered of the extent of job problems as they were perceived by the people in the sample. At their hospitalization, 165 of the total of 194 were formally in the labour market (i.e. they were within the national insurance system as employed people, rather than being a wife occupied with household duties, or a non-working widow, or a person defined as permanently incapable of any work). In fact, however, 8 of these were not in the labour market in any real sense, since they already regarded themselves as retired or (in the case of married women) returned to household duties and had no thought of working again.

The distribution of types of occupation of the 157 people truly in the labour market is shown in Table 6:1, and is compared with that found in Scotland by the national survey of the *Handicapped and Impaired* and also with the general

Table 6:1 Distribution of types of occupation (per cent)

	This sample			*Handicapped and Impaired* in Scotland (Harris, 1971)	*General Population* Scotland, 1971
	M	F	All		
Professional	4	8	5	3	3
Employers and managerial	10	0	7	8	10
Other non-manual	11	20	14	19	27
Personal service	4	22	9	7	6
Foremen and supervisors	8	0	5	5	2
Skilled manual	28	7	22	21	24
Semi-skilled manual	16	14	16	19	17
Unskilled manual	19	29	22	18	10
Armed Forces	0	0	0	0	1

national distribution (Scotland) of the Registrar General.

The agreement of this small sample with the National Survey is striking, especially since a greater proportion of these subjects might be expected to be *newly* impaired and disadvantaged. This would seem to suggest that those who become physically impaired are likely to be those who – perhaps because of a previous poor health history – are already disadvantaged.

Ninety-three of these 157 found that their physical impairment presented them with some difficulty concerning their work during the survey year. Less than half of these – 42 – found solutions to their problems by the end of the year, and a further 16 people decided to 'retire' or return to household duties. Thirty-five were left with unsolved job problems a year after this illness or accident. The characteristics of these groups are shown in Table 6:2.

Obviously, physical impairment is more likely to cause problems for manual workers than for non-manual ones, and semi- or unskilled workers are less likely to be able to solve their difficulties and continue to work. Unexpectedly, however, age did not appear to be very important, at least below sixty. Half the working women, and nearly two-thirds of the men, had some problem over their work. A crude categorization of the nature of the solved and unsolved job problems of these 93 people is shown in Table 6:3.

A very high proportion – 33 people out of the total of 157 in the labour market – were in categories (2), (3) and (4)

Table 6:2 Characteristics of those people who had job problems (at any time during the survey year, numbers of people)

	All those technically in the labour market (165 people)					
	Working, no problems (64)	Not truly in labour market (8)	Problems solved (42)	Problems unsolved (35)	'Retired' (16)	Total (165)
Sex						
Male	40	4	34	27	9	114
Female	24	4	8	8	7	51
Age						
<40	17	0	11	11	0	39
40–49	16	2	9	10	2	39
50–59	24	3	14	13	4	58
60–64	7	3	8	1	10	29
Work						
Non-manual	30	1	8	9	4	52
Skilled manual	17	3	21	10	3	54
Semi- and unskilled manual	17	4	13	16	9	59

Table 6:3 Nature of job problems and outcome (numbers of people)

	All those who had job problems (93 people)						
	Problems solved (42)		Problems unsolved (35)		'Retired' (16)		Total (93)
	M	F	M	F	M	F	
1. Already unemployed and anxious to find work	0	1	7	1	7	1	17
2. Dismissed from job and anxious to find another	4	1	3	2	0	0	10
3. Left job voluntarily and anxious to find another	2	1	1	0	0	4	8
4. Left job because physically incapable of it and anxious to find another	4	3	1	3	2	2	15
5. Demoted to job which was felt to be inferior	0	0	4	0	0	0	4
6. Problems about travelling to work	0	0	1	1	0	0	2
7. Retained job, but lighter conditions of work permanently necessary	8	2	10	1	0	0	21
8. Retained job, but lighter conditions of work required for a period	16	0	0	0	0	0	16

of Table 6:3, that is, they left their jobs as a direct result of this illness or accident. Forty-three other people retained the same job, or an adaptation of it, only with some difficulty. The categories of problem were spread across all age-groups and all types of occupation, except that a high proportion of those in categories (7) and (8), people who did not lose their jobs but were in need of lighter work for a temporary period or permanently, were in skilled manual jobs. Semi- or unskilled manual workers were more likely to be in categories (1) to (4), that is, to find themselves unemployed.

Employment and degree of impairment

Obviously the degree and nature of the physical impairment, together with the nature of his work, necessarily affect a man's difficulties in his job. A slight crippling disability might cause no trouble for a non-manual worker but make heavy manual work impossible, while few people's work would not be affected by complete paralysis. Excluding the two extremes of very slight impairment and total functional incapacity, however, it was very noticeable that there was no simple and direct relationship between degree of impairment and job problems. There were quite severely disabled people who nevertheless felt that their working life was very satisfactory:

Mr Hunter, a skilled worker in his 40s, had suffered from severe osteo-arthritis since adolescence. His back was severely bent and his walking ability very limited, but he had worked for the same firm for twenty years and was obviously a valued supervisory employee.

Again, James Hutcheson, a severely epileptic young man with slight deafness and slow speech, very firmly denied (as did his parents) that he had ever been stigmatized in his employment (as a 'disabled' person) or met with any problems, and certainly there was evidence during this particular illness episode that his manager and workmates were friendly and considerate, and thought highly of him as a worker.

There were many similar cases of people with a considerable degree of disability who were nevertheless at work without problems. On the other hand, quite minor impairments might frequently result in serious work difficulties: a single myocardial infarction, for instance, from which a man made an excellent recovery, could nevertheless cost him his job if he were a bus or lorry driver, and he might have difficulty in finding another.

Two common patterns could be observed: the abrupt discontinuity in the worker's career, where he suddenly found his whole life pattern altered, and the slow downward drift into ever less well-paid or enjoyable jobs, and finally into bored unemployment and invalidity. The first was likely, of course, to be associated with accidents or acute illnesses, and the second with chronic diseases, but the association was not invariable; it was possible for either to be the result of any type or time-pattern of impairment.

An example of the downward drift might be the career of Brian Wallace, whose chronic 'stomach trouble' had begun during Army service in the Far East many years before. For reasons which seemed good to him at the time, he had not sought a discharge on health grounds, so that the possibly advantageous label of 'service-disabled' was not available to him. He had an excellent record as an N.C.O. and on discharge had no difficulty about getting a supervisor's job. A long period of intermittent absence through sickness lost him this job, and he became a bus driver. Back trouble, apparently difficult to diagnose, was now added to his gastric complaint; he acquired an orthopaedic corset and lost his Public Service Vehicle licence. Eventually he underwent a partial gastrectomy, after which he became an attendant at a garage. His back pain did not improve, and he was passed without success from orthopaedic to neurological specialists. At the end of the survey year he had been unemployed for 14 months and spoke very bitterly of being 'thrown on the scrap-heap'. He applied for many sedentary jobs, always enclosing copies of his glowing, but by now rather old, service testimonials. 'You've got to face it', he said, 'I'm only a garage attendant now. Who's going to give a responsible office job to a garage attendant? I know I'm worth better than this but how can I prove it?' He felt he had slipped downhill very gradually and had not at any time been offered help from anyone. He was in arrears with his rent and threatened with eviction, and his wife, also chronically ill, could not help the family finances.

The sudden crisis which appeared likely to lead to the same sort of downward mobility might be a crippling accident, or the onset of a progressively disabling disease, but it might also be an unexpected illness which was not necessarily or intrinsically disabling:

James Andrews was a self-employed builder of 28, used to high earnings and giving the impression, at the beginning of the survey year, of a man who felt himself to be completely the master of his own life. A heart attack which he insisted was completely unexpected coincided with the birth of a third child to his young wife, and the world seemed to fall about this young family's head. At one point Mrs Andrews said explicitly, 'Everything's suddenly gone wrong. We're going downhill when it all looked so good. All the time it's getting worse – scratching for money, and he goes out to do a job and can't finish it and comes back so grey it frightens me, what are we going to do? What if there's a depression, with people down the street looking for food. We're not going to be caught like that – our children mustn't go without. I get frightened.' For the whole of the survey year the couple seemed to be thrashing about desperately, looking for overnight solutions to their problems, and planning and rejecting one ambitious scheme after another for retrieving themselves. To seek modest employment with someone else, or to accept the retraining which was suggested by the Department of Employment, seemed too slow and arduous a solution to be acceptable. The N.I. complications of the self-employed, added to some attempt at concealment of minor earnings, led to accelerating money problems, until debts accumulated which there seemed little possibility of ever paying off.

Unemployment

Table 6:3 showed that 17 people formally within the labour market were unemployed at this hospitalization. This is a high proportion, which underlines the effect of chronic illness or disability upon unemployment statistics. Thirty-three further people became unemployed as a result of this illness or accident, so that 50 men and women, or 32 per cent of all those in the labour market, were unemployed at some time during the year. As Table 6:4 shows, they were most likely to be men without skills, in their fifties.

Table 6:4 Characteristics of those people who were technically 'unemployed' (at any time during the survey year, numbers of people)

	The unemployed (50 people) who were		
	Looking for work (39)	Not expecting to work again (11)	Total (50)
Sex			
Male	27	4	31
Female	12	7	19
Age			
<40	8	0	8
40–49	5	3	8
50–59	19	3	22
60–64	7	5	12
Work			
Non-manual	6	2	8
Skilled manual	11	4	15
Semi- and unskilled manual	22	5	27

Ten people were dismissed from their job immediately after this illness, although there was no medical reason why they should not have returned to it. Most of them were casual shop, garage or labouring workers and few expressed any great surprise or resentment. They appeared to take it for granted that 'they'll have to get someone else' or 'they couldn't keep the job open for more than a few weeks'. There is, of course, no proof that the illness absence was the sole reason for their dismissal, and there was at least one case where it eventually became clear that the man had been about to be dismissed for other reasons, but the illness was at least the occasion of their losing their jobs. Eight people took the opportunity to leave their jobs voluntarily, deciding to try to change at this point from a job which they found unsatisfactory. Fifteen left by mutual agreement because the job was now impossible in view of their impairment, though they still wished to do some sort of work: three of these had been self-employed.

Sixteen of those people who were looking for work managed to find satisfactory jobs (those who 'retired' will be discussed later), though four or them had to wait for six months, and six were unemployed almost to the end of the survey year. Thirteen were still seeking work at the end of the year. Conspicuously, those who were already unemployed had less favourable outcomes than those who became newly unemployed.

It seemed that 'unemployed' was the dominant label being applied to them. The fact that they had been ill did not alter their status for the Department of Employment (except to relieve them temporarily of the obligation to 'sign on'), had no effect upon their income, and did not, it seemed, define them as someone whose working future the medical profession ought to be concerned with. 'Occupation: unemployed' was firmly written on their medical records (of course, some people, feeling that the label would be stigmatizing, concealed the fact that they were not working) and there was no example of anyone in this category reporting that doctors had asked them about their working future. Implicit categorizations available to those who were employed: 'a man who is going to have difficulty in doing his job, and needs advice', 'a man who may need help because his previous work will be impossible', 'a man who should be referred to the Department of Employment for special help' seemed never to be applied to the already unemployed, even though their position might in fact be entirely similar: this illness or accident might equally involve a change in the sort of work they were able to do. To become unemployed because of an impairment might not only set into operation helping mechanisms – from officials and doctors but more frequently from friends and relations – but also leave the patient determined to find another job himself. Circumstances offered him a natural timetable: 'As soon as this convalescent period is over I will find work', and often some resentment served as a spur: 'I didn't like that job anyway, and this gives me the opportunity to find a better one.' To become further impaired while already unemployed, however, seemed to have a depressing effect. The illness and convalescence were simply a holiday from the obligation to seek work, and the patient's confidence in himself was further shaken by any additional impairment.

The unemployed who are not actively seeking work – the 'work-shy' or 'voluntarily unemployed' – are sometimes believed to be a large and well-defined category, defining people with personality characteristics of a morally reprehensible sort. Doctors might use this category without overt condemnation as a mode of explanation, a psychological diagnosis. Employment officials might use it in a more explicitly censorious way. The survey subjects themselves used it very frequently, especially applying it to people younger than themselves, as a category overlapping with that of 'scroungers', 'people who milk the social security system'.

An examination of those people in the sample with a long-term formal label of 'unemployed', however, shows how arbitrary a category it is, where any physical impairment is involved. Various indicators were used to decide whether the patient was being considered as 'work-shy', by whom and with what degree of certainty – the willingness of the general practitioner to provide certificates of incapacity, the reports of examining doctors, the number and nature of the jobs the Department of Employment required him to apply for, his descriptions of interviews with employment and social security officials. It very rarely appeared that women or older men were being so categorized. Amongst younger men, however, there were several formally defined as 'long-term unemployed' when their physical condition might well have merited the category of 'invalid', while there were others with a lesser degree of ill-health who acquired the more favourable label with its less stringent obligations. Only the less seriously disabled are relevant here, of course, since they were considered to be in the labour market. At this level of relatively minor disability or chronic illness, the problems of defining 'fit to work' were at their most obvious. Fit for what work? Fit by whose definition? Was there in any case likely to be suitable work available?

There were several cases in which different agencies appeared to be applying different definitions:

> Mr Kinnaird (p. 94) appeared to be defined as having left his sheltered job ('without good cause') because he did not want to work, when in fact his object had been to find 'real' work and he found idleness intolerable. Medically he was defined as someone for whom work would be difficult to find, who had no real obligation to work, and so his idleness was taken for granted. He was in contact only minimally with any agency: in another case, that of Mr Robert Thomson, many different agencies were involved, each with its own categorization of the client. He had suffered for many years from a variety of symptoms, but a series of in-patient examinations could find no significant diagnosis. To the hospital doctors, he was a malingerer who was wasting their time: they dismissed him summarily. His own definition of his condition, however, was that he was quite unfit for work: he was caring, single-handed, for five school-age children and had little energy left over for anything else. A motherly home help encouraged him in a semi-invalid way of life. To his G.P., who was sympathetically generous with 'sick' certificates, he was a man who could certainly be allowed to define himself as ill at times, but not permanently nor all the time, for the inescapable clinical fact remained that he appeared to have no serious disease. To employment officials, with access to his medical record, he was certainly 'voluntarily unemployed' and in need of rehabilitation: he was in fact offered a retraining course but refused it on the grounds that his children would have had to be taken into care while he was away. To social workers, on the other hand, with no access to his medical record and a different professional viewpoint, he was a client for whom they had great sympathy. They accepted his own definition of himself as considerably disabled, and to them the central feature of the situation was the motherless children who might well have become their responsibility. Additionally, they did not necessarily share the Department of Employment's orientation towards the importance of gainful employment. Thus, every agency with which Mr Thomson was in touch was treating him in a different way: the result was that, although he was given as much financial and practical help as possible with the assistance of the social

workers, it was associated with repeated examinations, inspections, form-filling, and accounting. Since he was much too occupied with his day-to-day worries to remember dates or keep appointments, his affairs were perpetually on the brink of crisis.

In Mr Thomson's case, it was not easy to be certain that he genuinely believed himself to be seriously incapacitated, though the balance of evidence indicated that he did. There were similar cases, such as that of Mr William Kilgour, who was very definitely treated as 'work-shy' by the Department of Employment, but whose actions appeared to be motivated by his genuine conviction – remaining unassailed for some considerable time because of poor communication with the doctors dealing with him – that his long-term stomach symptoms indicated cancer.*

There was, of course, a small number of cases in which unemployment was unequivocally 'voluntary', in that it was a deliberate choice, not based on self-perceived incapacity to work. The stratagems employed in the exercise of this choice were described quite freely: one man said, for instance, after being sent by the Department of Employment to apply for a nightwatchman's job with long hours and low pay: 'I said to the foreman, "I get these black-outs, they've told you that, haven't they", and the foreman said, "Well, you're no use to us, are you!"'

It was not possible, however, to characterize these 'voluntarily unemployed' as sharing a common type of 'personality'; to avoid employment was a mode of response, a reaction (probably entirely rational in the light of personal circumstances) to a given situation, rather than the result of a psychological trait. Despite the frequently expressed myth about 'scroungers', it was of course virtually impossible for a man to be better off, in ordinary circumstances, if he were not working. Actual money income was not the only 'good' to be taken into account, however: there was also the value of leisure, or of not having to do work which was actively

*Towards the end of the survey year, Mr Kilgour at last became reassured. The thesis of the study would be better served if it were possible to say that his behaviour, and hence his categorization by the Department of Employment, immediately changed. Unfortunately, real people do not necessarily accommodate themselves to the researcher's purposes: in fact, he appeared to have acquired a taste for unemployment, and the subsequent months were a long story of attempts on the part of the Department of Employment to find him a job, which he continually frustrated.

disliked or which was known to be adversely affecting health. In these terms, many men would have been better off not working, but for the most part financial considerations had to be the deciding factor. Most of those who chose not to work had a small extra income from some other source, usually service or industrial injury pensions, and some had working wives. In the latter case, however, the cost of family and neighbourhood stigma at 'living off the wife' had to be taken into account, and in fact in every case in the sample where the wife was working and the husband was 'voluntarily' idle, marital relationships were so poor that the couple were virtually leading separate lives.

In general, however, the number of cases where there was any evidence that the unemployed man did not really want to find a job was small. Whether or not they actually found any pleasure, satisfaction or financial advantage in working, for the most part people made strenuous efforts to avoid the status of 'unemployed'.

THE SOLUTION OF JOB PROBLEMS

About three-fifths of those people who felt they had job problems managed to solve them during the survey year. Table 6:5 shows how these 58 people did so, including those whose only solution was to retire.

Some of those who managed to adapt their jobs to their impairment (they were more likely to be skilled workers) did so with the help of their employers. These were likely either to be small firms, especially those in which the employee had a family connection, or else large enterprises with a formal structure of light jobs specially reserved for convalescent, injured or aging employees. Typical of the first situation might be a young man who worked in a family motor engineering firm, who after an accident was 'promoted' to working in the office, or a man approaching 65 who was employed in a small business where the proprietor had been his friend since their schooldays. After a heart attack he was encouraged to work for two hours a day at first, increasing his hours gradually at his own discretion. Typical of the second situation were employees of paper mills or the docks, and as long as it was clear that the light job was only temporary, so that the worker could define himself as

Table 6:5 How people's job problems were solved (at any time during the survey year, numbers of people)

	All those whose problems were 'solved' or who 'retired' (58 people)					
	Sex		Work			
	M	F	Non-manual	Skilled manual	Semi- & unskilled manual	Total
Left labour force	9	7	4	3	9	16
Informal temporary adaptation of job	9	1	1	6	3	10
Formal but temporary 'light' job	7	0	0	6	1	7
Permanent adaptation of existing job	7	1	2	4	2	8
New and 'lighter' job, same employer	3	2	2	2	1	5
New job with different employer	8	4	1	5	6	12
Of those with new employers:						
Better job	3	1	1	2	1	4
Similar job	5	3	0	3	5	8

convalescent or undergoing rehabilitation rather than permanently disabled (even though in many cases his strength or abilities were permanently impaired), this appeared to be an arrangement which was satisfactory to the employee and favourable for his future career:

An example of a firm providing efficient structured provision for rehabilitation might be the employers of Mr Scott, a semi-skilled worker who had worked with them for 34 years, who was injured in a road accident. During the first month or two after the accident Mr Scott expressed very great anxiety about his working future; his particular injury would make his job difficult, and he felt insecure because of his age (late 50s) and was concerned about the prospects for his small pension. His worries came to a head, as so many men's did, about three months after he had left the hospital. At this point. he made special efforts to consult the hospital specialist and his general practitioner. The G.P. contacted the doctor employed by the mill, and Mr Scott was given appointments with the mill's nurse, the doctor, and his supervisor. He was completely reassured to learn that a light job would be waiting for him, and that special consideration would be given to matching any permanent effects of his injury to suitable permanent work. This appeared to have an encouraging effect on Mr Scott, who redoubled his own rehabilitative efforts and got back to work as soon as possible; by the end of the year he was working confidently at a slightly adapted job.

Unfortunately, of course, only a minority of employers came into these two categories: small enough and with a sufficient personal interest in the employee on the one hand, or, on the other, large enough to have formal rehabilitation procedures. Other employing enterprises in which people managed to find satisfactory temporary or permanent adaptations, though a formal structure might not exist, included conspicuously the Health Service itself, the University, and the City and County Councils.

A handful of employers were also instrumental in obtaining new jobs for people whom they could employ no longer: the skipper of a small fishing boat, for instance, was found a very satisfactory shore job in the industry by the owners. In other cases it was sometimes not altogether clear whether the employer was motivated by concern for the worker, or a desire to pass a problem on to someone else, but at least the employee escaped unemployment at that stage.

Other professional people or agencies were little help in obtaining adjusted jobs or new employement. A trade union was directly involved in only one case (a blind person), though of course unions might have taken part in the setting up of large firms' formal rehabilitation structures. (The role of the Department of Employment's resettlement services will be discussed later.)

Of the 42 people who found satisfactory adjustments or new work, hospital doctors had been directly concerned in four cases and general practitioners in another four. It was conspicuous that these medical interventions were particularly effective, for there were no cases in this sample where it was known that doctors had tried unsuccessfully to help. The cases were few, however, and this raises the difficult question of the medical profession's view of its role in the context of rehabilitation for work. The official view, promulgated in many reports, is that the working future of impaired patients ought very much to be the concern of, at least, hospital doctors, as part of a total rehabilitative service.[3]

The Piercy Report, for instance, recommended in 1956 that 'Rehabilitation must be a continuous process, beginning with the onset of sickness or injury, and continuing throughout treatment until final resettlement in the most suitable work and living conditions is achieved.' In 1972, the Tunbridge Report, finding that 'few of the important and practical recommendations [of the Piercy Committee] have been implemented,' recomended that a 'consultant in rehabilitation' should be appointed in each district general hospital, among whose duties would be the planning and operation of facilities for clinical, social and vocational rehabilitation.

No such post was contemplated at the hospital of this survey, however, and while consultants showed, in their discussions of the problem of employment help for the disabled, that they were not unconscious of the pressures such official views exerted upon them, in the absence of any formal structure (apart from the referral of a small number of patients to the Disablement Resettlement Officer) there was little that they could in fact do. Certain specialities might be very conscious of rehabilitation needs (rheumatology, orthopaedics), but even these clinicians could not be expected to be experts in employment, and there also seemed in many cases to be some reluctance to discuss with the patient any possibility of permanent impairment, so that the question of employment problems was not very often raised.

It must be added that very few patients themselves defined active help, as distinct from advice at a very general level, about employment as part of the hospital doctor's function. In fact, there were cases where it seemed obvious that the worker ought to have discussed his difficulties with his consultant, but admitted that not only had he never raised the question but that he had avoided the subject or been deliberately misleading. When asked about their reasons, people did not find this easy to explain. Usually they expressed some awkwardness or timidity, or they confessed to having been confused by the unfamiliar and intimidating setting of the consultation, with its seemingly rushed time-table.

In the four cases where a hospital doctor *had* been directly instrumental in solving a patient's job problems, it happened that the patients were all young, all severely and 'interestingly' disabled, and all professional or technical workers. This may, of course, not represent a general trend, but it is reasonable to suppose not only that doctors might naturally have more understanding and sympathy for such cases, but also that they would have more appropriate resources, in terms of personal acquaintances and career information, to offer.

In contrast to the general attitude to hospital doctors, a certain number of patients *did* define help with employment as part of their general practitioner's proper function. Several (particularly women) described at length how they had even asked their doctors to approach employers directly for them. There is no direct evidence about the doctors' attitude to patients' attempts to involve them in job problems, but it might well be thought to be an undue burden. The four cases where general practitioners had been directly responsible for obtaining new or adjusted jobs for patients all occurred in rural practices: an example was a farm-worker, suffering from bronchitis and a heart condition, who was advised to avoid dust and hay, and whose doctor rang up the local County Council offices in order to obtain a new job for him.

Informal help

It is obvious that in fact only a small proportion of those who solved their working problems did so with the help of professionals or formal agencies. Conspicuously, the greatest sources of help were the patients' work-group, or his network of kinsfolk and friends.

Many unofficial job adjustments were described:

Mr McLeod, a granite polisher who had been away from work for nearly a year, said, 'The other men are very good – they just don't let me do anything stupid and I know my limitations. If I think a job's hard another man comes to help me straightaway.'

Mr Hadden, a skilled worker in his 50s who had had several heart attacks and a badly fractured shoulder, was very grateful for the consideration of his workmates: 'There's no official . . . the job's not lighter, you understand, I'm supposed to be doing just the same, but I don't, I'm really having an easy time. The young ones – say what you like about youngsters nowadays – especially the young ones, they won't let me lift a thing, they take it from me and say, hey, you're not supposed to do that. They don't make me feel awkward a bit – they're a good lot, they know I've only got another five years or so to go.'*

Similarly, Mr McRitchie, a storeman who had also had two infarcts, expressed great appreciation of the kindness of his workmates and immediate boss: 'When I first went back they wouldn't let me lift a thing, and the engineer used to stand and watch me . . . he'd come up behind and clap me on the shoulder and say where's the fire, come on, we don't want you back in hospital!'

Mr McRitchie believed that whether or not it was possible to adjust a job depended very much more upon social factors within the work group – 'what sort of men there is there, whether it's everyone for himself' – than upon formal management policy, and indeed there were other cases where the firm's policy did not appear to be very helpful, but the employee got by because of his work-mates' help:

Mr Findlay, again suffering from heart disease, was away from his work for seven months and on his return was given a job which he resentfully felt to be a demotion. Instead of the indoor supervisory work which he had achieved after many years' service, and of which he was very proud, he was given (at the same pay) an outdoor job with some manual content. He said without much conviction that perhaps it was better for his health than sitting in an office 'but honestly I'm not really fit for it, anyway, I don't exert myself. If I feel tired I just take it easy, and no one to bother me. I can have a sit down, the other men cover for me.'

There were some indications that this pattern of peer-group help was not so common among non-manual and professional workers, and might even be resented if it did happen, as an attack upon status. Obviously, adaptation might be easier, if there were any need for it, but where a job was not physically hard there was also less obvious legitimation for concessions because of physical impairment. A teacher in the sample was quite convinced that his future had been prejudiced because he had been given a slightly easier job after a

*In contradiction to his praise for his specific young workmates, Mr Hadden, talking of rehabilitation generally, had some scorn and criticism for a vague class of 'those – usually the younger ones of course – who don't *want* to be helped. It's all made too easy. You have to help yourself and get down to it.'

heart attack, and an office worker described some ill-feeling between herself and colleagues about an adaptation to her work. In similar cases a manual worker, with a clearer conection between his health and his physical labours, would have been more likely to be grateful than resentful.

A high proportion of those who managed to obtain new and satisfactory jobs also did so with the informal help of family and friends. It may be, of course, that this is particularly characteristic of a geographical area where (on the evidence of this survey) kinship networks are still strong. At any rate, 8 of the 12 people who found new jobs in which they were happy said that kin or friends had been directly responsible.

> Mr Ellis, who had gastric and other conditions, had been poorly employed for several years after giving up a meter-reader's job. During the survey year his cousin retired as handyman at an educational institution, and managed to arrange for Mr Ellis to take the job over. A countryman who liked independence, and who was obviously a hard worker if allowed to go at his own pace, Mr Ellis found this the ideal job and at the end of the year was settled very happily.

> Another man typical of this group was Mr Gill, a self-employed man in his early 50s who was unable to continue his work after gastric surgery. For nine months he was very depressed and unhappy, unable (because of his age, he believed) to find a job. Finally a friend in his bowling club 'took him along' to a bakery, and Mr Gill said 'I'd never have got the job if he hadn't spoken for me – that's the only way someone my age can do it.'

The crisis as turning point

The emphasis earlier was on the crisis as a sudden fall into downward mobility. There were a few cases, however, where the crisis proved to be an advantageous turning-point, and these may be of special interest. In some cases the downward drift had already begun at a previous health crisis, and it seemed that this new event of another illness episode caused the man to pause and take stock of his future, and make a determined effort to arrest the drift before it was too late.

> Mr John Laing was perhaps representative. In his 50s, he had been a lorry-driver all his life, but two years before this hospitalization he

had lost the sight of one eye – a disability crucial to his existing job, though not necessarily important in many others. Like many men, he had thought at the time that fairly high pay was more important than finding himself a secure future, and he became a labourer for a builder, working very long hours at a physically demanding job. Now he had suffered a heart attack. He became registered as disabled and was found work as a dock night-watchman: more unsuitable work would be difficult to imagine, for the shifts were long, the winter weather unpleasant, and the pay unattractive. It might have been guessed that here was another inevitable slide into chronic unemployment. In this case, however, Mr Laing had a secure base in the local community, with many friends and relations nearby, and a determination to remake his life at this point. While working conscientiously at his night-watchman's job, he used his resources of friendly contacts to explore many other possibilities, and eight months after his hospitalization one of his applications was successful. He settled very happily into a physically less demanding, better paid, and more interesting machine-operating job in a firm near his home who were considered to be very 'good' employers. He summed up his philosophy as 'You've got to look out for yourself', and immediately ceased to speak of himself as 'disabled'. Previously he had accepted the label, with some misgivings ('Jobs arn't easy for us disabled') but now he described himself as 'recovered', as if disability were merely a temporary state.

A similar story was that of Mr John McGillivray, another long-distance lorry-driver who had lost his job and became registered as disabled after a serious accident some four years before. He had obtained work as a light-van driver, but had never been happy in it and the pay had been very poor. Now, at this hospitalization, he lost this job. He was very anxious to work, and called almost daily at the Department of Employment until he was found a temporary job in a garage. He worked at this with enthusiasm, though the pay was even poorer and he felt himself to be very under-employed. So far, the downward spiral had been accelerating. However, a certain amount of luck, added to Mr McGillivray's own efforts, had by the end of the year arrested the fall: through a friend, he moved to another firm with a better-paid and more interesting job, and he felt fairly secure.

In other cases, the crisis of this illness or accident resulted in a period of stock-taking, and perhaps an opportunity to break out of an increasingly unsatisfactory working life:

Mr John Allen, in his early 50s, had been a clerk and then a collector for a debt-recovery agency. His job meant a great deal of walking and climbing stairs, and had never been an ideal one for a man who was bronchitic and whose sight was poor; moreover he disliked it heartily. After the heart attack he made a determined effort to find more congenial work, although this was not a case where there was any advice or help from his doctors. After two months' convalescence he managed to obtain a job – as porter at a nearby public building – which he had 'hankered after' for some time, which offered easier hours, more security, and pleasanter conditions. At this point he said delightedly, 'I'm happier almost than ever before in my life, that's me settled for life now, I hope', and a year later he was repeating, 'I don't think I've ever been so happy at work. I knew this was the job for me. All those years – I hated it always – now I look back it's been a blessing in disguise, this heart trouble, I'd never have got out if I hadn't had to.'

These cases where an illness episode proved to be a turning-point upwards instead of downwards were few, and generalizations are hardly legitimate. It is obvious that particular determination and energy were required on the part of the individual: the argument would not be that 'motivation' or any other personal characteristic is the overwhelmingly important variable, for the mass of evidence tends rather to stress features of the environment and the economic structure, but rather that a few individuals can break out of the typical constraints. One characteristic which these people did have in common was a very supportive family or friendship network.

WOMEN AND JOB PROBLEMS

A slightly smaller proportion of women than of men found they had problems concerning their jobs. In part, this must simply reflect the fact that women's jobs may be less likely to be strenuous than men's, and so less likely to be affected by a physical disability, and in part it indicates the lower saliency of their jobs to women, many of whom will be married and not the major breadwinner. Nevertheless, it seemed that there was a genuine difference between men and women. Women were less likely to lose their jobs, less likely to have difficulty in finding a new job if they wished to change, and appeared to be treated with more flexibility by their employers – despite the fact (p. 137) that a high proportion of working women in this sample were in the least favourable job category, of unskilled manual workers.

The reasons appeared to lie in the relationship of women to the world of work, both at the formal level symbolized by the colour of their national insurance stamp and at the level of their own definitions of their working role. Married women and widows, having the right to choose to pay lower N.I. contributions, may be only peripherally within the system: this has certain disadvantages, as noted in Chapter 5, but it permits a greater flexibility, and opens up the possibility of genuine choice unfettered by the system's requirements. The actions of medical and administrative agencies seemed to indicate some uncertainty about which was the 'proper' role of women, with the result that both tended to solve the problem by saying, or implying by their actions, 'the decision is up to you, and we do not wish to influence you in either direction.' Notably, men in precisely the same position (in fact acting as housekeeper because of the incapacity of a wife, or caring for children) were treated very differently and not permitted a choice.

Women not fully within the N.I. system, since they did not receive unemployment or sick benefit, did not have (or present their doctors with) the difficult task of defining themselves as wholly sick on the one hand, or wholly fit for work on the other. The range of choices open to them was therefore much greater; they could consider working temporarily and giving it up when they pleased, or working part-time, or taking lower-status jobs for a time, without considering their N.I. position. The process of negotiation between doctor and patient for a definition of 'fit' or 'not fit' for work certainly could be seen to be taking place in the case of men, but it was often conducted covertly or indirectly, leaving a great deal of room for misunderstanding and conflict: in the case of women, the negotiation was explicit. Many women described conversations with their general practitioner in which the pros and cons of working outside the home were discussed:

> Mrs Malcolm, the 48-year old wife of a bulldozer operator, with four school-age sons, who suffered from myocardial ischaemia and other conditions, said at different periods, 'The doctor said why don't I stay at home for a bit', 'I told the doctor last week how bored I was

getting – I can't stand being alone all day and maybe I'll start work again', 'The doctor agreed it's bad for me, getting fussed and not knowing what to do with myself – it'll be grand to get out of the house and have the company.'

In fact, the choice, for women, was only rarely between work and idleness. As many of them pointed out, they were kept occupied with tasks whether within the home or outside it.

Mrs Robb, a 45-year old woman with arthritis who worked in a bakery, said, 'It's got very painful since I went back to work – but I don't know – I'll stay for a bit – if I stayed home I'd aye be doing housework, and that might be worse.'

Single women ought formally to have been in the same position as men, as far as their N.I. position and their relationship to their work were concerned. There were several cases, however, where single women appeared to be treated by doctors and by official agencies in a manner more typical of interaction with married women than with men. They described the same sort of discussions with their doctors as to whether they should 'stay at home for a bit' (a phrase unlikely to be applied to a man, at least before late middle age) and no woman reported any pressure from the Department of Employment or the D.H.S.S. about taking a job. The few instances of conflict which were described, such as the case of Mrs Baxter's daughter (p. 60) were over the receipt of benefits rather than whether the single woman should or should not be working. Nor did women express the same sort of uneasiness about not working that men did: they could more easily find other roles which were accepted by their family, their social group and (implicitly, if not formally) by officials as legitimate – doing the housework for parents, or for working daughters, or simply concentrating on their own housekeeping. These might not be the roles that they themselves would choose, of course, and several women expressed almost desperate unhappiness about being unable to keep their jobs, but this distress was based solely on their personal feelings and was never compounded by any pressures from their families, doctors or officials.

Additionally, the typical relationship between women, whether married or single, and their employers seemed to be a little different from that of men. A greater proportion described explicit negotiations with their employer about when they should return to work: it was not simply a question of 'the doctor may sign me off next month', but rather of 'the manager suggested I stay off until after the summer, my job'll always be waiting, and that would be most convenient for them, and I'm not in a particular hurry.' (Mrs Macandrew, who worked in a department store and was injured in a road accident.) In part, of course, this was due to the high proportion of women in service jobs or small enterprises where the relationship between employer or manager and employee was more likely to be a personal one – shops, bakeries, offices, domestic service. It may also be true that the structure of women's employment, often in semi-skilled jobs with a high labour turnover and part-time working, offered greater flexibility to the employer.

The result was that, for the temporarily impaired and for those with alternative occupations available, difficulties over their jobs were less likely: they found their looser relationship with the formal agencies of employment an advantage. For a minority of more permanently impaired women, however, it appeared to be a serious disadvantage. In particular, their rehabilitation was neglected and their long-term future given less consideration than would have been likely in the case of a man. Because most women had alternative roles available, and most women preferred to organize their own working lives in an informal way, it seemed that this was accepted by official agencies as the norm; women who were unable to solve their own problems received little help, or were encouraged to remain idle when in fact they did not wish to. If men and women with similar degrees of functional handicap are compared, for instance, it was much less likely that the woman would be formally registered as a 'disabled' worker by the Department of Employment, and the few women who were so registered described even less contact with the Disablement Resettlement Officer than registered men. If they had no obligation to report to the Department of Employment (because not drawing unemployment benefit) then there was no formal pathway of referral for help, and the women themselves simply had no knowledge of the D.R.O.'s function.

Even where there was contact with official agencies women's work seemed to be viewed rather differently from men's:

Wilhemina Simpson's history was a particularly clear example. She was a single woman in her 30s, who had a slowly progressive metabolic condition, and had worked at a succession of more and more menial clerical jobs. Her present position of apparently hopeless unemployment was due more to the fact that her working record was poor, because of sickness absences, than to any difficulty in actually working. She lived on supplementary benefit, in a tiny cottage, with an intensely protective and dominating widowed mother, and felt herself to be greatly in need of some occupation and some independent life. When in hospital she took the opportunity of asking for job help, and was referred by the consultant to the M.S.W. and thence to the Disablement Resettlement Officer. The combined accounts of the interview presented a picture of genuine anxiety to work on the patient's part, to some extent subdued because of her mother's presence, determination on the mother's part to retain her control over every detail of her daughter's life, and an initial helpfulness on the part of the D.R.O. which quickly cooled as it became apparent that Mrs Simpson was being 'difficult'. He said that it was unlikely that suitable work in open employment could be found for Wilhemina, and there were no vacancies at the occupational workshop. The patient and her mother appeared to be confused about the difference between sheltered work and occupational work, and reported that they had been 'put off' sheltered work because only pocket-money would be involved. A course of rehabilitative training in another city was suggested, and Wilhemina appeared to be attracted to the idea. At a second interview, however, her mother was adamant that Wilhemina was unfit to go away from home, and the suggestion was dropped. Because she had not asked for her name to be put on the waiting list for the occupational workshop, no referral was made to the social work department, and at this point contact with the Department of Employment ceased. Wilhemina had in fact certain talents, particularly for very skilled handiwork, but during the survey year her confidence and independence could be observed to deteriorate to an unnecessary degree. 'Sitting here with mother' had apparently been defined as a perfectly proper role for her to assume, and although there were one or two flashes of initiative when she went out on her own account to apply unsuccessfully for (highly unsuitable) jobs, by the end of the year she seemed to have sunk into complete dependence. In view of her mother's age, future problems seemed inevitable.

In several cases, the women concerned were grateful for their doctor's implicit offer of choice about whether or not to work, and glad that no pressure was put upon them. The other side of the coin, however, was that no one appeared to consider their rehabilitation.

> Minnie Fowlie, for instance, was a young woman who lived, with her small child, with her parents. She worked in a textile mill, and injured her back while lifting bales. Nearly two years after the accident she had still not returned to work, although an industrial injuries board had by now reduced their assessment of her disability, originally 15 per cent, to 3 per cent. It appeared that she had acquired a habit of slight chronic invalidism, rarely leaving the house, complaining rather vaguely but for the most part avoiding active medical treatment. Obviously, she preferred to stay at home, and her general practitioner sympathetically and routinely signed certificates of incapacity. She had accepted the formal label of 'disabled' (if only to the extent of 3 per cent) and seemed happy to adopt that role, even though it appeared to be hampering her own rehabilitation.

THE ROLE OF 'RETIREMENT'

Eight people had, in effect, 'retired' from work before the survey began, and a further 16 did so during the year. Seven of these people were women deciding to give up work outside the home, but 17 were men or women, the youngest of whom was 52 and the oldest 64, who were in fact putting themselves into a similar category to 'old age pensioner', by admitting that their working life was over, and making the permanent adjustments in both their attitudes and their practical affairs which are more usually made at the age of 65. There were, of course, several other people in the sample whose future careers seemed likely to take this pattern sooner or later. Although no one under 65 (men) or 60 (women) can formally be a retirement pensioner, official agencies collaborated with these people in allowing them to take up this role (their formal role, if they were within the national insurance system was that of invalidity pensioner); once the definition of 'unable to work again' had been agreed upon by the medical profession and by administrative agencies, and accepted by the patient, then it appeared that they were left alone by the Department of Employment, their affairs were routinized by the D.H.S.S., and they were likely to be among those whose 'needs' – for such varied things as housing, discretionary benefits, free prescriptions – were given some consideration by both doctors and officials. This meant that their affairs were likely to be a little more settled and straightforward than those of people whose 'retirement' had not been legitimated or had not been accepted by the patient and his family themselves. On the other hand, the acquired definition seemed to be an irrevocable one in practical terms; there was no instance during the survey year, nor anywhere it seemed likely in the future, of someone revising his decision to retire, even if his circumstances changed slightly – if, for instance, his health improved a little, or employment prospects became better in his particular trade, or he found that he enjoyed retirement less than he had anticipated.

This group of people would seem to be of particular interest in the context of questions about old age and retirement from work, withdrawal or disengagement from active social roles, and the connection between age and physical impairment. Was the role of 'retired because of impairment' felt to be very different from the role of 'retired because of age'? Was it perceived as a stigmatized or disadvantaged state? Did these people in fact appear to disengage, either voluntarily or enforcedly, from society at large?

The 'disengagement' theory suggests that the process of aging is an inevitable mutual withdrawal between an individual and the social system to which he belongs.[4] Successful aging requires voluntary disengagement, and various institutions of a society may have the function of assisting this process. This theory has been the subject of much controversy: on the one hand it has been suggested that it may be true for North American society but not for other less youth-centred ones;[5] on the other, it has been suggested that such disengagement is enforced in all societies where technology is advancing rapidly, as it is convenient in such societies for the old to withdraw. The theory has its echo in practical social administration in the debates between the principles of 'segregation' and 'involvement' and in the ambivalent nature of policies concerning retirement: debates and policies which concern the old and the disabled equally. As far as the old are concerned, the emphasis in Britain is usually, at the level of welfare policy, towards as much involvement in the community as possible. On the other hand, many people are not allowed to work beyond the watershed age of 65, even if they wish to do so, and the provisions of the national insurance system make it clear that all but modest part-time work is expected to stop at 65.

There have been few empirical studies in Britain of how the retired actually do see their role, but one study of 99 'secure and healthy' couples at the time of the husband's retirement concluded that although a variety of patterns could be discovered disengagement was not a particularly frequent process, and where it did occour not a happy one.[6]

The subjects of the present study had very different characteristics, since they were retiring prematurely, were not healthy, and were not necessarily financially secure. Conspicuously, they were likely to be semi- or unskilled manual workers, since it was more likely that impairment would not preclude work for non-manual employees, or that their employers, or the employers of valued skilled workers, would be willing to offer adjustments in working conditions so that permanent retirement was not necessary. A few of the 17 men and women who retired were people who became so disabled that any work was impossible, but a larger group were those who although not wholly disabled were unable to continue their present manual work, which was physically heavy or in some other way unsuitable for their particular condition.

How did they adjust to retirement? Notably, for many it was a very gradual process, beginning at a point where they defined themselves as unable to work, forced into unemployment against their will, and ending many months later at a point where they defined themselves as having *chosen* to retire. Often it seemed that in this process they had been gradually and tactfully guided by general practitioners, who appeared by their actions to understand that a bald directive to give up all thought of work, at a time of crisis, would have been unacceptable.

This may be illustrated by quotations at various stages during the year from Mr Cruikshank, a storeman of 60 who had a history of poor health, principally bronchitis, ever since suffering from tuberculosis 30 years before. One month after this hospitalization he said, 'I'll have to stop work for the time. The doctor said to take it easy till summer-time. I'm always better then.' Two months later he said, 'I'm still not fit to work – maybe if a suitable job turned up I'd take it – but my doctor wouldn't let me start.' Eight months after the hospitalization he was reluctantly becoming reconciled to giving up work permanently: 'I'm not looking for work now. I've given up the idea, really – it was always a very forlorn faint hope. I'd rather, but there's no point in thinking about it. Days like this when it's windy I couldn't go out. My doctor agrees, though I'm only seeing him every three months now, for the certificate.' At one year he seemed quite content; in reply to enquiries about his health he replied 'Fine – better than I've been for years, only one or two very mild attacks lately. Yes, I'm really very well.' But he had entirely given up any thought of working: 'I'd get ill again if I tried; the doctor agrees. No one's bothering me, I saw the insurance doctor and he said, "Don't worry, we'll fix them [the Department of Employment] across the road." '

Several people described a similar process of gradual negotiation for a 'retired' role between patient and general practitioner, and placed an emphasis on the element of choice they felt to be involved.

The existence of a legitimate role of retirement pensioner appeared to offer many advantages to the group of people being considered. It would not, of course, be possible to give an exact age which was the dividing-line between the state which was felt to be stigmatized, 'disabled and unemployed', and the unstigmatized state, 'retired', but certainly all the relevant people in the sample under 50 years of age placed themselves in the first category, while people in their early 50s spoke quite proudly and contentedly of having retired. Mr Johnstone, for instance, a blacksmith with a rather unsettled history of emigration and changing occupations, used to date events from 'the year when I retired', when he had been 54. Several people had been eased into their premature retirement by the same sort of ceremony that marked 'normal' retirement: a party and a small cheque for Miss Hird, a large clock and the management's grateful thanks for Mr Rennie. Having been legitimized in this role, by doctors and officials as well as employers and friends, they no longer felt it necessary to think of themselves as disabled or dwell on their impairment for work. Despite the recurrent or chronic complaint which their doctor continued to certify, they often described themselves as '100 per cent fit now', 'never better in my life', or 'enjoying being my own master now I'm retired.'

It must be remembered that almost all of these men and women were manual workers, many of whom had never enjoyed work particularly. Their career-patterns were more likely to have dwindled in middle age to ever less attractive jobs, rather than progressed in a way which gave them satisfaction. Towards the end of their working careers, poor health had made their work difficult or painful, and although the shock of the first realization that perhaps their working life was over sometimes caused an initial reaction of denial and bitterness, most of these people were eventually happy to accept their doctor's suggestion that perhaps society did not require them to work any more.

There was no case in which the decision to retire, of itself, caused any long-term distress, though there were cases where contentment was marred by the ensuing financial problems. The people whose retirement appeared to be spoilt by money troubles were, however, few, for in most cases their self-defined 'needs' were modest; their rents were likely to be low and their grown-up children a help rather than a liability. Also, they were the people who appeared to receive the most sympathetic attention from the D.H.S.S.

For the most part, people slipped into the role of 'retirement pensioner' contentedly. In many cases the spouse would also be in poor health, and the couple found routine household and family tasks – cleaning and shopping, visiting children and entertaining relatives – a satisfying joint occupation which filled all their time. There was little evidence that work-groups continued to be a social resource after retirement, and one or two men did mention missing the contact with 'mates'; on the other hand, neighbour and family groups became more important. A few men living alone, who happened to have no close family, had become socially isolated, but for the most part there was no feeling of disengagement evident in this group; physically their world might have narrowed (although many took the opportunity to travel to visit relatives) but within the confines of their neighbourhood and family they took on new roles with enthusiasm:

> Mr Marshall, for instance, who 'retired' at 60, spoke at first a little gloomily about the prospect. Six months later, he had become absorbed in the job of the single-handed daytime care of an infant grandchild (his rather younger wife was working), displaying his expertise to interviewers with obvious pride and enjoyment.

IMPAIRMENT AND THE ECONOMIC STRUCTURE

The evidence which has been given seems to suggest that the physical nature of a man's work may be less important in the context of impairment than certain other associated factors: the size and structure of the employing firm, the amount of autonomy he has in the working situation, the structure of his working group. The difference between those for whom a crisis meant disaster, and those who managed to arrest a potential downward drift, was often that the more successful man had (or managed to find) an individual job, not necessarily formally classified as skilled, which he could learn, which made use of whatever special experience and talents he had, and in which he was or became a valuable person not easily replaced at a moment's notice. He could be regarded, and regard himself, as an individual who happened, amongst all his other characteristics, to have a physical impairment, rather than an undifferentiated member of the category 'disabled worker'.

It is true that when the sample was analysed by the conventional categories of socio-economic class, some of the expected variations appeared: non-manual workers appeared to have fewer working problems and semi- and unskilled manual workers the most. This over-simple analysis does not, however, explain why the circumstances of some manual workers were very similar to professional workers, and why some people in professional and managerial jobs had post-impairment careers typical of unskilled workers. There was, for instance, a road-sweeper who was paid while he was away from work, who felt entirely secure in his job, and who adapted it wholly satisfactorily when he returned. There were cleaners, shop assistants and porters in similar situations. On the other hand, there were self-employed professional people with little security or room for manoeuvre when misfortune occurred. The relationship of job problems to socio-economic class is obviously not clear-cut, though on commonsense grounds it would seem that a man's place in the economic structure must be an important variable in this context. It could be suggested that the conventional grouping is perhaps out of date, and that – at least for this purpose of examining the effect of misfortune upon 'careers' – a more precise description of the relationship of the individual to the economic structure of the society in which he lives is required. The important characteristic of a man's job appeared to be the nature of his contract with his employer – its scope, time-scale, the extent to which it was formalized or casual.

Two classes of people had conspicuously unfavourable post-impairment careers – those who were self-employed, on a fee-for-service basis, whether they were highly skilled professionals or window-cleaners and taxi-drivers, and those whose bargains with their employer for their work were entirely individual and casual, with no progressive pattern or long-term arrangements, no effective trade union or cohesive work-group. Many shop workers, garage workers, drivers, and labourers for small firms came into this category. When they, or the self-employed, became physically impaired, unemployment and immediate financial troubles were more likely, and they were more likely to accept a general label of 'disabled' as the most advantageous one at their disposal.

Those people whose relationship with their working world was more formally structured were in a more favourable position. They were more likely to receive some support while sick, and to keep their jobs or be able to adjust them. They could see various alternatives before them, and could keep their options open for their convalescent period. Any permanent impairment was likely to lead to a period of great uncertainty and insecurity – not immediately, but some months after the illness episode or accident – and people were apt to consider actions during that period which they would afterwards regret. To be part of a known structure cushioned these uncertainties, and such people were more used to looking ahead into the future. The important difference appeared to be not so much practical job security as a more future-oriented attitude. Such people had no need to accept a 'disabled' label at once: they could wait until it became certain that it would do them no harm.

Typical of enterprises with bureaucratic, structured conditions of employment were the Health Serive itself, the University, the Civil Service, education, and local government, and although there were of course exceptions the general trend was for these employees to be able to solve their job problems, even though the job itself might be less skilled (porters, labourers).

Another group of employing enterprises, almost exactly opposed to these in structure but very similar in effect, seemed to be those which could be called 'paternalistic'. Like the 'casual' enterprises, these provided entirely individual contracts with the employee, but on both sides the contract was envisaged as long-term rather than from week to week, and the employer accepted some responsibility for his worker's welfare. Examples of this type of employment were small offices, some family retailing businesses, farmers, and rural estates. In these circumstances, too, the employee seemed to be more likely to feel that he could remake his future gradually.

Intermediate between these unfavourable and favourable working situations came the employees of large factories, mills and docks, where the conditions of work were firmly structured but unlikely to be progressive, and the worker was likely to be paid for work done (shiftwork, piecework) rather than on a salaried basis. Here the patterns were erratic, and favourable or unfavourable outcomes depended on the particular firm's practices and the circumstances of the impairment. The outcomes of industrial injury tended to be particularly unfavourable, and this will be discussed in Chapter 7.

The 'dual labour market' hypothesis[7] is of interest in connection with this analysis of favourable and unfavourable types of employment structure – the suggestion that it is the 'insecure' part of the market that attracts young men, while older men are interested in more secure jobs. Simple 'security' is an inadequate description of the difference between the jobs which have here been called 'casual' and those which have been called 'bureaucratic', for the difference lies in the whole relationship of the man to his work, and the extent to which the working situation provides a structure supporting other aspects of his life. The 'casual' nature of many women's jobs did not necessarily present the same problems to them. This survey does provide evidence, however, that men with low skills will face particularly chronic problems if, when advancing years and physical impairment reduce their attractiveness to employers, they are still in the 'youthful' and insecure part of the market. Ideally, official resettlement services should be designed for this group as well as for the rather different needs of the young or congenitally disabled.

THE OFFICIAL RESETTLEMENT SERVICES

It is obvious that in the sample as a whole little use was found to be made of the special services of the Department of Employment. These services, based on the Tomlinson Report of 1943 and the subsequent Disabled Persons (Employment) Act of 1944, and found by the Piercy Committee in 1956 to be 'suitable' and 'comprehensive', 'needing little change or development', represent policies which were by the 1970s over 25 years old and generally agreed to be in need of revision. Nevertheless, the services are, in principle, comprehensive.

The central figure is the Disablement Resettlement Officer, found at all larger Employment Offices, whose duty it is to help the disabled to find work, and to maintain the register of Disabled Persons. From this register, all employers of more than 20 people are statutorily obliged to fill a quota of 3 per cent of their work-force, so long as there are suitable registered applicants for vacancies. The objectives of this 'quota scheme' are admitted to be largely educative, in making clear to employers that they have a duty to consider disabled people: in practice, enforcement has never been practicable and compliance on the part of employers has fallen steadily (from 38.6 per cent of firms with a quota obligation not fulfilling it in 1961, to 57.8 per cent not complying in 1972). Two occupations — electric-lift operator and car-park attendant – are 'designated' as reserved for registered disabled workers.

For those judged too severely handicapped to be capable of jobs in open employment, 'sheltered' work in special workshops may be provided by Remploy Ltd, or by local authorities or voluntary bodies. Facilities in the City of the study included a Remploy factory employing about 80 disabled workers, and the Blind Workshop, with about 100 blind and other disabled employees. Local authorities also have permissive powers to organize home-working schemes for the housebound.

For the disabled person who needs rehabilitation for work or retraining in a new trade, short courses at Industrial Rehabilitation Units* designed to help restore working fitness and provide assessment for suitable work are available, and also vocational courses at Government Training Centres, though both, in this City, would mean going away from home. There is also a wide range of special services available within the system: vocational training at residential centres run by voluntary organizations, training in technical or com-

*Now named Employment Rehabilitation Centres.

mercial colleges, professional training, and individual training arrangements with employers willing to offer subsequent employment.

The world of the people of this sample, however, seemed far removed from the world of this comprehensive and not unimaginative system.

Registration as disabled

The sample supported the evidence, of the Department of Employment itself among others, that registration as a 'disabled' worker is very arbitrary. There were more people eligible for registration, and not registered, than there were registered. Some of those who were on the register (and probably on their firm's quota) had no problems and had been working successfully for many years. Some of those to whom registration had never been suggested were badly in need of special help. Two of the registered had long been defined as incapable of work (though both would have liked some occupation).

Table 6:6 Those people eligible for registration as 'disabled' (at the end of the survey year, numbers of people)

	All those eligible for registration (47 people)				
	Employed		Unemployed		
	Satisfac-torily	Not satisfac-torily	Wanting work	Not wanting work	Total
Registered	10	2	7	2	21
Not registered	6	9	6	5	26

The arbitrary nature of the register is usually explained by the fact that registration is voluntary, and so will never represent all disabled workers. As a matter of fact, few people in the sample appeared to appreciate its 'voluntary' status: no one had ever *asked* to be registered, and only one person (unsuccessfully, but rather unrealistically in his case) had ever asked to be taken off the register. Most workers in the survey represented registration as an administrative procedure arranged by medical and employment authorities together, without much reference to them, or something which happened automatically if, because of health problems, they remained too long amongst the 'ordinary' unemployed. Particularly if they had been registered at school-leaving age, they did not see it as a matter over which they had much choice: they had always been defined as a 'handicapped child', and the label of 'disabled adult' had, in their case, automatically followed. A typical explanation was, 'Well, I was put on the register when I left school because I'd been to the special school, see.' This does not necessarily prove, of course, that no individual was conscious of having been offered a voluntary choice: to have been *given* the label of 'disabled worker', and to admit to having *chosen* the label, might be different things.

The word 'disabled' took many people aback. The small proportion of the sample who had been handicapped since childhood were used to hearing it, although they might not like it, and another small proportion of people who were suddenly, unequivocally and seriously incapacitated – by, for instance, a severe spinal injury or a stroke – had no choice but to agree that they were functionally disabled. Registration for work would be unlikely to be relevant for the latter group, however, and for the great majority of those people who found themselves on the register, this was the first time that anyone had actually applied the word 'disabled' to them. They seemed to see it as an administrative term without real meaning, and many tried to explain what it did imply: a young man suffering from coeliac disease said: 'The register is meant for . . . well, it's all right for them that have crutches, say, or one leg – people like that sooner than someone like me. I'm not really *disabled* – I'd be much better off not on the register at all.' Another man spoke of 'us people they call the "disabled" – it just means we can't do a hard job', and another said, 'It means going on what they call the disabled list. Well, if you can't do your work you *are* disabled, aren't you. The list doesn't mean you're really disabled, like you had no legs or something.' The problems of explaining their interpretations of the official category led many people to avoid the use of the words 'disabled register' altogether and substitute 'on a green card', the inference being that this was simply an administrative category of the national insurance system, comparable to that distinguished by the colours of the cards of some working wives or widows.

There is no doubt that a strong general feeling existed that to be 'on a green card' was a practical disadvantage. The unanimous opinion – sometimes based on the worker's perception of his own experience, but more often general lore of the 'everybody knows that' kind – was that men on the register would find it *more* difficult to get employment, would have a very limited range of jobs available to them, and would be discriminated against with regard to pay and conditions of work.

Some men who were in fact registered tried to do without the D.R.O.'s services. One young man, for instance, refused to ask for help because of his complete conviction that 'if you get a job as a disabled person, then you only get the disabled pay, which is never more than £14 or so, even if you're working beside other men getting twice as much and doing the same job as them.' Pressed to explain what he meant by 'the disabled pay', he showed that there was some confusion in his mind between sheltered work, 'designated' work, and work in open employment as a registered person. Other people were clear that registration ought not to affect pay, but nevertheless believed that in fact it did: Mr McGillivray's account was, 'The manager of the garage said, "Oh yes, you're the one from the D.R.O.," and you could see him thinking, "That's lower pay I can offer",' and this was supplemented by the long story of a friend who had accepted a job at £17 and was immediately dropped to £14 when, at the end of his first week, he produced a previously concealed 'green card'. Similar stories were told by other people, and though there is, of course, no proof that the allegations were true, it is certain that many men believed them to be true, and one at least had felt strongly enough to write to the Prime Minister about it. It is also true that of the 12 registered men at work, there was proof about rates of pay in 9 cases, and most had earnings which seemed very low.

It was also felt that the range of jobs the D.R.O. might have available was very limited. A typical comment was Mr Hamilton's: 'Being on the disabled register's no advantage. It's just that if they can't get rid of a job at [ordinary employment office] they send it on up to the disabled – what's the use of that?' Making the distinction which appeared to exist in many people's minds between 'disabled' and 'chronically ill', he added: 'They don't have many jobs for people like me who aren't very fit.'

In fact, the job into which Mr Hamilton finally settled happily was obtained through the D.R.O., though only after a long period of moving from one unsatisfactory job to another. At some time during the survey year, eight men were found jobs through the disabled register, though some of them were unsuitable and did not last long.

The survey subjects gave the impression that the Department of Employment's most important categorization, as they saw it, was between those whose 'motivation' was good – the 'keen' and co-operative – and those whose attitude to work was 'poor'. A good client was one who was ready to accept the assessment made of his impairment, desperately anxious to obtain work, not over-ambitious with regard to salary or responsibility nor over-fussy about hours and conditions, and grateful for the service offered. If this impression were true, it might easily, of course, be explicable in terms of the sort of resources that the D.R.O. had available: it was, after all, necessary for him to fit people into the jobs at his disposal. Clients who were ambitious, or who had ideas about improving their skills, or obviously resented what they felt to be a categorization as second-class employees, felt that they were not popular. Several men said that to refuse a job on the grounds of low pay or unsuitable conditions marked them out as 'not really wanting to work at all'.

Their reaction to this depended on their own assessment of themselves as workers, and their own definition of their physical condition. Men to whom impairment had come as a sudden blow, especially if they had been in skilled and highly paid jobs, found the categorization traumatic. Some accepted the label immediately and used it to explain and excuse the fall to a lower status. Others might simply ignore it as an irrelevance, and expect little in the way of help. Others, especially those who had been registered for a long time and who 'knew the ropes', might very deliberately judge whether or not they would get what they wanted by falling in with, rather than fighting against, the stereotypes, and chose to present themselves in ways which matched the categories they perceived.

This was most clearly described by the worker who said: 'I really wanted a job, and I wasn't prepared to be fussy just now. I'll have to see what I can make of it later. If you want any service you've got to show you're really keen, and above all the important thing is you mustn't be sorry for yourself. It worked, because the D.R.O. picked up the phone and said, "He's here now, and he can be up in five minutes – we know him, he's really keen to work." '

Problems of the resettlement service

It must not be supposed that these findings represent any particular local problems or inefficiencies, for they match many much larger-scale enquiries closely. In the National Survey, only 66 per cent of the handicapped who were formally unemployed were registered.[8] In the survey of *Men out of Work*, where more than a quarter of the whole sample said they were disabled, about equal numbers of these were registered and not registered, and it was common for people to say that they thought registration would limit their job opportunities.[9] In October 1970, the Department of Employment analysed all those unemployed people 'who were being dealt with by the Department as disabled' – a group known as the 'Disabled Live File'. They numbered nearly 100,000, of whom three-quarters were formally registered as disabled, and 65 per cent of them had been unemployed for more than 6 months.[10] The rates of unemployment of registered disabled people have commonly been compared with general unemployment rates:

Unemployment rates, per cent

Year	*Registered disabled*	*General, Great Britain*
1968	10.3	2.9
1970	11.8	3.3
1975	12.0	3.0

it is obvious that such figures have very little meaning, since the relationship between being disabled, being employed, and being registered is not really known, and so many people are formally known as 'long-term sick' when in fact they would be capable of work if any were available.*

*The unduly high proportion of unemployed registered disabled in the present sample is due to the fact that so many were newly impaired. If they had been followed for longer, some might have been expected either to find work or to leave the labour market.

The Department of Employment itself is, of course, very conscious of the problems of the resettlement service, and at the time of the survey had instigated a detailed review. One of the factors leading to problems was held to be the changing pattern of disablement, historically, though it could be argued that it is the *definition* of disablement, rather than the distribution, which has in fact changed. Certain relatively minor changes are, of course, real: the decline in the numbers of those with amputations and injuries as First World War veterans die, the decline in tuberculosis, or the increasing likelihood of survival for those born with certain congenital disablements. More important, however, is the change in what is seen as registrable: in 1950 there were 6,391 on the disabled register suffering from 'mental handicap' and in 1971 (in a register smaller by one-third) 12,477.

The growing significance of age-related impairments, and of mental conditions, and the widening of the whole concept of what disability is, in the working context, 'tends to blur the distinction between disabled people and other disadvantaged people'.[10] Thus, 'it is clear that we should to an increasing extent think of the employment problems of unemployed disabled people as being either connected with personal or psychological problems or related to adverse movements in the labour market that affect older and unskilled people generally.' The Department of Employment has therefore suggested that it might be desirable to 'think in terms of one specialised resettlement service for all people with special employment problems', the 'socially handicapped'.

It seems that a paradoxical situation, similar to that noted in the field of practical welfare, is developing in the field of employment services. In an attempt to avoid stigma (the 'disabled' are not only the halt, the lame, and the blind, but ordinary people) and introduce some equity and rationality into the system (a man with chronic bronchitis or mental handicap may be just as much in need of special help as one more visibly disabled), in an attempt to find categories which are neutral, true, and fair, in fact new categories are being developed which may be even more stigmatizing. Only those physically handicapped people who do have job problems will find themselves in this category, singled out as a 'problem' group.

A similar development is the creation of a new team of 'Unemployment Review Officers' by the Supplementary

Benefits Commission, to deal with the unemployed in long-term receipt of supplementary benefit. The authors of *Men out of Work*,[11] while recognizing that the *intention* is to develop a sensitive and supportive role for U.R.O.s, comment on the fact that the distinction is increasing between the temporarily unemployed, and 'those whose unemployment results from a seriously disadvantaged position in the labour market', and it is invidious that the latter should become 'the prime concern of the organisation which has taken over the legacy of the Poor Law'.

The analysis of the Disabled Live File showed that the clients categorized as disabled tended to be elderly (53 per cent over 50 years of age), male (89 per cent), with additional 'disadvantages' (71 per cent), judged untrainable at various recognized levels (67–88 per cent), and unskilled (75 per cent). Obviously, the employment services find this clientele difficult to help. Since they can no longer be defined in terms of clear-cut clinical categories, it is necessary to define them in terms of the effect of their characteristics *for the defining body,* that is, in terms of the task they present to the employment services. They become a 'problem' group, when in fact the problem lies not in the group itself, but in fitting people with different characteristics of all sorts into a given economic structure.

Work rehabilitation and training

It is not possible to make any evaluative comment on the Department of Employment's rehabilitation and retraining establishments – the I.R.U. and G.T.C. – simply because so few of the sample had any experience of them. Three people had attended I.R.U.s some years before (all men, all under 40, two now working in sheltered employment and one in a 'designated' job) but none had any experience of G.T.C.s. The Rehabilitation Unit was suggested or mentioned to two people after this hospitalization, and the Training Centre to three: all declined to go. One young man himself raised the question of retraining after reading leaflets in the employment office. Except in the case of the blind, no one in the sample had any experience of, or indeed any knowledge of, other special training facilities or provisions for work at home.

There was some confusion, amongst the small number who did know about retraining facilities, between the I.R.U. and

G.T.C. The concept of non-vocational 'rehabilitation' was difficult for them to grasp, except in terms of physical medicine, and while they might readily admit to needing physiotherapy, on the one hand, or training in a skill, on the other, they were unlikely to define themselves as needing 'rehabilitation for work'. The men who had been to I.R.U.s, or their families, tended to have had mistakenly practical and specific expectations and so had been disappointed:

> Mr and Mrs Hutcheson, for instance, described at length how their son had been sent to an I.R.U. some years before, which they had seen as a great opportunity, the opening of a new life for the young man. They had expected him to learn some marketable skill and had been bitterly disappointed when, in their view, he had 'learned nothing – wasted his time.'

When people were asked why they had not enquired about retraining at a G.T.C., or had turned down the D.R.O.'s suggestion, they offered explanations in terms firstly, of the practical difficulties of leaving their homes, and secondly, of the poor reputation that they felt the Training Centres had. Some of the practical difficulties, like Mr Thomson's over the care of his children, were real, but it was the 'uselessness' of government training ('everybody knows that') that was usually stressed as the major reason for refusing retraining. The same stories were repeated by man after man: that there was discrimination by employers against workers who had been to G.T.C., and that 'the system's no good anyway because the unions won't accept it'. These were usually supplemented by tales of 'a man down the street' who had been trained in a skill but was unable to find work – tales so similar in detail that it seemed likely that they were an example of folk-tales in creation. It was widely held that the training centres were full of those who were work-shy and difficult to employ, and that disabled people would be stigmatized by contamination: it seemed that, again, the attempt not to single out the disabled was having an effect opposite to that intended, and was resulting only in the creation of a devalued class of the generally 'disadvantaged'.

In fact, however, there were indications that the reluctance to go away from home might be the more salient problem, and the ritual stories about the training centres an excuse and rationalization. The few people who were debating whether or not they might consider retraining displayed a great deal of anxiety and timidity about leaving the security of family and home for an unknown situation in which they might not 'make the grade':

> Although Richard Kinnaird's community support was minimal, he said, 'The trade I fancied, the centre's in England — I don't want to go to England, I'm a bit feared of going so far away and leaving everything.' A month or two later, he said, 'No, I've given up the idea, I daren't go all that way. I'd have to give up my digs, and then if I couldn't get a job there I'd have nothing here either. I want to stay independent. This is my home. It's too dangerous to give it up.'

Amongst doctors and officials, the reluctance of the City's people to go away from home was commonly cited as the major reason for the under-use of rehabilitation and training centres, and the building of local centres was thought to be the only possible solution. There is no doubt that a local centre would have been advantageous, but it is also possible that this emphasis on the unwillingness of local people to leave home resulted in a self-fulfilling prophecy. No one reported having been actively encouraged to consider retraining: rather, lack of interest seemed to be taken for granted.

In any case, training courses were thought of only in relation to a restricted range of jobs. There were several people in the sample (an example might be Mr Wallace, pp. 140–1) who had drifted downwards to unskilled manual work, but who would have been quite capable of learning a non-manual job.

Sheltered employment

The question of sheltered employment, equally, was relevant to few people in the sample: the obvious question raised is why the system touched so small a number. Again, it was largely the limited nature of sheltered jobs that was the restricting factor. It has long been argued that the emphasis on craft skills in blind workshops is out of date, and in the workshop of the City as elsewhere the range of work had been greatly expanded beyond the traditional basket-work. Nevertheless, the emphasis remains in almost all sheltered workshops upon industrial work, and it could be argued that this is equally out of date in the post-industrial society.

The patterns of the present system of sheltered employment were established by the recommendations of the

Tomlinson Committee in 1943. Building upon the earlier charitable provisions (especially for the blind) and upon war-time experiments – the Lord Roberts workshops of the Boer War, the governmental instructional factors for disabled ex-servicemen set up in 1917 – the Committee recommended a system which, embodied in the Disabled Persons (Employment) Act 1944, remains substantially unaltered. In an attempt to avoid the stigma of charity, the Committee had stressed the advantages of directing sheltered employment away from welfare towards as 'normal' an industrial structure as possible. The workshops should, for instance, manufacture 'articles required for war or other public purposes, and not fancy or semi-luxury articles dependent for their sale on the charitable public'. Historically, the clientele for the workshops were the sense-deprived and those injured by war, largely the orthopaedically disabled.

In fact, these are the groups that *open* industry can most easily cater for. There were examples in this sample of the blind, and of severely crippled people, working very efficiently outside sheltered employment. For the orthopaedically disabled, a machine may have to be adapted or the work environment considered, but the work itself does not have to be de-skilled. The sort of sheltered work that was required by those people in the sample no longer able to continue in their jobs was work with shorter hours or less physical exertion, but not necessarily less skill or dexterity, than open industry, and in particular work where some inevitable absenteeism through sickness would be tolerated. The restricted range of sheltered jobs, and the industrial emphasis, were suitable for only a minority. On the one hand, many others would have liked and been capable of white-collar work, and on the other many people used to being out-of-doors all their lives described the idea of a 'shut-in' Remploy factory as intolerable.

Another reason for the low level of demand for sheltered work was because it was seen, by potential clients, as a final and last-ditch solution, a life-sentence from which there could be no escape. In part, again, this seemed to be a true reflection of the practice – if not of the principle – of the structure, viewed historically. Although the Tomlinson Committee had laid stress upon the rehabilitative possibilities of sheltered work, and had envisaged the transfer of many people into open employment, the definition of eligibility laid down by the 1944 Act (and still in operation) virtually precluded much movement from sheltered to open jobs. Those who were eligible were those whose disability made open employment *impossible*, either permanently or 'for a substantial period'. Nor could those who managed workshops be expected to find it easy to reconcile two incompatible roles as manager of an efficient industrial enterprise on the one hand, and of a therapeutic rehabilitation service on the other. One situation implied a stable workforce, in which productive employees should be encouraged to stay, and the other a high turn-over, with the 'best' employees encouraged to leave.

A third barrier to the potential client arose out of the rather confused and easily misunderstood system of administrative provision, again a historical legacy. The principle of building upon existing structures had created a tripartite arrangement, with responsibility divided amongst local authority, the government-supported company Remploy, and voluntary agencies. Although people were clear that jobs at the Blind Workshop or the Remploy factory were subsidized, they were often not sure whether it was by government or local authority, and the complicated, indirect and unpublished methods of financing were a fruitful source of misunderstanding.* In general, the Blind Workshop was still looked upon as a charitable organization by those with no personal experience of it, and the Remploy factory as a commercial enterprise.

Another source of confusion was that, again as a legacy of a pragmatic history, rates of pay varied between the different sheltered workshops. Blind workshops were known to pay most generously, and local authority workshops usually the least, with Remploy in an intermediate position. These differences reflect the history of provision in very concrete terms: the strength of the early pressure for one special group, the blind, the original governmental emphasis on the

*Remploy is subsidized directly through the Department of Employment. Local authorities have a statutory duty to provide employment for blind people, but only permissive powers for other disabled people. In cases where they supplement Remploy's provision, government aid comes largely through specific grants, taken into account in assessing general rate-support grant. Where (as in the case of the Blind Workshop) the voluntary organization is acting as the agent of the local authority in fulfilling its statutory duty, financial arrangements are entirely local. Subject to a maximum, the Department of Employment pays 75 per cent of whatever the local authority contributes (with other arrangements for capital costs).

war- and industrially-disabled, and the reliance upon the vagaries of local decisions for the rest. Those few (sighted) disabled people in the sample who considered sheltered workshops at all expressed a clear preference for the Blind Workshop.

Another set of distinctions within the system, again a source of confusion, concerned the different status of the work provided by 'designated' or 'disabled' jobs, sheltered work, and diversionary 'occupational' work. Few people appeared to understand the distinction or to have had it adequately explained to them, and this led to many (mistaken) comments about 'only pocket-money in sheltered work', or 'the disabled rate of pay you get in registered jobs'.

In general, the official resettlement services might be seen as a rich mine of historical residues. For the most part, people saw them as irrelevant to the problems described in the earlier part of this chapter.

SUMMARY

Of the 157 people who were truly in the labour market, well over half found that they had some problem concerning work during the survey year. Less than half of these found solutions to their problems. A large number of people, 33, had to leave their jobs because of their current illness or accident.

There was no simple and direct relationship between job problems and degree of impairment: many severely disabled people nevertheless found very satisfactory working lives. Those who did have problems were more likely to be male, and manual workers, and to be already unemployed. In some cases physical impairment had led to a sudden discontinuity in the worker's career, and in others to a slow downward drift into increasingly less well-paid or enjoyable jobs. To be already unemployed was conspicuously unfavourable, for it seemed that the category of 'unemployed' took precedence over that of 'ill' or 'disabled' as a master label.

Only a small proportion of those who solved their working problems, by finding adaptations to their jobs or new work, did so with the help of professionals or formal agencies. The greatest sources of help were work-groups, kinsfolk or friends. Though interventions from the medical profession were effective where they occurred, they were rare; indeed, the procedures and time-tables of the clinical world sometimes seemed to the patients to run counter to those of their working worlds.

Whether or not problems could be solved depended upon the relationship of the individual worker to the economic structure of society, and the actual nature of his work, rather than simply upon his socio-economic class. Women found their looser relationship with the world of work to be an advantage, leaving them more freedom of action. They, and older men who could be encouraged to retire, were presumed by agencies to have an alternative role available to that of 'worker', and so there was less pressure upon them to accept the formal label of 'disabled'.

This label, in its clearest form as the disabled register of the Department of Employment, was generally held to be a stigmatizing and disadvantageous one in the context of work. Registration was found to be very arbitrary, and the selection of clients appeared to relate more to the problems of the agency in carrying out its formal functions than to a response to 'need' or 'demand'. Official resettlement services were seen as very limited in character, and the quota system designed to encourage employers to consider disabled people was felt to be ineffectual. It is suggested that positive incentives for employers to provide light jobs, to retrain impaired workers, or to adapt working conditions for the disabled, might be effective in a way that negative sanctions (in any case never applied) are not.

People were found to react to their categorization as 'disabled for work' in an instrumental way. They found it essentially meaningless as a general category: whether or not they had job problems depended on a complex interaction of their state of health with the nature of their job and with their social setting. If, as a formal category, it offered any advantages they would accept it, but they resented its extension into areas of life where they did not necessarily accept that they were disabled. If the category came to be seen as synonymous with 'unemployable' or 'socially disadvantaged', then it would be avoided, just as in the field of social security 'disabled' would be rejected if it became confused with 'the poor', or in the field of practical welfare would be resented if it seemed to be treated in the same way as 'social problem'.

REFERENCES

1. See, e.g., Sinfield, A., *The Long-term Unemployed*, Paris, O.E.C.D., 1968; Hill, M. J., Harrison, R. M., Sergeant, A. V. and Talbot, V., *Men Out of Work*, Cambridge University Press, 1973; Daniel, W. W., *A National Study of the Unemployed*, London, P. E. P., 1974.
2. Buckle, Judith, *Work, Education and Qualifications* (Part II of *Handicapped and Impaired in Great Britain*), London, H.M.S.O., 1971.
3. e.g. *Report of the Interdepartmental Committee on the Rehabilitation and Resettlement of Disabled Persons* (Tomlinson Report), London, H.M.S.O., 1943; *Report of the Standing Committee on the Rehabilitation and Resettlement of Disabled Persons*, London, H.M.S.O., 1946, 1949, 1958; *Report of the Committee of Enquiry on the Rehabilitation, Training and Resettlement of Disabled Persons* (Piercy Report), London, H.M.S.O., 1956; British Medical Association, *Report on the Rehabilitation and Resettlement of Disabled Persons*, London, H.M.S.O., 1954; *Report of a Subcommittee of the Standing Medical Advisory Committee, D.H.S.S.* (Tunbridge Report), London, H.M.S.O., 1972.
4. Cumming, E. and Henry, W. E., *Growing Old*, Basic Books, New York, 1961.
5. e.g. Rose, A. M., 'A Current Theoretical Issue in Social Gerontology', *The Gerontologist*, May 1964.
6. Crawford, M. P., 'Retirement and Role-playing', *Sociology*, 6.2, 1972.
7. See, e.g., Bosanquet, N. and Standing G., 'Government and Unemployment 1966–70: A study of Policy and Evidence', *Brit. J. Industrial Relations*, 10.2, 1972.
8. Buckle, Judith, 1971, op. cit., p. 37.
9. Hill, M. J. *et al.*, 1973, op. cit., p. 46.
10. Department of Employment, *Resettlement Policy and Services for Disabled People*, London, H.M.S.O., 1973.
11. Hill, M. J. *et al.*, 1973, op. cit., p. 148.

7
THE INDUSTRIALLY INJURED

The category of 'industrially injured' is a special one. It may or may not coincide with the category of 'disabled', but, since it is a matter of legal definition and has concrete consequences in the form of money benefits, it might be expected to be a clear label in a way that 'disabled' is not. There may be no practical difference in condition or circumstances between a man cripplied in a road accident and one injured at work, or between a man whose chronic back pain is due to a lifetime's manual labour and one whose back injury was caused by a single identifiable accident. Nevertheless – for reasons concerned with the historical development of welfare and with the economic value of the work ethic, sketched in Chapter 1 – most industrialized societies have chosen to treat the traumatically work-injured (and the war-injured) rather differently from the rest.

The industrially injured not only receive special national insurance benefits, at a higher rate than ordinary sickness benefits (for a period of up to 26 weeks) but may also subsequently receive a temporary or permanent pension, or a lump sum, designed to recompense them 'for loss of physical or mental faculty' sustained in an accident. This disablement benefit may be increased by a number of allowances, notably a 'special hardship allowance' which is payable if the injured person, returning to work, earns less money than before his accident. The injured employee may also, and quite separately, seek damages as compensation if his injury is caused by a civil wrong or 'tort'. The majority of employers are compelled by law to insure against liability, and the litigation is usually carried out by insurance companies. Trade unions frequently act for employees.

This common-law system of compensation has come under considerable criticism, on the grounds that it is extremely costly, subject to uncertainty and delay, and not efficient in providing sanctions against negligence.[1,2] It has been widely suggested that a comprehensive system of social insurance would be preferable, replacing both tort liability and special national insurance benefits for industrial injury, and treating all incapacitated people alike;[3] such a system has been introduced in, for instance, New Zealand and some Canadian Provinces.

There is, however, little evidence on the practical effects of the existing system upon the lives of individuals. In this sample there were 19 people who believed that their injury was directly caused by their work. They are few in number, but these people may be of particular interest. Did the existence of this legal category, which might be presumed to be straightforward, affect the processes of definition? Did it influence their behaviour, or that of agencies towards them? How were their careers affected by the special payments they might receive as support or compensation?

The definition of industrial injury

In fact, the processes of defining an injury as industrial did not appear to be wholly straightforward. In the 19 cases where the patient believed, and was supported by some clinical evidence, that his injury was caused by his work, 13 were formally categorized as industrial injury at once, two after a considerable lapse of time, and four were never so defined. There were also, of course, other cases where the evidence was ambiguous and the patient himself uncertain. It was only vaguely understood that an 'accident' had to be distinguished from the impairment caused by a 'process' over many years of work, and in any case the distinction was felt to be unreal.

> Mrs Leask, for instance, was a machine-operator whose work involved continually using her knee to press a lever sideways. The knee suddenly locked at work, and eventually she underwent surgery for cartilege removal. The consultant expressed the opinion that this was due to her work, but Mrs Leask felt that this would not be defined as an accident and never applied for any injury benefit, though she was away from work for three months.

For the most part, however, people were naturally eager to blame their work if possible. They felt the distinction between work and non-work injury to be arbitrary and unjust in its effects, but were usually clear about their right to special treatment if the injury did take place at work. It would not have been reasonable to expect anyone to query the basis of that right; rather, they sought to suggest ways by which it might fairly be extended. Mr Stott, for instance, who was knocked down just outside his factory gates, spoke ruefully many times of how 'it would have been different if I'd *started* work – it isn't really fair, is it, the difference it makes whether it was five to eight or five past.' Other people who had suffered simple accidents at home frequently said, 'If *only* I had done it at work!'

The fact that special compensation existed would obviously encourage people to define themselves as industrially injured, if possible. There were several (not included among the 19) who speculated whether or not they might claim that their condition had been caused by their working conditions, and an atmosphere of conflict might well have built up: 'It *could* be due to work, but my employer says that's nonsense, and of course, the doctors are in cahoots with the employers, they say no-one can tell what caused it.' It was, in fact, the conflict setting – employee against employer, or employee against the D.H.S.S. – which, by an ironic twist, caused the few people who were definitely eligible for injury benefits but refused to apply for them to act so apparently irrationally. One worker, whose accident had very definitely taken place at work, had previously had a diagnosis of alcoholism applied to him, and it appeared that his reluctance to have the injury defined as industrial was due to his feeling that 'they' would be prejudiced against him and his medical history would be disclosed.

Other reasons why an employee might be reluctant to engage in what he saw as a conflict situation with his employer were exemplified in the story of Mr Shand. This married man of 22 was employed by a builder. He was working with a fork-lift truck when (according to him) 'one of the other blokes accidentally knocked the brake' and the fork-lift came down upon the fingers of his right hand. He was off work for 7 months, and one year after the accident two fingers were still badly distorted and without feeling, with chronic ulceration which was receiving out-patient treatment. He was very embarrassed by the ugliness of the hand and had developed various awkward concealing techniques.

For 6 months following the accident he was receiving ordinary sickness benefit, made up to full pay by his employer. No injury benefit was ever received. The patient has some idea during this period that it might be possible to 'take the employer to court' and his wife tried to encourage him to make enquiries, but neither of them had any knowledge of the relevant national insurance benefits nor any understanding of the distinction between N.I., disablement compensation and tort damages. He decided against taking any action because 'I asked some of my mates and they said it would mean my cards on the spot.' He and his wife discussed the possibility that there might be legal safeguards for his employment, but they came to the conclusion that 'the employer will always win somehow' and were nervous of any 'tangles with the law'. In any case, the employee thought that his employer was generous in making up his pay, and did not see how any compensation would improve his financial position. An additional complication was that the family lived in a tied house at a very low rent, and were frightened of losing it. He was not a member of a trade union.

Industrial disease

The problems of deciding whether or not an injury is 'industrial' and whether or not it is, in the employee's eyes, reasonable and in his best interests to suggest that it is, are of course repeated in an exaggerated form in the case of industrial disease. If the definition of an industrial injury was held to be arbitrary and sometimes equivocal, the definition of an industrial disease was thought by the subjects to be derisorily unjust. It was obvious and 'only fair' that employers should compensate employees in the most reprehensible cases, where the disease was caused by negligence or the flouting of regulations for the processing of dangerous materials. Any more general principle that compensation might exist under national insurance for certain industries or certain diseases was merely an irrational quirk of the system. Was not the rheumatism or bronchitis of a man who had been an outdoor manual worker all his life equally caused by his work? The definition of industrial disease was simply felt to be too arbitrary to be relevant, and although there were two or three people in the sample who felt strongly that, for instance, their work as granite-polishers was the cause of their lung disease, there was no instance in the sample of anyone formally seeking the official categorization.

It appeared that doctors too found the concept of industrial disease difficult to deal with. Several people reported that doctors had told them that their disease was industrially induced, though this was hearsay, since there was no case of a definite statement in medical records. It may be noted, however, that the fact of a man's employment as – for instance – a granite-polisher, might well be commented on in records as though it were relevant.

The assessment of industrial injury

Dating as it does from an early period in the history of provision for the disabled, the principles on which industrial impairments are assessed represent a limited and clinically oriented view of what it is to be disabled. One of the themes throughout this study has been the way in which assessments of need based on objective clinical measures are giving way to assessments based on functional measures of the social consequences of impairment – and the problems which this presents. The original problems of the older ways of assessing eligibility for services, against which the emphasis on social functioning is a reaction, are amply illustrated in the measures still used for assessing industrial injury.

The principle of compensation, rather than providing for need, underlies the British system, although ostensibly the national insurance system purports to recompense for lost earning capacity rather than to compensate for pain, disfigurement or loss of function. This means that a sliding scale of recompense is appropriate, for obviously, the loss of an arm merits greater compensation that the loss of a finger. In some countries* benefit is assessed directly in terms of reduced earning capacity, the simplest system being based on an examination of actual earnings before and after disablement. In Britain, however, with a tradition of preferring to rely on professional experts for assessment, disability is still measured on purely medical grounds. Thus, the system still persists in which impairments are 'scored' in percentage terms: 30 per cent for one eye or one foot, 50 per cent for four fingers, 90 per cent for one arm.

The survey subjects were unanimous in finding this system ludicrous. Amputations were at least easily defined, but for the majority of less definite and irrevocable injuries there was a great deal of room for conflict.

The comments of George Leslie, a single dock-worker in his thirties, who had received injuries when a winch wire had snapped back upon

*e.g. Germany, Sweden, Norway, Netherlands.

> his neck, were typical. After 6 months away from work, his residual disability was assessed at 2 per cent. He was very resentful, and complained: 'Two per cent of what? It doesn't make any sense, does it. I'm still on the light shift [special work for convalescent or disabled workers] and my pay's still a third of what it was. I make that 33 per cent! I don't understand their arithmetic. How disabled you are means what you can earn.'

Workers were placed in a dilemma. They rarely had any wish to exaggerate their disabilities: after all, this might affect their jobs. On the other hand, no matter how objective the medical assessment might purport to be, they certainly felt that their presentation affected the decision made: they would be foolish actively and voluntarily to relinquish the income which was their 'right.'

> A particularly clear illustration of this conflict, and of the disadvantageous consequences it might have, was the case of John Duthie, another unmarried dock-worker. He fell from an insecure loading platform, injuring his back and legs, and was in hospital intermittently for 14 months and away from work for 16. Two years after the accident he still considered himself very impaired, with constant back pain and difficulty in walking far or standing for long. On his return to work he too was given a light job which (with no overtime permitted) cut his earnings by at least half. At first he was assessed as 30 per cent disabled, and after a year as 15 per cent. During this year he expressed growing worries about his future. He had been a vigorous man, proud of his physique, but he now felt himself placed in an equivocal position where to minimize his disability might prejudice any additional disablement benefit, while to emphasize it might mean that at best he could never earn more than his present reduced wage. He was unable to make up his mind whether or not to seek further specialist treatment: on the one hand, he felt that his present condition was barely tolerable; on the other, that further hospitalization might lose him even the light job. A relatively minor dispute over a 5 per cent deduction from his disablement benefit for a 'pre-existing condition' assumed a disproportionate importance to him and he became very bitter about it, insisting that this ten-year-old back condition had also been a dock injury, although his general practitioner's records were unclear about it. As the year went by he became more and more aggrieved and aggressive, and it seemed that the conflict over the official assessment of his disability was not only affecting his whole attitude to his working life but also prejudicing his medical rehabilitation.

A more trivial example of the way in which assessments were viewed was given in the comments of Mr and Mrs Coull who had both sustained injuries. Mr Coull had lost the thumb of his right hand and was defined as permanently disabled to the extent of 35 per cent, with an appropriate weekly income. His wife, a fish-worker, had cut the left forefinger with a knife and some years later still found the finger quite useless. She had been assessed as one per cent disabled, and her finger had been valued at a lump sum of £4. While laughing at the stupidities of 'the system', and agreeing that his injury was the more serious, they still felt strongly that the difference between £4 and (over a probable lifetime) several thousands seemed disproportionate.

Small lump sums such as this* almost always caused great offence, whereas pensions however small did not: the former seemed to the injured to be an insulting 'paying off' for a disability which would be of permanent importance to them and which they disliked having evaluated in monetary terms, while to be awarded a pension offered them a continuing recognition in an acceptable way. The differences may be epitomised by typical comments: on the one hand 'They gave me £99 for my finger – that's what a finger's worth; would you sell a finger for that?' and on the other 'Of course, I've got a pension – it's only small – for my thumb.'

The dual system of compensation

A complicating factor affecting people's definition of themselves as eligible for compensation for their industrial injury was, of course, the existence of a dual system of recompense: benefits through their national insurance on the one hand, and 'damages' or tort compensation from the employer on the other.

The main drawback of the dual system highlighted by this survey was a very simple one: that it was very rarely understood. It was quite commonly believed that disablement benefit, particularly when paid in lump sums, was the same as civil damages obtained through the courts and 'all came out of the employer's insurance.' People rarely knew the correct name of the benefit they were receiving, or

*Lump sums may be paid in place of weekly pensions if the disablement is assessed at 20 per cent or less.

understood the difference between injury benefit, disablement benefit, and hardship allowance, and these confusions not only resulted in loss of potential benefits but also fostered aggressive discontent in some individuals and apathy in others.

The confusion between N.I. benefits and civil damages was the cause, in a few cases, of reluctance to apply for any injury benefit at all. When asked why they had not applied, these patients offered reasons which might have had some force in practical terms as far as tort damages were concerned, but were irrelevant to N.I. benefits: they were frightened of losing their jobs or antagonizing their employers, or believed that the question of fault was relevant. In the case of Mr Shand, already quoted, he was in a tied house he was fearful of losing, and he was anxious not to offend a 'generous' employer who was making up his full basic pay. In the case of Mr McCall, a contributing factor to his dislike of the idea of 'trouble' was the local shortage of employment opportunities, and again his family and housing were relevant:

> Mr McCall lived in a rather remote country area with his wife and five young children. During the six months following his injury he received varying weekly sums without at any time understanding the reason for the variation or the basis of the calculations. He was a quiet, shy man, unused to either telephones or correspondence and with no easy way of reaching officials. It is certain that he received no injury benefit for the first two-and-a-half months, and indeed it was probably the questions of the survey itself that eventually persuaded him to make a claim; he had expected that 'they' would automatically allow him all that he was entitled to. Since he had not claimed within the statutory period he lost the money which he would have been entitled to. It was not until 9 months later, when he returned to work and began to talk to workmates, that the idea of claiming compensation from his employer (for an accident caused wholly, he believed, by others' negligence) occurred to him; he had thought at first that by applying for national insurance compensation he would automatically set a claim against his employer into motion if 'they' thought it appropriate. He did start proceedings, through his union, but very half-heartedly, for he was afraid of losing his job and of 'trouble' with officials and the law. Well over a year after the accident occurred, the claim had barely started, and it seemed doubtful whether he would pursue it.
>
> Mr McCall's story was also an example of the way in which the

system fosters antagonism and suspicion. At the beginning of the survey year he had few complaints about his employment as a crane-driver: it was 'quite a good job' and though the pay seemed very low the family appeared to be content and comfortable. In this as in other cases, however, the employee's attitude to his work could be seen to change gradually over the survey year, as initial optimism and thankfulness because 'it could have been worse' gave way to disappointment at slow improvement and a dawning recognition that some impairment would be permanent. At first, all Mr McCall wanted was to get back to his job: by the end of the year he was convinced that his employer was forcing him to do exactly the same work as before, though he found it difficult and painful, 'because now I've started to put in a claim for damages, he wants to be able to say I'm doing the same as before, so I can't really be disabled, whatever the doctors say. I'm caught, see, if I don't do the job then I've got no job, and if I do I'm not injured.' How much truth there was in this is not relevant to Mr McCall's behaviour, since he believed it to to be true. Gratitude had given way to suspicion, and instead of trying to minimise his disability, Mr McCall was beginning to exaggerate his difficulties.

Another example of the growth of jealousy and resentment concerned the cases of the two dock-workers, Mr Leslie and Mr Duthie, who happened to be neighbours. Mr Duthie had received damages of £1200 from his employer, which he regarded simply as compensation (in his view inadequate) for his lost earnings during the lengthy period off work. Mr Leslie, who got no damages, knew some of the circumstances of his neighbour's case and was very aggrieved by the difference between them. While he acknowledged that Mr Duthie was by far the more seriously injured, he insisted that 'he got a hardship allowance for that, national insurance hardship is supposed to be compensation for the suffering and so on, I agree he was due that. But for *compensation*, that's for being off work, losing your earnings, eventually I got £6 [six months' disability benefit for his 2 per cent injury] and he got *thousands*, I heard. When I asked they said the difference was the winch wasn't anyone's fault, but both accidents were more or less the same, just things that happen.'

The system of tortious liability was, in general, strongly felt to be simply a lottery. Tort damages, relying on the proof of some 'fault', were of course relevant to road accidents as well as industrial accidents. Of the 19 work accidents, 5 were the subject of tort actions, and in the 8 road accidents in the sample, two people received compensation.

In many cases no rational cause could be perceived why an accident should have been in one category rather than another. The militancy of the individual, his level of information about the possibilities, trade union membership, the attitudes of employers, and adventitious circumstances (in particular, the presence or absence of witnesses) all appeared to be more salient than the actual facts. Many accident victims reported having been told by their unions, by the D.H.S.S., and in one or two cases by solicitors, 'it all depends upon having had witnesses.' It appeared possible that unions and other advisors were using this as an excuse to avoid involvement in doubtful cases; it was a tactful way of saying that the facts might by disputed. The use of this invocation of the necessity for witnesses inevitably, however, made the patients resentful and cynical about the legal system.

The concept of fault seemed also to be difficult to accept. There were few instances where it was clear that there had been negligence on the part either of the injured person, or the employer or vehicle driver, and in most cases the necessity to talk in terms of fault appeared to offend some sense of natural justice. One man expressed this clearly by saying, 'It was an *accident*, wasn't it, and an accident's nobody's fault by definition. I didn't do it on purpose! My boss wasn't out to injure me intentionally either.'

Compensation and rehabilitation

The limited evidence of this survey (few large sums were received in compensation) was that lump sums tended to be of little benefit to the injured in the long term. No individual received compensation, whether as disablement benefit or civil damages, which actually matched his loss of earnings. Larger sums were quickly spent, often in ways (for instance, buying motor-cars) which were more likely to lead to future problems that to provide any lasting benefit. Mr Duthie had spent part of his compensation on a car, but had owned it for only a matter of months when it was so badly damaged in an accident that it was written off.

Another man, Mr Downie, a labourer in his 50s, was injured while on demolition work, and had received a smaller lump sum disablement benefit with which he was quite pleased. He also spent the money on a car and its running expenses. Although he had been assessed as only 10 per cent permanently disabled, he himself was very dissatisfied with his condition, with chronic ulceration of the leg which had been injured by an iron ball, and (he claimed) considerable pain and unsteadiness. After eight months treatment he returned to work; his employer had arranged, without consulting him, that he should take a new job with a building firm. He found the work difficult and painful, and valued the car very much as a means of at least travelling to work easily. However, he was poorly paid and frequently off work – on two occasions he fell, receiving further minor injuries – and maintaining the car proved to be too expensive. Towards the end of the survey year he was running into debt and had regretfully decided that the car must be given up. This, combined with his dissatisfaction over his job, was making him increasingly resentful and depressed. He appeared genuinely anxious to continue to work, if a suitable job could be found, but it seemed very likely that he would either be dismissed, or choose to stop working, before very long.

There were other cases where it seemed that the complications of compensation systems were not helpful to the patient's career, simply because they caused delay. Both physical rehabilitation and consideration of a man's working future might be delayed until his compensation position was clarified: this required a definite prognosis, and in cases where such a prognosis was difficult to make the patients often felt themselves to be 'only marking time until someone makes up their mind' or 'just going back and forward' for many months.

Mr Dalgarno, for instance, a young semi-skilled worker in a paper-mill, with a wife and three small children, was still idle a year after the accident in which both legs had been broken and lacerated. There had been no discussion with his employer, with the Department of Employment, or with doctors, about his future. It appeared to him that he was merely drifting, and he became increasingly discouraged as successive examinations and assessment boards produced 'wait and see' results. His own feeling was that the question of compensation, which he rather vaguely thought 'the union is looking after', and which was held in abeyance because of his slow recovery, was blocking any serious consideration of his working future.

In general, despite the fact that the category of industrial injury is ostensibly one of the clearest labels that can be applied to disabled people, and moreover one which offers practical advantages in terms of benefits, the survey subjects did not find it a very comprehensible or advantageous category. On the contrary, the industrially injured were amongst those who found themselves most vulnerably and helplessly enmeshed in the system, and their histories strongly support the criticisms which are increasingly being levelled at mechanisms of compensation. The existence of a legal category including so great a variety of people, from those with very minor but permanent impairments to the totally incapacitated, served only to confuse the concept of 'disability'. A man's income and his job are areas of life which are obviously connected, and if he is in need of help they ought to be considered together. It seemed to many of the industrially injured that the two systems of help were operating quite independently of each other, or even sometimes against each other. There were exceptions: some employers had considerate and efficient schemes for the rehabilitation and re-employment of their injured workers. For the rest of the injured, it was understandable that their immediate concern should be for their compensation or their pension; by the end of the year, however, some were already beginning to realize that the relatively small sums of money involved were of much less importance than prompt and realistic help in organizing their working future.

SUMMARY

Nineteen people in the sample were injured at work, though only 13 of these injuries were immediately defined as industrial. The survey subjects, while naturally anxious to have the advantages of injury benefit or compensation, found the concept of work injury (and still more, disease) to present practical problems. The simple quantitative measures of physical impairment used in assessment appeared to them inequitable and inappropriate.

The dual system of compensation for injury – national insurance benefits and civil damages – caused considerable confusion. The concept of fault, central to the system of tort liability, was often felt to be inappropriate, and the system in general caused resentment because it was thought to be capricious. Relatively small lump sums of money paid as compensation seemed particularly pointless, when what was really needed was expert job help and advice.

REFERENCES

1. Harris, D. R., 'The Legal System of Compensation for Death and Personal Injury Suffered in Accidents', in Lees, D. S. and Shaw, Stella (eds.), *Impairment, Disability and Handicap,* Heinemann Educational Books, 1974, p. 30.
2. Doherty, N. and Lees, D. S., 'Damages for Personal Injury: Some Economic Issues', ibid., p. 56.
3. Lewis, R. and Latta, G., 'Compensation for Industrial Injury and Disease', *J. Social Policy*, 4.1, 1975, p. 25.

8
PROBLEMS OF FAMILY RELATIONSHIPS AND SOCIAL LIFE

Amongst the self-defined problems of this study, it was the practical troubles of money, work, daily living, discussed in previous chapters, that the patients were, in general, most anxious to talk about at first. It is not, of course, possible to say whether these 'really' loomed largest, or were simply offered as more easy to explain or more likely to be soluble. Eventually, however, it became clear that in a number of cases the problems were largely social – problems of marital relationships and family roles, or alternatively of isolation and loneliness, problems of boredom and lack of social interaction. These were some of the unhappiest people in the sample.

These problems, in particular, raise in its most obvious form the question of stigmatization. This has been one implicit dilemma complicating the helping services discussed in previous chapters: the major overt problem has usually been the difficulty of deciding, for a given purpose, who 'the disabled' *are*, but running behind it – and sometimes used as an excuse for avoiding it – has been the question, 'Even if we know who the people are whom we are required to help, and can define them in suitable administrative categories, do we wish to single them out and label them "disabled"? Might it not be better to categorize in some other way?'

Where more purely social services are concerned – the provision of occupation, recreation, social activities, case-work help in adjustment to handicap – the stigma which may be thought to attach to physical disability is even more relevant, since it lies behind the central arguments about integration and segregation. Is it better to provide special care and special facilities which mark out groups of people as 'different' or to try to integrate them into the community? In most countries, the tendency has always been to structure a social segregation, providing separate facilities and encouraging the disabled to interact primarily with their own minority group. Increasingly, this practice is being questioned, not least by disabled people themselves,[1] and it is being suggested that the justifications of segregation as 'best' for the handicapped may be a rationalization of society's unease and guilt.

The evidence which has been given shows without doubt that the *consequences* of physical impairment may place the sufferer in a stigmatized category, identified with the unemployable, the poor, or the dependent. Many people objected strongly to specific administrative variants of the 'disabled' label which they had found to be stigmatizing, such as 'handicapped child' in the field of education, or 'registered disabled' in the field of work. It remains to be asked, however, whether the survey subjects perceived that the disability itself led to any problem of social stigmatization, and whether they felt that any segregation was being imposed on them. It was felt that to enquire too directly about patients' perception of stigma would be impertinent, but indicators were selected to give some measure of their experience – whether the circle of friends had narrowed, willingness (taking practical problems into account) to engage in social activities, opinions of the 'helpfulness' of neighbours, and whether the patient volunteered any anxiety about his interaction with others.

A complex pattern appeared to exist. Those with common and not readily visible impairments would, of course, be unlikely to find the question of stigma relevant. In late middle age, chronic bronchitis or heart conditions might be considered almost 'normal'. Amongst young people with obvious orthopaedic disabilities there was rarely any indication that social interaction presented them with problems. Practical difficulties aside, no crippled, paralysed or limb-deficient patient reported that his circle of friends had narrowed or his social activities ceased; indeed (depending of course on age) many of them prided themselves on taking part in all the social and sporting activities that were within their capabilities.

Ann Duff, a young woman with an amputation, described how she had applied for her first job: 'I felt people had spoilt me while I was training, looked after me, you know – now it was the crunch: out into the real world! I'll never forget that first interview – they never even mentioned the disability. I suppose they were looking at me, to see how I managed, but they didn't make it obvious. I came away on top of the world! Later on, I saw the personnel report in the files, and of course I read it. It said – I've always remembered the words – "a very pleasant young girl with a slight limp!" Now wasn't that a generous description? It gave me confidence at once, to see that people didn't make too much of it. I think perhaps people with a visible handicap, when you can see they're coping, are better off perhaps than people with a condition which can't be seen. It's more of an unknown quantity to others.'

Three of the most severely disabled young men in the sample, who would need permanent personal care, became engaged to be married (in all three cases to nurses) during the survey year, and there were no other unmarried men under 40 with incapacitating disability. It must be added, however, that of the – rather few – severely and visibly disabled young women, none was married or engaged.

Perception of stigma appeared to depend very much upon the nature of the impairment, and was strongest in all those conditions which threatened the taken-for-granted world of everyday interaction. The limited range of 'normal' physical characteristics on which the rules of social interaction depend could, it seemed, encompass to some degree the lack of mobility of those with crippling conditions, but any condition which made communication difficult, or involved unusual and unpredictable behaviour which disrupted the customary pattern of social life, fell too far outside the accepted range. As Hilbourne has suggested,[2] these characteristics 'disabled the normal', putting non-disabled people at a disadvantage because their ordinary social equipment was inadequate for coping with these new situations. The people in the sample who felt most strongly that their disability was a stigma were those suffering from ataxias, spasticity, severe multiple sclerosis, deafness, blindness to a lesser extent, and epilepsy. It may be conjectured that severe disfigurement, of which there was no example in the sample, ought to be added to the list.

Epilepsy came into a special category. In fact, none of the sample's epileptics gave any evidence at all that they had experienced any social stigma, but each one expressed surprise and gratitude at this and all told generalized stories about the problems which epileptics 'usually' faced. The condition was 'known' to be one against which there was particular prejudice, but in this sample at least no actual examples of prejudice could be cited by any of the people who spoke in this way.

> Mr Rennie, for instance, described with gratitude how his workmates had 'looked out for him' during the years before his steadily worsening condition had forced him to stop work. Alexander Kennedy insisted that, despite fairly frequent grand mal seizures, he had never met with any discrimination during his schooling ('No – the other kids soon got used to me – it was the janitor they'd run for, I was his pet') or his employment. In this case it was the young man's mother who talked at length about how 'lucky' he was, since 'everyone knows' that epileptics are usually shunned.

This limited evidence suggests that epilepsy may be a special and interesting case. Publicity and education may have had some effect in altering people's behaviour towards epileptics (several people mentioned television programmes) while at the same time leaving them very conscious of 'the way it used to be' or 'the way *other* people behave.'

In the case of the other conditions felt to be stigmatized and socially damaging, in part the problems were simply practical ones. The focus of this survey was on interaction with agencies, rather than purely social interactions. Yet, even in the case of communication with agencies, where both participants usually wished primarily to convey information, it appeared that the inevitable misunderstandings which arose caused the client to feel that he was not being given sufficiently close attention. At this point he might withdraw, or he might become belligerent, setting up a vicious circle of irritation on one side and resentment on the other. The affairs of Mr Collie (p. 202) were a typical example of this. Conspicuously, all those people who like Mr Collie had difficulty in making themselves understood had antagonistic relationships with at least some of the agencies with whom they had to deal.

It was also notable that all those people in the sample who were severely hard of hearing had problems, and were likely to find it difficult to solve them. It appeared that this was a group whose special needs – for extra time and patience on the part of officials, for special care to see that they did not become socially isolated – were being conspicuously neglected.* Their disability's lack of visibility was, it seemed, almost a drawback to them. Whereas other 'invisible' handicaps (from epilepsy to cardiac disease) leave the possibility of normal social interaction for most of the time, deaf people may try to conceal their disability and yet still be unable to interact normally. The results were obvious in the many examples of misunderstanding on the part of the patient (who would not admit that he had not heard) and on the part of agencies (because the deaf person answered questions almost at random).

> Typical was Mrs Law, a lady of 60, living alone, who had suffered severe fractures in an accident. She was very concerned about her health in general, and anxious that some gastric symptoms should be diagnosed, but seemed unable to take any initiatives or to understand the investigations that eventually took place. She had no contact with the M.S.W., or with any welfare agency, and little with her general practitioner, and admitted that because of her deafness she disliked contact with any professionals and hated being in hospital. Because of some misunderstanding at the physiotherapy clinic, causing a scene which she found unpleasant, she refused to return to it. She felt herself to be completely socially isolated, and said to the interviewer at one point – 'I've seen nobody but yourself for a month – if it wasn't for the lassie [daughter] I'd never see a soul.' She talked at great length of her husband, who had died 23 years before.

> The case of Mrs McHardy (pp. 95–6) was particularly interesting because she was permanently crippled as well as deaf. It did not seem that she felt her orthopaedic disabilities as a potential stigma: she had, after all, gone out to work all her life. It was her deafness, rather, that caused the muddle she got into over national insurance, and prevented her from seeking the practical help that she needed. She explained that her deafness got worse when she had to speak to strangers, 'If I don't know the person's voice I get nervous which makes me not able to hear so well', and over the years had lost contact with everyone except her workmates. She was at the same

*Because, precisely, of the problems of communication, wholly reliable accounts about what medical and other help deaf people had received were sometimes difficult to obtain. The impression was, however, that more might have been done for many of them medically as well as socially. Several had no hearing aid. Some said it was very many years since they had seen any sort of specialist about their hearing, and in a few cases it seemed that a gradual deterioration had simply been accepted fatalistically without any attempt to seek medical advice.

time anxious for, and afraid of, social contacts, 'I'm scared of ending up knowing no one. People like us end up in asylums.' It had been suggested by 'the girls at work' that she join 'the disabled club' but she refused to consider the idea, not apparently because of the label (she spoke quite readily of 'hard of hearing being a *real* disability – the worst one there is') but because of her fear of strangers. She and other subjects strenuously avoided the word 'deaf': 'I'm *very* hard of hearing, but that's different from being deaf, isn't it?' she said. She had heard that it might be possible to learn to lip-read (through the Society for the Deaf) but was very insistent that she might consider this only because she 'hadn't known it was for the hard of hearing, not only for deaf people.' In fact, she did not during the survey year pluck up sufficient courage to go.

Even where no practical difficulties of communication existed, however, social problems were notably likely to arise for all those people whose diagnoses came into the category of neurological. Social relationships appeared to be adversely affected by the popular connection which existed between 'the nervous system', 'the brain', 'character' and 'intelligence'; many of these patients seemed defensive about their condition, and expressed the feeling that both agencies and social contacts treated them as 'different' by such phrases as 'people treat you as though you're daft', 'it's a *physical* condition, but people don't understand that', or 'I'd get more sympathy in a wheelchair'.

The clearest demonstration of inability to come to terms with a neurological diagnosis, and the quite disproportionate ill-effects upon the patient's life, was the case of Mr Petrie. This architect in his 40s, with a slight congenital disability, suffered an unexpected neurological 'accident' with temporary ataxia, and a residual but gradually improving loss of co-ordination. When he was first discharged from hospital, he expressed himself as very happy with the explanations of his condition that he had been given, but as time went on it became obvious that he and (particularly) his wife were beginning to worry. He understood *what* had happened, but not *why* – and especially, why to him. What could he do to avoid its happening again? Might the condition be hereditary – what about their children? Mrs Petrie, especially, eventually expressed vividly her uneasiness about anything to do with 'the brain': 'I know it's silly, but somehow one wouldn't be frightened if it was his stomach – I've always been nervous of anything like this. Of course, I realize it's a *physical* thing – it's not the thinking part of the brain, you understand . . .' During the next two months it became obvious that her worries were becoming an obsession, although Mr Petrie's symptoms improved. Then Mr Petrie had a relatively minor, but messy, accident: two weeks later, while he was still convalescent, his wife left him, taking the children with her. There is no evidence, of course, that the marriage was a secure one before these events, but appearances suggested that it was, and certainly Mr Petrie blamed the 'shock' of his illness entirely. During the following nine months there were many vicissitudes as he tried to put pressure upon his wife to return, but at the end of the year he was still alone, free now from neurological symptoms but very unhappy and in need of practical help. In his determination not to let the house 'go to pieces', he had tried to do a cleaning job which his congenital disability made him clumsy at; he had injured himself in a fall and had remained alone and unable to care for himself for several days. His own summary of events was: 'Everything fell in on that day I had that attack – it's unbelievable, how there was no warning how things were going to go wrong. It started out as a medical problem but it's turned into a social problem now.' The sheer physical contrast between the house that the interviewer had first entered, lively, comfortable, full of children, and apparently secure and happy, and the desolate place that was left at the end of the survey year, was a particularly eloquent demonstration of the truth of his summary.

Many of the conditions which were 'undiagnosed' or imperfectly understood by the patient (which were often also neurological) were felt to be particularly stigmatized for similar reasons: because they were strange and difficult to understand. Several people with early multiple sclerosis provided examples of this.

The process of stigmatization is, of course, self-reinforcing, for the negative reactions of other people continually provide new grounds for stigma:

Mr Collie did not seem to feel that his severe and progressive ataxia of itself caused people to shun him; he described his neighbours as 'friendly enough'. What he did feel as stigmatizing was the fact that his wife had left him: 'They must think it's queer, her going and all. I don't know what they think. But to leave a man crippled like me – it looks bad, it makes me out to be a sort of monster. It wasn't like that at all, really, it just wasn't possible. But it makes you feel rejected, being left like that. You've been thrown down, just thrown down, you're no use.' It seemed that Mr Collie's fears might be

> justified, and that his wife's reaction to his condition might indeed affect the way in which other people viewed the condition itself. Two representatives of agencies, discussing the services offered in this case, both mentioned, quite gratuitously: 'Of course, his wife left him . . .', one adding that they 'didn't blame her'. The fact of his wife's desertion seemed to be accepted as evidence that he was 'really' of an unattractive character, with his severe and frustrating disability an irrelevance.

Another comment about Mr Collie was, 'Oh, yes, that man with the nasty disease . . .' The adjective might be taken to mean no more than 'serious', of course, but there were certainly overtones of 'unpleasant', easily transferred from the disease to the man. It was precisely this sort of process that the people who felt stigmatized objected to. They defined themselves as normal except for a handicap which was entirely physical, but it seemed to them that they were being defined as abnormal in character, or intelligence, or mental condition. They were being labelled in ways which they felt to be entirely wrong and 'unfair'.

Problems of family relationships

Within a stable group of family and neighbours the stresses of interaction may be eased by familiarity over time, and a new 'normal' established with a new set of taken-for-granted rules. The process of 'disabling the normal' may, however, take on a new dimension, for the family structure is no longer normal within the larger structure of the society:

> To say that Mr Brown is the husband of a woman with multiple sclerosis is to do more than label the person to whom he is married or endow him with a 'courtesy stigma' which arises because of his marriage. It is to recognise that he himself is disabled by his wife's disability and the constraints placed upon him because of it.[2]

The helping professions, recognizing this, have readily accepted the concept of 'the disabled family'. Little is known, however, about the ways in which family dynamics are affected by the advent of chronic illness or disability. The present study can offer only limited observations on family interactions, and it is suggested that there is a great need for more intensive research in this area.

Certain patterns were, however, obvious. There was much

evidence about the strain which impairment can put upon marital relationships. This seemed more likely in the case of the husband's disablement than the wife's, though it may be only that wives were more willing to talk about it. In only a few cases did a wife's disablement cause a complete change in the family's way of life, however (when, for instance, the husband had to give up his work to care for her); for the most part the wife 'managed', with varying degrees of hardship, with the formal or informal help of other women. A husband's disablement, on the other hand, meant a radical change; he might have to stay at home and adjust to 'idleness', or change his job or conditions of working in ways which affected the whole family pattern. Many wives described how discord developed: 'This place isn't big enough for him to be home all day', 'The children get on his nerves, he isn't used to them all the time', 'It irritates me to see him sitting there doing nothing, though I know it's not his fault.'

This was particularly true if the couples were young, and the disability completely unexpected:

> Mr Scott, for instance, a young industrially injured man who remained unable to work, and very unsure about his future, during the whole of the survey year, admitted that whereas he had previously been 'happy-go-lucky – not one to bother', he had now become bad-tempered and violent. He found himself completely unable to adjust to life in a two-roomed flat, overcrowded with small children and a large dog. His wife took a part-time job, but gave it up because she was unhappy about his care of the children, and the household became full of stress.

> Mrs Mann, another young wife with four toddlers, vividly expressed the strain of living with a husband whose heart condition permitted only intermittent work: 'He gets attacks of rage – I know it's only because he's worried – but the red begins to rise in his neck and I get the shakes when I see it. His illness is making me ill – I can't sleep either – it's the children that suffer.' Mrs Mann was advised by a health visitor to consult the Marriage Guidance Council, but she decided against it because 'that wouldn't do any good, because it's his health that causes it. It's a medical thing, not a social sort of thing.' Eventually she decided that the best person to consult would be 'a doctor at the hospital'.

Mrs Mann was one of several wives who mentioned the effect of a father's chronic illness or disability upon the children. Irritability where young children were concerned, and lack of sufficient energy to take an interest in, or sometimes to discipline, older children, were frequently spoken of as characteristics which had developed since the father's impairment.

There were only a few cases in which young families were being given social work support. In one case a new gratuitous tragedy had been superimposed upon the problems of a family with a severely disabled breadwinner, and the family acknowledged gratefully their social worker's efforts to prevent total disintegration. Social workers were likely to know families with disabled members, however, only if and when there were *other* problems – problems of practical need, or problems brought to their attention by some other agency (for instance, the housing department because of unpaid rent, or the police because of child delinquency). Before these problems had time to accumulate, or if in fact interpersonal relationships were the only problem, social workers were unlikely to be considered by the patients themselves or by those in contact with them as an appropriate source of help. This difficulty is not easily soluble, for even if social work resources were sufficient for a routine offer of support to all disabled families – which of course they are not – there would still be some resistance on the part of the potential clients to a service which seemed to assume that they might need case-work help, simply because of the association of social work with economic deprivation, and with social control agencies. It may perhaps be noted that the routine enquiries of medical social workers in the hospital setting were, on the other hand, never resented because they were seen by the patients as a service within a medical, rather than a social, context. There were, however, no sample cases where the medical social workers had remained in contact with the family for very long, and at the point of hospitalization few people could anticipate the nature of problems of family adjustment.

One of the most perceptive accounts of how people felt that impairment affected their relationship with spouses, parents and children is Sainsbury's, in *Registered as Disabled*,[3] where it was found that marriages were more likely to break up if it was the wife rather than the husband who became disabled, and that marriages tended to break up soon after the onset of a condition rather than after a long period of strain induced by disability. In the present survey – in, of course, a different geographical area and with a different population of, on average, less severely handicapped subjects – it was found that wives were more likely to leave disabled husbands. Considering only those cases where the couples had separated since the onset of impairment, there were five separated or divorced men, and only one woman, and three men were left by their wives during the survey year.

Sainsbury's second finding, that marriages were at risk soon after the onset of disability was, however, supported, and it seemed ironic that those husbands or wives who had been deserted occupied so much of the time of social workers (because of the practical problems), while none of those for whom the problems were just being created – the newly impaired whose marriages were obviously cracking – had been referred for the practical help or emotional support which might have averted the crisis.

These were, however, all younger couples. The marriages of middle-aged or elderly people appeared to be less subject to strain, perhaps simply because it is less contrary to normal expectations to find oneself caring for a spouse in later years.

> Mr Cheyne, a man nearing 70 who looked after his rather younger, completely handicapped, wife devotedly, explained simply, 'I never did mix much with people – I don't miss going out – me and the wife were always together.'

Older couples would often both be 'in poor health' and would develop elaborate routines of caring for one another, sharing out household tasks without regard for the conventional roles of the sexes. There were a few couples in the sample who were both so severely disabled that neither could have managed to remain in the community without the other; problems were inevitable when one of them died, of course, and they expressed this as an ever-present worry.

Many middle-aged wives went out to work for the first time, or after some years outside the labour force, when their impaired husband gave up work. Most of them said, sometimes a little guiltily, that in fact they enjoyed it.

> Mr and Mrs Ironside, for instance, both in their 50s, began to discuss in joking fashion how they were 'getting on each other's nerves' about two months after Mr Ironside, who had been a dustman, had undergone arterial surgery. The flat was small, and Mr

Ironside, a man with a very masculine image of himself who was used to spending his evenings in pubs and was very scornful of 'women's putterings', admitted that he was getting surly, 'I can't help it – the wife goes *on* all day!' After five months, Mrs Ironside took a job from one to six each day, ostensibly 'to help the budget', but in fact she seemed delighted to be at work, 'I did work before when I was younger, and I must say I'd rather than guddeling around all day here. The place isn't big enough for us both!' The arrangement was a success in that the couple appeared to regain a warm and comfortable relationship, though Mr Ironside was lonely and a little disconsolate about 'a man's wife having to work'.

Occupation and recreation

Mr Ironside was representative of a group of men whose main social problem was their lack of occupation. Housebound women did not appear to feel this: no matter how difficult their disability made it, they were rarely without some household occupation and they often occupied themselves with handicrafts, and most women of middle-age described very frequent social contacts with daughters, other relatives or neighbours. Very few appeared to regret their lack of social activities outside the home. The only general complaint that was made by those who had no access to private transport was that they missed 'going shopping' and found buying clothes or large household items difficult. Many might manage short expeditions to neighbourhood food shops, but be unable to cope with public transport to big central stores. They said they missed 'looking round' or 'window-shopping', and easy transport for individual expeditions would have been the service they would have appreciated most. On the other hand, men who had been used to working, and to a social life which took place largely outside the home, felt very isolated.

Mr Ironside had been a gregarious man, and he was very articulate about the hardship of being reduced to the wholly female company of his wife and women relations. He explained: 'Men don't go visiting in houses. It's the women natter over the cups. You couldn't have men coming here, could you – they'd be awkward. So I do miss my pals.' During his housebound year of the survey, he was observed to change greatly, from an aggressive and humorous man full of small practical plans, to boredom and resignation. By the end of the year he had forgotten all his plans and had retreated into fantasy:

> what he would do if he won the pools, or how different a life he might have led. 'Always fancied being a big game hunter. Do you know that's what I would have liked – driving a land-rover around Africa. I think often now of what it would have been like.'

There were several other middle-aged men who were badly in need of occupation. Hobbies and interests cost money, and they were likely to be living on very reduced incomes. Even if they were not housebound, part-time and easy 'wee jobbies' were less easy to come by for men than for women. Occupational centres or workshops were designed for a different clientele – the obviously 'disabled', permanently incapable of ordinary work, not working men who because of deteriorating health were unable to do the full-time manual work they had been employed in all their lives. In any case, these men were crucially affected by the 'earnings' rules, which meant that their benefits would suffer if they earned more than a limited amount. The administrative distinction between work and occupation seemed unreal to them, and their feelings about the 'unfairness' of the system – 'If I can earn the money, why should they take it away from me?' – prevented some from even trying to find part-time work.

There were a few seriously disabled younger people of both sexes who were also unhappy because of boredom and inactivity, though the needs of housebound younger disabled men for occupation were usually, it seemed, given some consideration. One young man was given some work to do by his previous employer; in another case an Army Welfare Officer was very helpful in assisting a paraplegic to organize light work which he was interested in and could do at home. Those who lacked occupation were the few whose family resources were inadequate to help, and who were unable to work in open employment but not so seriously disabled as to be housebound. The major problem was that there was no money for either social activities outside the home or the materials for hobbies within it.

Loneliness and isolation

The small but distressing group of people who were found to be completely socially isolated were of both sexes (though rather more likely to be men) and of any age: the characteristic which distinguished them was simply that they had no close family nearby, and no firm base in the community. They might be single, or divorced or widowed but without children, or with children who had moved elsewhere. If, in addition, they were too severely disabled to work, or to take part in social activities, and particularly if they had conditions of the nervous system or sense organs which hampered social communication, then it appeared possible for them to sink out of sight completely into a withdrawn and lonely world.

One such patient was George Cowie, still in his early 40s, with a progressively disabling disease, who had remained at home for eight years at the time of the survey. The only people whom he saw regularly were his home help and social workers, his only social contacts were visits from a teenage daughter who lived with his estranged wife, and his only outings were twice-weekly visits by ambulance to the hospital physiotherapy department. He expressed himself as quite desperate: 'What do I do? I just sit here night after night. I'm a prisoner. You have to be like this to know what it's like,' and he looked forward to the inevitable day when 'It'll have to be a Home in the end.' He remembered his stays in hospital with some pleasure because of the company – 'We had a laugh or two there' – and his hope for the future was a place in one particular residential home for ex-servicemen, about which he had heard glowing reports through an acquaintance. He could not, however, find anyone to advise him about an application, for everyone in professional contact with him was determined to 'keep him in the community'. Unfortunately, as he ruefully pointed out, he *had* no community, and he felt very much that he was simply marking time, wastefully waiting to get worse.

The process of becoming isolated was perhaps most vividly described by Mrs Crombie. Widowed for ten years, she had no close relatives in the area and had moved twice since her husband's death. She was fiercely independent and would not contemplate an old people's council bungalow, though her two tiny rooms were up several flights of stairs and without any amenities. There was one son, who lived a long way away and did not have much contact with his mother. A neat and tidy person who set great store by 'manners', her increasingly messy surroundings embarrassed her considerably, and she explained, 'I haven't many friends now – no, none really – I don't like anyone coming and seeing me like this.' She described how, after her husband died, 'I was lonely for a time. But I could get out then, and I did have one friend, we used to go out for a coffee or a drink. People used to say, "I don't know what you see in him, Maggie," but we suited each other, it was someone to talk to, we were in a group. But then he died, it was four years ago now, and since then I've let myself go. They never bothered with me after I began to be ill [Who?] The group we used to go around with. No one cares now. You've got to have ties with people at this time of life.' Mrs Crombie's neighbours were constantly changing and it seemed that her increasing blindness had caused her to become awkward and suspicious of people: she complained of harassment by neighbours and was on poor terms with her landlord (who would obviously, in fact, have liked to get rid of her).

It was only after a second hospitalization for a myocardial infarction that Mrs Crombie was registered as blind and various welfare workers began to visit her. By now, however, it seemed to be too late: she was locked into isolation by her own despair, and only confused and irritated by the multiplicity of agencies.

The problem of acute isolation among some disabled people is at once one of the most distressing and the least easily soluble. These are people whom it is difficult to help, and it is idle to suggest that they would necessarily welcome the eruption into their lives of either professional social workers or voluntary community helpers from, for instance, churches, youth groups or other organizations. Many people in the sample did find friendship and support within their church, but they were by definition not isolated.

To be disabled and isolated almost inevitably means practical problems, however, and these at least can be solved. The varying degrees of success of the attempts eventually made to help Mrs Crombie seemed to point to important factors about the acceptability of potential helpers. Mrs Crombie would accept routine services from professionals if she saw them as something she was entitled to, but if she was to accept the help she most needed – individual services tailored to her needs, given with friendship or affection – then the role which the helper could assume was crucial. The most successful, in Mrs Crombie's case, was a young man from a church group who could assume a 'son' role, performing small practical jobs and treating her with easy familiarity. In other cases elderly men seemed to accept young women as daughter-like helpers, if they did not seem too briskly professional or 'superior'.

Relationship with general practitioners

The only professional with whom Mrs Crombie and other isolated people like her were automatically in contact was their general practitioner. He might not, of course, define it as within his function to attempt to help a patient's social isolation, nor might he have found it easy to know how to help. In any case, however, it was unlikely that help would come from this source, since Mrs Crombie was an example of a general finding that there was a strong correlation between the existence of social and other problems and a poor relationship with the medical profession in general and the general practitioner in particular.

No direct questions were asked of the patients about their perception of their relationship with their general practitioner. Unsolicited comments were invariably made, however, and a crude attempt was made to categorize these. Forty per cent of the sample appeared to have exceptionally good relationships with their G.P., and expressed special gratitude to him. Fifteen per cent were dissatisfied. The remaining 45 per cent were satisfied and expressed no complaints.

Of course, no legitimate conclusions can be drawn from this about the quality of service offered by general practitioners, though it may be noted that a high proportion of patients spoke of their doctors in glowing terms. What is of interest, however, is the fact that the 15 per cent categorized as having 'poor' relationships were more likely than others to have social problems, and also practical problems. Over half had social problems (compared with about a quarter of those with an excellent or good relationship).

It cannot be necessarily inferred, of course, that people's problems were due in any way to poor relationships with their G.P.: it might equally well be that their problems affected the relationship. The practical hardship, extreme isolation, and neglected state of health of people like Mrs Crombie could obviously have been alleviated by the active intervention of a doctor: on the other hand, she had a complex and long-standing general antagonism towards the medical profession as a whole and cannot have been an easy patient. In other cases it was obvious that the patient's problems were the cause of his poor relationship with his G.P., where overburdened families were trying to use their doctor as a source of help for difficulties – money or practical problems – which he doubtless felt unable to deal with, and so were being treated as difficult or demanding patients.

There was a small but clearly distinguishable group of families themselves defined by social welfare agencies as 'problems' who were very likely to be on bad terms with their G.P., or to change their doctor frequently.

Mrs Burnett's family was an example of such a family, where it appeared from their actions that every agency with whom they were in touch was finding them to be a problem in terms of that agency's functions; any contact or referral between agencies served only to reinforce the label. To the housing department, they were poor and dirty tenants. To the health visitor, they were a family who had refused to accept help for the needs which *she* perceived (for advice in the management and care of children). To welfare agencies, it appeared that Mrs Burnett's daughter, an apparently able-bodied and aggressive woman, was defined as a 'scrounger', for she had little success in obtaining the basic necessities which she eventually asked them for. Her mother, so obviously in need, might have been more successful, but she was unable to make her applications in person. To the G.P. they may well have seemed troublesome and unco-operative patients. Thus, when the time came that 'needs' were very real and urgent – advice and help about diet, chiropody services, financial help, assistance with laundry and nursing care during a terminal illness – community services were conspicuously absent.

Others among the group on poor terms with their G.P. were neither 'difficult' isolates nor 'problem' families, but cases where conflict had arisen because of disagreement over the seriousness or nature of the disease. Whatever the cause, it was a notable general finding that a bad relationship with the general practitioner was a very good indicator of the likelihood of serious social problems.

SERVICES FOR OCCUPATION AND RECREATION

The statutory responsibility for providing for the social needs of the disabled rests with the local authority, in collaboration with (or sometimes using as their agency) voluntary bodies. The rationale for this is obvious: the feeling that the local community ought to be involved in deciding what the social needs of its disabled members are, and how they should best be provided for in local conditions. Also, this is an area in which it has traditionally been accepted that the use of voluntary or charitable resources is appropriate. Nevertheless, the evidence of this sample would suggest that these provisions for the prevention of social isolation, the provision of occupation, or the general support of families are wholly inadequate. In this, the City of the survey is not in any way unusual.

The problems of any general definition of social needs are great. The pattern of provision was traditionally laid down by voluntary organizations, who might obviously vary considerably in their definition of what it was proper or practicable to provide, and their view of who their clients were. Provision by the local authority for social and occupational activities was first based on Section 29 of the National Assistance Act (1948), but the legislation was permissive, not mandatory, and the services unspecified. In 1960 the provision of welfare services for the handicapped became mandatory, but delineation of the form and purpose of the services remained at the generalized level of the Piercy Report: 'The chief object of a welfare service must be to ensure that sufficient aid is given to any handicapped person requiring help to enable him thus aided, to have some share in the life of the community.[4] The Social Work (Scotland) Act (1968) was equally unhelpful about the precise duties of the reorganized social work departments in the field of physical disability, and though the Chronically Sick and Disabled Persons Act specified certain facilities which were to be provided ('recreation in the home', and 'lectures, games, outings or other recreational facilities outside the home') local authorities were left to deal as best they could with defining what 'recreation' the handicapped might want or need.

The result was, not unexpectedly, a great unevenness of provision, and a certain amount of despair at the gap between provision and potential need. Where occupational centres are concerned, for instance, the National Fund for Crippling Diseases survey reported typical findings: 'A London borough which expects to have 5,000 handicapped people in their area currently has day centre provision for 60 physically handicapped and 200 mentally handicapped' and 'One of the Northern counties with an active construction programme has three day centres and is now building five more. The centres will have a total of 400 places, but this county has a population of one million, and expects next year to have 20,000 disabled on its register'.[5] In the National Survey, 2 per cent of the sample had attended local authority centres.[6]

The provision of purely recreational facilities is likely to be on an equally minuscule scale. The problem of deciding what is wanted or needed may well be solved by using the simple criteria of what existing organizations are willing to provide. What sort of activities or facilities do 'the disabled' as a general category require? The question is meaningless, and so there is a great temptation to rely upon those who believe that they do know part of the answer – the voluntary organizations, who can at least define their own functions, as they see them, in relation to their own chosen clients. Eight per cent of the National Survey sample attended clubs for the disabled or handicapped.[7]

It is not, therefore, surprising that none of the present sample were attending the local authority occupational centre, and none were members of general 'disabled' clubs, though two had tried a club for disabled young people, and one couple and one single person had attended (and enjoyed) an annual Christmas dinner for 'the handicapped' provided by the City. Five people belonged to disability-specific voluntary societies, with varying degrees of enthusiasm; in general, their transport services were valued (as were those of the W.R.V.S. and Red Cross) but there were few sample members who were attracted by outings or social evenings.

Amongst the non-members, there was little interest expressed. The occupational centre and general 'disabled' clubs suffered from the stigma – from the point of view of the physically disabled – of too high a proportion of mentally handicapped participants. One young man explained his rejection of a youth club by saying, 'They're all *too* disabled – I'm not as bad as that.' The vast reservoir of goodwill and community effort represented in the voluntary organizations appeared to reach but a tiny proportion of the potential clients, and it seems of interest to ask why this should be so.

The voluntary organizations

Eleven disability-specific voluntary societies were known to exist in the City at the time of the survey, and the officers of nine of them were interviewed. Most represented themselves as very 'successful' and flourishing in terms of financial support: for instance, organizers of three of the societies said, 'We built up very quickly, and were rolling in money – thousands of pounds – it was most embarrassing, so we decided to send most of the money to Edinburgh for them to distribute', 'We are well supported by legacies and donations and fund-raising – we have more money than we need, at the moment. We resist sending legacies to London [to the parent organization] because the people want to help the people *here* and it's not fair on them to send the money down there. But we do send donations regularly to London on condition that they're used for research', and 'We're not short of money – we contribute to less well-off areas, like Glasgow. In fact, I suppose we're too successful, because they're talking of splitting the branch into two, which of course we don't want.' One or two societies with declining membership, on the other hand, presented this equally as 'success': 'We shouldn't attempt to be as flourishing as before – now there's less need for us, people are much better catered for now – we can fade out.' Most of the societies' officers had a tendency to talk as if their membership represented the total population of people in the area with a given condition, though if challenged they might be willing to agree that this could not in fact be so.

Referrals to the societies were described as being made in a variety of ways: on the one hand, those societies in which medical consultants were active relied upon the patient being told about the society at the hospital, and on the other, some societies complained that the principle of medical confidentiality prevented their finding their clients at the most obvious source, the hospital clinic. One official explained, 'We realize there must be people we don't know of, and who don't know we're there. But the clinics won't give us names, of course, that's confidential. So what can we do? We have to rely on people hearing about us by word of mouth – anyone interested in the disease who meets a sufferer will see if he wants to be put in touch with us.' Social workers were described by most of the societies as 'asking us to help with particular problems'; that is, they often referred their clients if they perceived that the society's particular activities would be of help. In general, however, societies were not well informed about statutory provisions or the functions of the social work department (several officials confused the department with the D.H.S.S.) and so rarely instigated referrals in the opposite direction.

Hospital sisters, medical social workers, and health visitors were mentioned by various societies as sometimes telling patients about them, but no society said that it was common for general practitioners to refer their patients.

Voluntary organizations for the disabled are not, of course, all alike. Some of the societies were started by, and continued to be supported by, the interest of medical specialists; these tended to emphasize information and education, and saw themselves as helping not by practical measures but by communication and sharing of information among their members. There were one or two rather similar 'self-help' societies, begun as pressure-groups by the families of people suffering from a given condition. Others saw themselves as social clubs: 'The over-riding function of our society is providing a friendly group, someone who cares – meeting other people and getting out.' The major activities of this particular society were a monthly 'social', twice-yearly outings, a Christmas dinner, and the provision of holidays. Still others stressed a 'welfare' function. The societies for the blind and for the deaf, having statutory duties as the agent for the local authority, had clearer functions, and both saw themselves as providing (in different manners) total care and support for the special needs of those registered as their clients. Both were observed to offer efficient and comprehensive services.

Thus, each society defined its own functions, and defined its clients according to those functions. One of the representatives of a club which was represented as largely 'social', said: 'We have a rigid rule that we only do things for members. Some people say we ought to be ready to help any sufferer, but our own members must come first, don't you think? If they're not a member, I have to say I'm sorry, but they don't seem to be on our list, we can't help.'

This process of defining the clients was seen at its most interesting in the categorization of 'the blind' and 'the deaf'. Although there were over 700 registered blind people in the area, the partially-sighted, whom the local authority had equally a duty to register, formally numbered only 14. It was obvious that this categorization – for which legal and clinical definitions exist – was in fact a social process. Those involved in it (the society for the blind and ophthalmic specialists) had developed unstated but largely agreed-upon procedures. In view of the services provided, a category of 'partially-sighted' was not useful; only if people were called 'blind' could full services swing into action. Which of the partially-sighted were called blind depended on a complex of factors – age, economic circumstances, other disabilities, degree and nature of residual sight and its functional effect on the individual's life – relevant to the usefulness of the services which could be offered, and in particular, to the society's historical view of its function as primarily teaching and training. 'Blind' could also be an anticipatory definition, for those who were going blind were urged to register on the grounds that they could benefit from teaching while they still had some sight.

Statutory definitions of blindness have to exist because specific goods (including a money allowance) are involved. Who the 'deaf' are, administratively, is even more problematic. Locally, they were defined solely as the congenitally deaf and dumb, or those who became deaf in early childhood. This was the group for whom the officers of the society for the deaf had particular training, and their resources (in this case, inadequate for the society's perceived needs) could not extend their comprehensive and devoted service to an unknown but very large group of hard-of-hearing. Nevertheless, they wished to extend their coverage, and had formed a club for the hard-of-hearing, concentrating on trying to find the elderly isolated.

The result of these processes by which clients were defined was a lottery. To be eligible for the services of a specific society a patient must suffer from disease X *and* want a social club, or from disease Y *and* be attracted to informative meetings, or from disease Z *and* have welfare needs, or be hard-of-hearing *and* elderly. Only a few of these combinations turned up in the present sample so that, for instance, a young woman dismissed the hard-of-hearing club as being 'only for old folks', or others said about the society for 'their' disease, 'outings and such; not for me', or 'I do know people who belong and they say they're very nice, but meetings aren't my cup of tea.'

A general problem of providing recreational clubs for the disabled is, of course, that they are not a homogeneous group, but include as wide a range of personal characteristics – age, interests or education – as an able-bodied population. If an attempt is made to provide for special subgroups, as in clubs for the young disabled, great disparity remains in degree and type of impairment. The only circumstances under which any sort of mix, especially of degrees of impairment and of social classes, seemed to be achieved was when the more fortunate or less severely disabled could see themselves as having joined clubs in order to help 'the poor people who are worse off than I am'. The secretary of one society, herself disabled, seemed to imply that *all* her members took this attitude when she said, 'It makes everyone better to see other people worse than they are – I think that's why our socials are so friendly and so cheerful. Everyone is in it to *give*.' A member of another society had worked for it for many years, until – her disease worsening – she herself became urgently in need of welfare help. She alleged that an official of the society had responded to her tentative requests by saying reprovingly – 'We're not in the association for what we can get out of it, you know.'

In general, and excepting the societies for the blind and the deaf, the officials of voluntary organizations seemed uneasy about their welfare functions. Many placed great emphasis on delicacy in money matters, which may have been appreciated by their members, but might also be felt to reinforce the 'charity' image of voluntary organizations which some survey subjects appeared to hold. The secretary of one society explained, for instance, how what she described as 'deserving cases' were excused from payment for excursions by a 'confidential' committee, and 'when it comes to paying for the dinner, the members are told the cost but left to contribute what they can – we don't even issue receipts, and no one but me knows.' Few officers appeared to have much knowledge about statutory welfare provisions or about, for instance, the details of the Chronically Sick and Disabled Persons Act. Only a very few organizations (for instance, the Multiple Sclerosis Society) offered total supportive services defined by their perception of the individual family's needs rather than by the society's own categories of 'the things the organization does'. In any case, any attempt at a precise definition of the difficult concept of 'social needs', which could be universally applied to 'the disabled', would have been resisted by the potential clients. They were happy to admit that they might be disabled in some particular area of life – might need transport, or a job, or an income – but they rarely saw themselves as socially disabled.

SUMMARY

Although the practical problems of work, money, and daily living seemed to be most prominent amongst the patients of this survey, it was social problems – family relationships, isolation and loneliness, lack of occupation and recreation – which were perhaps the most distressing. They were conspicuous amongst people with diseases of the nervous system or other conditions affecting communication, who felt that they were particularly stigmatized by society.

The sample produced clear evidence of the strain which impairment can impose upon family relationships, especially if it were the husband who was disabled and the couple were young. Social work support for emotional and family problems tended to be available only *after* a crisis situation had developed, when help might be too late. In part, this was because families did not see social workers, whom they associated with 'problem families', as the appropriate source of help.

A strong association was found between the existence of social and other problems and a poor relationship with the medical profession.

The problems of any general definition of social needs, and thus of the design of any services to fill them, are obviously even greater than those associated with practical or employment needs. Additionally, it has always been felt more appropriate to leave the definition and provision of these services to local communities, and especially to voluntary organizations.

REFERENCES

1. See, e.g. Hunt, P. (*ed.*), *Stigma: the Experience of Disability*, London, Chapman, 1966.
2. Hilbourne, J., 'On Disabling the Normal', *B. J. Social Work*, 2.4, 1973.
3. Sainsbury, Sally, op. cit., 1970, pp. 108–25.
4. *Report of the Committee of Enquiry on the Rehabilitation, Training and Resettlement of Disabled Persons*, Cmnd. 9883, London, H.M.S.O., 1956.
5. Murray, Joanna and Orwell, S., op. cit., 1973, p. 32.
6. Harris, Amelia I., op. cit., 1971, p. 109.
7. ibid., p. 123.

9
DIAGNOSIS AND DEFINITION

The preceding chapters have attempted to trace out the ways in which the categories applied by different agencies influence the patient's own definition of himself, his condition, his needs and his eligibility for help. Obviously, another very important component of the individual's view of himself as ill or well, handicapped or normal, permanently disabled or temporarily incapacitated, will be the clinical definitions he is given – not only what formal diagnostic label he is being treated under, and what he has been told about diagnosis and prognosis, but also how he perceives that he is being treated, and how he interprets what he has been told. This, too, will affect his presentation of himself and his behaviour.

In attempting to describe some features of the processes by which patients developed views of their own medical condition, there is an obvious danger of unwarranted generalizations. Patients are individuals, who differ in their education, medical knowledge, experience of illness, modes of expression, and responses to stress or to uncertainty. Nevertheless, the general impression in this sample was of similarity of response rather than diversity. Education or social class, for instance, did not appear to make a great deal of difference: the highly educated were just as likely to present a 'wrong' diagnosis as the poorly educated, though the vocabulary in which they could discuss it might be more technical. Explanations of differences in health perception and health behaviour have often been sought in simple and easily described variables of social position, but this survey would support the view that they are more likely to lie in the complex areas of social interaction.[1] With only a few reservations, then, this chapter will discuss the reactions of patients to their own diagnoses in a generalized way.

There were two conspicuous findings: firstly, that patients' own accounts very often differed markedly from those written on medical records, and secondly, that patients' accounts frequently underwent a process of change as time went on. Both of these findings are, of course, commonplace knowledge. But the analysis contained in the final chapter of this report will suggest that one of the circumstances in which problems of adjustment and rehabilitation were very likely was when the patient's own view of his condition differed from that of his doctors, and thus it seems important to attempt to show the ways in which this situation arose. The patient's rewriting of his medical history will be discussed first, since showing what patterns the patient *wants* to make, what he prefers to see as cause and effect, may shed some light on the interpretation he puts at the time on what he is told.

The strain towards rationality

The major feature of patients' accounts of their illness condition was their strenuous attempts to see their medical history *as a whole*, to connect together everything that had happened to them in an attempt to provide a coherent story, in which effect followed cause in a rational way. They found it difficult to accept that one of their physiological systems might 'go wrong' this year, and another the next, in an altogether disconnected fashion, and therefore tended to telescope together in time different illness episodes in an attempt to connect them causally. To them, their bodies were an entity, and malfunctionings must be connected. (In many cases, of course, this may have been objectively true, but it ran counter to a system of medicine in which different physiological systems might be treated quite separately and by different people.)

There seemed to be a deep need for people to be able to make sense of their world. They could cope with the idea of the future only if they could understand the past as a continuous story, and if necessary the past would have to be revised. Many people began their accounts with 'It all started with that accident a few years ago . . .' or 'I see now that the stomach trouble last year was the beginning . . .' or 'I had chest pains three years ago, and the doctor said it was fibrositis – of course, it must have been my heart.'

The idea of illness simply 'happening' was too threatening: it took all order out of the world. People were therefore very concerned with 'causes', and a great deal of friction with their doctors was due to the fact that authoritative statements about cause were often not available.

The parents of a severely epileptic son, for instance, ascribed his condition, at various times, to childhood illnesses, to a fall causing a head injury, to air-raid warnings during the war, and (as the mother's last resort): 'It must be something in the family, I suppose. But I was one of seven and there was never anything wrong with my family. Of course, my husband was an orphan and I don't know his family.' Another patient understood that 'calcium had been removed from an artery' and he had developed a complex account of how this could have had a connection with chemicals handled at his work. He was extremely annoyed when doctors dismissed his explanations without offering him, he thought, any equally rational alternative 'cause'.

Conspicuously, people preferred to think in terms of environmental or behavioural causes if possible, rather than physiological ones. This was even more true of spouses than of patients themselves: wives in particular frequently explained at length how (usually) overwork, stress or work that was heavy, or (less frequently) the husband's bad habits (drinking, too little exercise), had caused his disease. It seemed that to blame some behavioural cause was less frightening than to accept the disease as a physical characteristic, though of course these 'explanations' could also be interpreted as indirect attacks on the husband, recriminations for his alarming failure of health. A common way in which husbands explained the illnesses of wives, which seemed based on rather similar principles, was to invoke the menopause, even in women in their late 30s or very early 40s – 'Of course, illnesses often start at this time of life for women.'

The preference for environmental causes was shown at its most extreme by one couple who explained with a wealth of circumstantial evidence how the husband's chronic stomach trouble was caused by 'something going wrong' with the local water supply – 'There's been a lot of stomach trouble round here.' For the moment, they seemed genuinely to forget that (as medical records showed) this condition had first been treated many years before, and it was not until many months after a partial gastrectomy had been performed that they began to speak of the husband's 'ulcer' rather than his reaction to the water supply.

Overwork and stress were favoured explanations of chronic disease. Popular accounts of the relationship between stress and ill-health appeared to be well-known, and often a circular causal relationship was created: in stressful situations which were obviously the result of ill-health (such as unemployment), the stress itself would be blamed for the ill-health continuing.

It is of interest to note that this supports the findings of Wadsworth *et al*, in their survey of self-reported illness; when their subjects were asked to ascribe causes to their disease, it was found that only 4.4 per cent of doctor-diagnosed conditions were thought to have environmental causes, while 30.2 per cent of self-diagnosed (or other-diagnosed) conditions were so described.[1] 'Causes' obviously varied by condition, but 'work' and 'stress' were quoted for many types of disease. In this survey, as in Wadsworth's, patients were willing to consider that some of their physical conditions might have psychological causes, but only as a residual explanation if all else failed and if the psychological condition could be seen to have an underlying environmental cause. Several patients expressed some scorn of 'doctors' psychologizing, if they felt that the physical basis of their symptoms had not been adequately investigated.

There were interesting cases, however, where both patient and doctors gave evidence of suspecting that the 'cause' of an illness lay in fact in social problems, but where, since the problem had been presented in a medical context, it had to be treated as though it *were* a clinical problem. Thus, the patient was presented with the framework on which he could build a diagnosis which, though without clinical foundation, might come to have a very real and important status.

> Mrs Forsyth, for instance, explained her 'real' troubles very explicitly – an alcoholic husband who was unemployed and who left her for a time, an obsessive hatred of the place she lived in, severe money difficulties – 'I get nervous just because things get too much.' Looking back, after her circumstances and her health had both improved, she said, 'I think the trouble started when I found the empty bottles around the house – and the place, and him not working – I couldn't see any way out of it – we had hit rock bottom.' Yet, once she had presented herself for medical treatment, her condition had to be considered within a clinical category. In fact, no firm diagnosis was made, and her consultant noted as a significant fact that 'I gather there are problems over housing.'

> Nevertheless, the symptoms that had brought her into hospital had to be investigated clinically. Thus, it appeared, arose the construct of 'thyroid trouble' which structured her own and, later, her husband's presentation of her condition for almost the whole of the subsequent year. As she had asked for a medical diagnosis, there had to be one available – though Mrs Forsyth's medical record stated categorically that her thyroid function was normal. She developed complex accounts of the causes of her fluctuating health – it was due to her thyroid being 'like a wee red flower that comes out and then goes in again' – and when she was rehospitalized for weight loss (it must be noted that at the time she was living on £6 a week, of which at least £5 was spent on rent and other non-food expenses) she was convinced that 'it is going to mean surgery on the thyroid this time.' At the end of the year, when the social problems seemed less difficult, Mrs Forsyth could admit that she now believed there never had been any thyroid disease, and that the whole episode had probably started because a young doctor in the hospital, presumably knowing only that she was to have tests of thyroid function, had introduced her to some students going round the ward as 'Mrs Forsyth, who is having a little trouble with her thyroid.'

Mrs Forsyth's was a case where she managed, for a time, to forget the social or environmental causes of her health problems. In other cases, where there was no obvious cause available, people tended to speak of a malfunctioning as if it were a disease which one 'catches' – not that they thought it to be infectious, but as if it were a condition out there somewhere waiting to attack them, rather than a characteristic of their own physiology. Thus, several people talked like Mrs Forsyth, of suffering from 'thyroid', or 'blood pressure', or 'gastric stomach'. Another favoured way of dealing with the frightening advent of impairment, and providing a comprehensible structure into which it might fit, was to connect it in some way to heredity or 'family failings'. This, again, seemed to be a useful device for producing order out of malignant chaos – many heart conditions, terrifyingly unexpected at first, were as time went on incorporated into such a pattern. These structures were often developed post factum, through long family discussions and enquiries which established how many uncles or cousins had also suffered from 'heart'.

In cases of sudden and unexpected impairment, a common pattern over time was observed. At first, people's definitions of their own condition would be extremely fluid, influenced almost from day to day by what information they were given or by the way in which they perceived that doctors were treating them. At this point it was often difficult to be sure what they 'really' thought, for apprehension might easily be concealed behind a rejection that anything was seriously wrong. On the one hand, several people who were formally diagnosed as not having had a myocardial infarction insisted that they 'must' have, since they had been in the intensive care unit; on the other, some people presented their condition as very much less serious than it was.

Mr Buchan, for instance, a man of 54 who had suffered a severe infarction with ventricular failure, talked during the weeks after his discharge from hospital of nothing more serious than 'bad rheumatic pain' in his arm, and appeared to be more interested in his chest than his heart: 'It didn't really affect the chest; I was very lucky.' That his expressed intention of returning to his work (manual, though not particularly heavy) four weeks after leaving hospital was genuine was attested by the fact that the family adjustments (concerning the temporary stay of a daughter, his wife's working hours) were planned on that basis.

Similarly, people who had suffered severe injuries, though they might be particularly depressed about the future immediately following some explicit information from medical personnel, or after comparing other people's cases with their own, tended on the whole towards over-optimism about their future. By about three months after their sudden impairment, however, people's fluid definitions of their condition had hardened.

It was at this point that Mr Buchan began to mention his 'heart attack' for the first time and said rather ruefully: 'I think I'm becoming a bit of a hypochondriac – worrying over every little pain – it's easy to do.' Within a short time he was presenting his illness as very serious: 'I was very nearly gone, you know – I have to take care I never get tired – I'll never be the man I was.'

This was the point at which many people would have particularly liked support, and the point at which quite trivial failures in communication might have disproportionate consequences.

Mr McLeod, a man of 50 who had had two infarctions, was at first very happy with his treatment and felt that communication had been excellent: 'They told me straight they couldn't say when I'd be recovered, well, it stands to reason they can't lay down hard and fast rules, they treat everyone as an individual.' But three months later he was perturbed at his seeming lack of progress, and after an out-patient review hastened to his general practitioner to 'hear the verdict'. When he was told that no report had been received, he felt that this was very sinister: 'Something's being kept from me. I think it's worse than they let on,' and began making gloomy plans for a premature retirement. At the end of the year, however, when he felt recovered, he was again minimizing his illness and preferred to forget his period of worst despondency.

Similarly, this point, three or four months after discharge from hospital, was commonly the most depressed and hopeless time for people whose accident left a permanent disablement. When first convalescent, they had been able to see distinct progress – from perhaps being immobile to being able to get about, from being a patient to being a man back in the community. As progress seemed to slow down, however, and practical decisions about the future assumed more urgency, the reality of permanent disability induced apathy and lethargy in some people (depending not only upon personality but also and perhaps more importantly the circumstances of their life), so that they sank back into depressed inability to plan for the future, and in others a wild determination to take some action, often inappropriate and ultimately disadvantageous.

How the story would then be seen as developing, both retrospectively and prospectively, would of course depend upon subsequent events. If the eventual outcome was seen as relatively favourable, then the period of the most pessimistic definition might be forgotten, or the actions taken then represented as deliberate and not forced choices.

Understanding and communication

Obviously, this tendency on the patients' part to rewrite their medical history, and to try to make a coherent and manageable story of it, was not only affected by their communication with their doctors but also affected the meanings they found in what they were told. Communication was, in fact, the one subject about which a great deal of dissatisfaction was expressed. It must be made clear that the patients' (unsolicited) opinions about the treatment offered by hospital and by general practitioner were, in the great majority of cases, wholly and enthusiastically favourable. Very many people insisted on expressing their gratitude to doctors and other hospital staff, and few had complaints about treatment. Several individual consultants were singled out for praise as 'approachable', 'kind', or 'a real gentleman'. The only consistent pattern of complaint concerned information-giving practices.

> This was not confined to any one sort of person, or any one kind of disease. A civil servant in his 50s said: 'The doctors won't answer direct questions, you get the feeling they don't want you to know anything, what tests have shown, or what the cause of a thing is. I asked what precisely it was that smoking did that could harm a stomach ulcer, and the doctor just didn't answer.' An unemployed labourer complained similarly: 'They're a closed shop, doctors are, you can't get past it, You can't talk their language so can't talk to them at all, anyway they don't want to tell you anything – stand at the bottom of the bed and mutter!' A rural carpenter's summing up: 'They don't tell you anything because they think us countryfolk is fools,' can be compared with the conclusion of a police sergeant in the city: 'Doctors really are incapable of making any clear statements at all. All you get is flannel. If you asked a doctor whether that fire there is on, he would never be able to give you a yes or no. They're terrified they may be wrong, I suppose – well, we know they're only human and can make mistakes, but why can't they say what they *think*. On the other hand, I've got some sympathy for them, being in an Aunt Sally profession the same as I am.'

Despite these strong feelings on the part of some patients, however, it may be assumed that the majority of cases where misunderstanding had occurred, or the patient felt that information had been inadequate, arose not from lack of care for the patient's worries, but from one of four causes: organizational failures, misinterpretations by the patient, genuine clinical uncertainties, or (occasionally) deliberate therapeutic management of information. The effects of these will be considered in turn.

Organizational failures and misinterpretations

Many of the patients who appeared to be confused about their own diagnosis, or unhappy because their definition did not seem to match what they perceived as the medical definition, were those whose condition was complicated and involved several different consultants or departments of the hospital.

> A patient who had been immobilized with back pain and had undergone orthopaedic, neurological, digestive system and other examinations described his impression of this clearly: 'The trouble is these specialities are all in boxes, and you have to fit into the boxes. It's just a roundabout – you go round and they do their tests, and if they can't find anything you just get off and onto another one.'

Delay in referrals from one consultant to another contributed to the uncertainty and distress: in several cases the patient had gathered that he was to see another consultant 'as soon as possible' and, clinging to this as the next stage in his career towards diagnosis and treatment, found himself quite unable to adjust to an indefinite wait.

> In one case the period extended for ten weeks, and the patient appeared to spend this time almost entirely in brooding over, and discussing with her immediate family, questions about her exact position: am I ill? will I become more ill? what do these symptoms mean? will I be permanently disabled? Her conversation was full of conflict, at one moment dwelling on her symptoms as an excuse for not fulfilling her obligations, and at the next trying to rationalize them out of existence in terror at the prospect of losing her role as wife and mother by prolonged hospitalization or serious disablement. The practical consequences included some deterioration in her relationship with her young husband, who obviously found her behaviour difficult.

Where more than one consultant was concerned, the patients were apt to interpret the different things they were told, not simply as different parts of the truth about their condition as seen from various points of view, but as disagreements or confessions of ignorance among the experts. In such cases they were likely to expect their general practitioner to adjudicate. In fact, they were usually much more likely to remember or think that they understood what their community doctor had told them, in all cases where the diagnosis was not simple and straightforward, perhaps because of the lesser strain of the more familiar consulting environment. It was also notable that they were more likely to believe their general practitioner, in all cases where there was, or was perceived to be, any conflict between the two sets of information – although, in fact, in several of these less well-defined cases, it appeared that it was the consultant who had given the more precise diagnosis.

In a few cases there was evidence that there was some confusion about whether general practitioner or hospital was managing the information-giving procedures. Several patients waited with increasing anxiety and dissatisfaction for their G.P. to 'tell them the results' of their hospital investigation or treatment. On the other hand, there were cases of long-term complex conditions where it seemed that the G.P. felt strongly that information-management should be kept in his hands, and where, if the patients' accounts were to be believed, it appeared that he was offering a revised version of the hospital's diagnosis. Usually this was a softer and less threatening account, though there was one case in which the G.P. had written out a certificate of incapacity, shown to the interviewer, which named a condition considerably more serious than that which had been diagnosed and stated unequivocally on the hospital's discharge note. This patient was worried by the discrepancy with what he had been told while in hospital, but thought at the time, 'He's maybe trying to frighten me – perhaps he thinks it's the only way to stop me smoking and drinking'. It was notable, however, that by the end of the year he had come to accept the G.P.'s rather than the hospital's version.

Another case where the patient clearly perceived discrepancies in information-management, not in this instance about the diagnosis itself, but about prognosis and the meaning of symptoms, was Mr George King's. The account of this young man, who had suffered for eleven years from a fluctuating and potentially disabling disease which required careful management, was 'I went and asked my doctor if I should wear dark glasses – it was being used as a demonstration patient in the hospital that showed me what these headaches and eye trouble were all about. I hadn't understood before that it was normal with this condition. Then I watched a medical T.V. programme and it gave me the idea of glasses. But they don't like you to know too much, do they – certainly the doctor didn't like my having watched it – he said I'd only get morbid! But I'm trying the glasses.'*

*It must be added that this patient had found his general practitioner exceptionally kind and helpful in practical matters, and expressed great gratitude to him for his general support.

Other conflicts arose not because of discrepancies between the information given by different doctors, but because of discrepancies between what patients perceived as being done to them and what they were told (or more usually not told). One simple administrative practice which caused a great deal of worry – and consequent creation by the patient of diagnoses without foundation – was not being told 'the results' of investigative procedures, especially if they were negative. People rarely understood that one of a battery of tests might be a routine measure unlikely to be of any real importance, and spent a great deal of time wondering what the fact that a certain test or X-ray had been performed might 'really mean'.

Mrs Hendry, for instance, was a rather excitable woman in her 40s, who had been hospitalized for the investigation of stomach pain in fact diagnosed as a reaction to the drugs which she was taking for a chronic condition. She had been recalled for repeat X-rays when other patients examined at the same time were not, and was convinced that this meant serious trouble. (In fact, of course, the most likely explanation was simply some trivial error.) After her discharge from hospital she had been required to return for a barium meal X-ray, and this further confirmed her fears. Four weeks after this, having heard nothing about the 'results', she was in a panic condition which was seriously disrupting the family life; they were due to travel away for business reasons, but 'couldn't go until they heard', and emergency preparations were being made for the care of a son. Eventually her husband persuaded their G.P. to telephone the hospital, and it was discovered that, since the results of all tests were negative, the routine procedure would have been to discuss the situation with her only at her out-patient appointment, two months after discharge. Meanwhile, defining herself as 'possibly very ill', she was conducting her life in accordance with this definition.

In another and much more serious case, the patient's misinterpretation of investigative procedures helped to reinforce his antagonism to the medical profession, with unfortunate consequences. This patient had been diagnosed as alcoholic and suffering from cirrhosis, though the diagnosis had never been properly understood by the patient or his wife, in part because he had in fact stopped drinking. It seemed to him that he was being judged in moral terms for what he defined as a physical illness, and when, following an episode of hepatic encephalopathy, he was given an E.E.G., he found this very sinister – now 'they' were trying to prove him mad as well as bad, simply because they did not know what was 'really' wrong with him!

In the same way that 'tests' assumed a perhaps disproportionate significance, so 'drugs', another visible and concrete aspect of treatment for the patient, were invested with special meanings. That a presciption was given was taken to be proof that something was wrong: if at the same time no clear diagnosis was given it was proof that the doctor knew (or how would he know what to prescribe?) but was not disclosing what he thought. For one doctor to alter the drug regime prescribed by another was frequently taken as indicating disagreement about diagnosis or treatment. (It may be added that there were several cases in which it was observed that the patient did not understand that drugs prescribed at the hospital were meant to be substituted for those already obtained through the G.P., and went on taking both.)

The ward of the hospital in which the patient found himself was another clue to his condition which was sometimes open to misinterpretation. In particular, many people found their experience of a neurological ward frightening; they might not have thought themselves seriously ill (with, for instance, sight disorders) and of course might not have been in fact, but to find themselves amongst many patients who *were* seriously or permanently impaired was a shock and raised doubts which might subside only slowly.

Of course, information-giving procedures might be expected to differ from ward to ward, and from one individual consultant to another, not only because of personal differences but because the nature of the task in hand differed. It was notable that the patients who were most satisfied with the information they had received were those who had undergone surgery (excluding neurological surgery), and though it may be simply that surgical procedures are easier to explain, it also appeared to be relevant that the pattern of events automatically structured the information-giving procedure: before an operation, the patient is told what is to be done, and immediately after surgery may well ask for further details himself. In the long drawn-out course of a complex illness, such a natural explaining-point may never arrive. Many patients from surgical wards expressed great appreciation of the way in which X-rays had been shown and explained to them or diagrams drawn for them in order to make clear exactly what was happening.

Even in the case of complex illnesses, of course, it was often evident from the patient's accounts that doctors had certainly made attempts to explain their condition to them. Misunderstanding or rejection were, however, not uncommon. Sometimes misunderstanding appeared to have arisen because the consultant's explanation had been an attempt to present the condition in accurate physiological terms, which meant nothing to the patient: what he wanted was a simple label together with an explanation in functional terms. One multiple sclerosis sufferer, for instance, could give an accurate description of the physiological causes of his symptoms, but did not know the name of his disease; another young woman had had epileptic attacks well 'explained' without the use of the word epilepsy. Often it seemed that the implied or explicit request for information had been interpreted as meaning, 'what is happening?', and had been answered in precise physical terms – a lesion here, or a malfunctioning there, was having such and such effects. In fact, the question had meant, 'why is it happening?', and the patient listened only perfunctorily to the description; what he was really interested in was the much more difficult question of cause – why did the lesion or the malfunctioning occur, and why to him?

Where neurological conditions were concerned, general practitioners in particular appeared to favour rather vague explanations involving the word 'nerves'. Usually the intention seemed to be actually to refer to the nervous system, but this was not the interpretation the patient imposed. To him, 'nerves' meant an emotional or psychosomatic disorder. The effect in two or three cases was very distressing. The patient felt that his condition must in some sense be his own fault; he spoke of his efforts to 'pull himself together' and did not expect (or, as far as could be observed, receive) much sympathy from his significant others. The ambivalent attitude to any diagnosis understood to involve 'nerves' can be summed up in a woman's description of her sister, clinically defined as suffering from serious organic disease: 'The doctor says it's her nerves; of course she can't help it, poor thing, but we don't *encourage* her.' People in this position were particularly likely to have practical problems which could be seen to arise very directly out of their inability to define their condition and their role.

Uncertainty and management

The cases so far discussed have been those where misunderstandings arose inadvertently. A conflict of definitions can also arise, of course, from genuine diagnostic uncertainty.

It has often been pointed out that adaptive strategies which doctors must develop for dealing with the necessarily probabilistic nature of much diagnosis and most prognosis are a source of strain in their relationship with their patients. 'The problem of uncertainty is a basic component of many medical decisions, and every physician must learn to live with this.'[2]

'Real' uncertainty as a clinical phenomenon may, however, be distinguished (analytically, though not necessarily in practice) from what Davis has called 'functional' uncertainty as a mangement technique. In his classic study of children with paralytic poliomyelitis, Davis[3] found that there was necessarily a period of 'real' uncertainty in this case, but though this virtually ended at a given point (if never perhaps completely) there was no parallel change in the parents' understanding of the prognosis. He suggested that this 'functional' uncertainty is maintained by both doctor and patient: 'On the one hand, the pretence of uncertainty serves to reduce materially the expenditure of additional time, effort and involvement which a frank and straightforward prognosis might entail,' and on the other, parents tended to maintain and even exaggerate the idea of uncertainty, since it can represent hope.

Davis was looking at a situation in which 'real' uncertainty was soon resolved as far as diagnosis was concerned, and largely resolved at a certain point with regard to prognosis. If varied conditions are observed, however, it is obvious that the two may be separated: diagnosis may be certain but prognosis uncertain, or on the other hand the doctor may be sure, for instance, that symptoms are unlikely to prove permanently disabling, without being able to be certain of their diagnosis. When the third variable of time is added, and it is remembered that patients are particularly anxious about 'causes', and apt to base their own definition of the present and their own expectations of the future upon their perception of cause, then it is obvious that the possible patterns of medical/self-defined certainty/uncertainty are complex.

Some patterns were observed to be advantageous, and some disadvantageous. 'Real' uncertainty about diagnosis was almost always disadvantageous: unable to offer a legitimizing label, people found themselves floundering. How were they to present themselves for help if they wanted it? What role-obligations could they properly relinquish? Housewives and mothers were usually in an even more equivocal position than employed people, who at least had a certificate saying that they were 'ill' which released them from their main obligation, to go to work. The difficulties of doctors were not helped by what seemed to be a great faith, in the abstract, in medical science: the more articulate or thoughtful patients might talk generally about the limitations of medical knowledge, but when it came to their own condition it 'must' be possible to find a cause (it must be remembered that these patients' symptoms were not, by definition, trivial) and any failure to do so was likely to be ascribed to inefficiency. Thus doctor–patient relationships became strained, and the dilemma was difficult to resolve: several patients *said*, 'I wish they'd say when they don't know', but no patient in fact accepted for long, and without criticism, a clear expression of real clinical uncertainty.

Uncertainty about prognosis, whether 'real' or 'functional', was readily accepted in the early months following a suddenly impairing episode. Grateful to be alive, and obviously improving, people talked often about how 'it might have been worse'. If there was permanent disability, time was needed for a gradual redefinition of self, and doctors were frequently observed to be guiding the process along. This uncertainty must not last too long, however, for the moment would inevitably arrive when uncertainty turned into despair (with the practical result that rehabilitation facilities were not taken advantage of) or was resolved by the creation of a firm, but possibly mistaken, definition of the patient's or his family's own making. The time-table might be structured by routine clinical procedures ('I will know after my out-patient appointment next month'); on the other hand, the precipitating events in the individual patient's life (an interview with his boss, the decision whether or not a holiday or a wedding should be postponed, the advent of financial problems, the limits of his family's tolerance, the sudden realization that he could no longer take part in some valued activity) might have a time-table which matched ill with the routine timing of hospital review and follow-up.

To say that 'functional' uncertainty as a management tool, if carried on beyond an initial period of adaptation, was observed to have disadvantageous effects for the patient is not, of course, to suggest that the manipulation of information can never be shown to be a valuable therapeutic procedure. What the patient requires is a label which will satisfactorily explain the situation as he sees it, and will legitimate the adoption of a role which he is able to play. One woman in the sample, whose whole family life had been in sad disarray, was observed to change her behaviour radically when given the diagnosis of 'stomach ulcer' in place of the more serious condition which had, in fact, been diagnosed but not disclosed to her. This was a label which she could accept and which provided a role which she felt was suitable to her physical capabilities – not so ill as to be bedfast, but nevertheless excused from some household duties and granted some special consideration by her family.

If 'uncertainty' is prolonged, however, so that an acceptable role cannot be defined, the effects are likely to be unfortunate. One case may be described in detail as illustrating very clearly the effect of the patient's understanding of his own condition upon his self-definition, and the effect in turn upon his behaviour, especially his help-seeking behaviour.

> John Stuart was a young man with three small children (one aged two years) who had been diagnosed as suffering from multiple sclerosis three years before the survey. He had not been told this, and defined himself as intermittently and 'unluckily' ill with a series of different (though perhaps connected) things. This had many consequences: he felt himself stigmatized as being odd, and spoke bitterly of 'the old body who put it about the scheme' that his ungainly walk was due to drink. What explanation could he offer? Only 'I can't help it; I don't quite know why.' He felt himself isolated, unique: 'The doctors keep on looking at me but they say they can't cure me.' His G.P. had mentioned 'nerves', and therefore he was slightly apologetic: 'I'd never thought of myself as a nervy type'. He did not see himself as entitled to any particular help, and had not approached any welfare agency, though the family were in desperate financial straits. He still saw himself as under an obligation to support his family like any other man though employment presented problems, and he had struggled to work at a factory where he was a packer at times when his fluctuating disability made it barely possible, in order to keep alive or renew national insurance entitlements. He had in fact been registered as a disabled worker when, because of sight difficulties, he lost his job as a van-driver, but

he regarded this as a formality connected only with his sight. He did apply for certain welfare benefits (welfare milk, family income supplement) for which poverty, rather than disability, made him eligible, but on none of the forms which he filled in did he mention his health.

Mr Stuart's seemed to be one of the clearest cases where lack of a clear clinical label (as far as he was concerned) led to an inability to define a legitimate role for himself, and where his presentation of his condition crucially affected his help-seeking behaviour.

SUMMARY

Illustrations have been drawn from these patients' histories of the way in which they interpreted the clinical information they were given and tended to write their medical histories in a form which seemed to them rational and coherent. The information-giving practices of doctors were obviously an important component of the process of creating a self-definition.

Communication was, in fact, one subject about which a great deal of dissatisfaction was expressed. Misunderstandings appeared to arise because of organizational failures, for instance between different doctors, or misinterpretations of procedures or explanations. Genuine diagnostic uncertainty, or occasionally deliberate therapeutic management of information, also created difficulties for the patient. Because he could not define his own condition clearly, or disagreed with the clinical definition which he perceived as being applied to him, he found it difficult to know what obligations he could properly relinquish, or what help he could legitimately ask for.

REFERENCES

1. Wadsworth, M. E. J., Butterfield, W. H. and Blaney, R., *Health and Sickness: the Choice of Treatment*, London, Tavistock Publications, 1971.

2. Mechanic, D., *Medical Sociology*, New York, The Free Press, 1968, p. 179.
3. Davis, F., 'Uncertainty in Medical Prognosis – Clinical and Functional', *Amer. J. Soc.*, 66.1, 1960, pp. 41–47.

10
PROCESSES OF DEFINITION

The histories of these 194 patients have shown that society's expressions of its desire to help 'the disabled' are in a state of considerable confusion. The confusion is not simply practical, to be cured by more efficient organization, but is more fundamental: the desire to care for the vulnerable becomes mixed with secondary motivations which are the mechanisms by which society actually puts desires into practice. What may be a genuine moral impulse is muddled because it has to be mediated through bureaucratic and professional structures. It is easy to decree, for instance, that an allowance should be paid to alleviate hardship for the severely disabled, but as soon as the decree finds form in practical services other considerations intervene. Who is to get it, and how can equity be assured? What name will it have: how will its name influence its distribution? Who is to adjudicate eligibility, and do they want the job? What is the largest amount – and it is likely to be very small – which can be paid without upsetting the intricate differentials of existing payments for those who have or have not an insurance entitlement, or those who can or cannot or will not support themselves? How can the qualifying regulations be so framed that there will not be too many applicants? How does this particular measure fit in with the operational philosophies of the agencies who will be involved in its application?

To say that the system, as it eventually affects the individual client, may seem to owe more to the requirements of institutional structures than to the original intentions, is not necessarily any criticism of individuals within these structures, who have been placed in several dilemmas. There is the dilemma of singling out an undesirable characteristic – physical impairment – without appearing to stigmatize; the dilemma of persuading people to accept a label, 'disabled' or 'handicapped', which although it may be offered with the intention of helping may be rejected because potential clients find it meaningless, or alternatively because they find it too full of unwelcome meanings. There is the dilemma of determining 'needs' for an essentially heterogeneous group, and the dilemma of designing criteria of eligibility for services.

Since the cause of need in this context lies within the sphere of medicine, then the medical profession are the obvious adjudicators: yet the content of these needs is social and the mechanisms provided for their alleviation are those of welfare administration. The medical profession is required to fit its clinical categories to other sorts of defining systems which may well be incompatible.

Ideally, the medical profession has a one-to-one relationship towards its clients, and the doctor is strongly socialized into seeing his function as directed solely towards 'the best interest of the patient'. He is not, in ordinary clinical practice, supposed to see the welfare of society, or prevention of fraud, as overriding considerations. Social workers may share this professional ideology, but in other parts of the welfare system the orientation may be quite different. Administrative categories are necessarily dichotomous and designed for large groups of people. Administratively, a man is sick, or he is not; his injury is 'industrial', or it is not; he has a condition conferring eligibility for a particular benefit, or he has not. Clinical labels, on the other hand, are not usually dichotomous or rigid, and in many cases it may be supposed that the medical profession will dislike being forced into situations where they are required to make unqualified prognoses. They have learned that every patient is an individual and every prognosis may be confounded: the 'facts' of clinical practice are more properly estimates of probability, based on experience and subjective judgement. They have adapted to working in what Mechanic has called the context of uncertainty.[1]

To administrators, however, uncertainty is an awkward environment. The administrative structure forces doctors to choose between 'sick' or 'well' for a certificate, to adjudicate whether a man 'is fit' for work (and not whether he wants to work or whether it would be best for him to work), to say whether a patient is able 'to leave his residence' (and not whether the crux of the question is some other residence or some other means of leaving it). By convention, the actions of doctor's are given arbitrary meanings: a patient has to wait for the final review of his condition before he is 'recovered'.

The administrative structure also necessarily imposes its own time-tables. 'Short-term sickness' lasts for three months; illness of up to three days' duration does not count as sickness and need not be legitimated for national insurance purposes. Up to his sixty-fifth birthday, a man may be chronically ill but still 'in the labour market'; after that date he is a retirement pensioner and his illness is no longer administratively relevant. Roth,[2] in particular, has shown how the medical profession, too, may develop 'time-tables' to structure the patient's career in the way that best fits their own organization. The patients of this survey, making their ritual monthly visits to a doctor, or waiting three months for a review of their case, were very well aware of this. Ideally, however, the formal ideology of the medical profession is in terms of individual time-tables, and in any case, these medical structurings of time, though less arbitrary than administrative ones, may equally bear little relationship to the patient's situation as he sees it. They may also be in direct conflict with administrative time-tables, as the patients' histories have shown.

The obvious translator of medical categories into social, and the obvious definer of social needs, is the social worker. As the patients' histories have shown, however, the efficient use of social workers in this field can be confused by demarcation disputes between 'health' and 'welfare' and by the difference in status between the medical and social work professions.

The most difficult dilemma of all, however, is the problem of attempting to loosen definitions at the legislative level and yet avoid the vagaries of 'discretion' at the level of service-delivery. It was suggested in Chapter 1 that there is a strong movement towards wider concepts of who the disabled are, and towards more functional measures of what their needs might be. The inefficiencies and inequities of the older and more rigid categorizations, depending heavily upon clinical definitions, have been well illustrated in those parts of the system where they persist – for instance, the selection by clinical category of those entitled to a disabled person's vehicle or those eligible for free drugs, the singling out of those defined as 'blind' or 'deaf'. The assessment of industrial injury is perhaps the best example of the way in which criteria so particularistic about the disability itself (the exact position of an amputation, for instance) and so vague about its actual social consequences for the patient, in his particular circumstances, naturally breed conflicts about definitions. The elaborate structure of boards and medical or legal tribunals erected to deal with disputed cases bears eloquent witness to this.

Many examples have been given of the trend, in some parts of the system, towards looser categories and more comprehensive services. The provision of vehicles is extended to housewives; attendance allowance is provided for people outside the national insurance system; it is recognized that people living on supplementary benefit may have special health expenses; services for the 'disabled' seeking employment are extended to new groups; the Chronically Sick and Disabled Persons Act offers specific services to a very vaguely defined clientele of all those sick and disabled people who may need help.

It was also suggested in Chapter 1, however, that this widening of the clientele for services would be likely to make agencies' own processes of categorization more important, and these processes might well be more dependent upon the agency's own history, personnel, organizational structure and perceived function, than upon the needs of the clients. Thus, by a paradoxical process, categorizations might become even more arbitrary than before. In a system so fragmented, the patient might well be faced with a multitude of labels, and find even less congruence between the definitions of his situation being imposed upon him and the reality of his life as it seems to him. Examples of agencies defining their function and clientele in terms of their own structure and ideology have been manifold: local authorities' choices of what services they would offer to whom, doctors' definitions of the relevance of social circumstances, housing departments' practices, the definition of the proper client of the disabled employment register, the services and clients chosen by voluntary societies, the social security system's categories of people who might legitimately stay at home instead of working and those who might not.

Each agency defines its own market for clients, in part according to the resources available. Medical social workers in hospital, for instance, will readily admit that though their market is largely defined for them by medical personnel, by exerting some persuasive effort they could easily enlarge the number of potential clients by two-fold or more. But their workload is already adjusted to just the amount (or probably a little more) that they find practicable. Any agency in this field could expand its clientele, but if the expansion is not controlled within administrative limits the system will collapse. In the long run, of course, new systems would have to be erected – the number of medical social workers would have to be doubled – but no practical worker can be expected to sacrifice present clients, and allow his own organization to be destroyed, in order to demonstrate that some other organization might be an improvement.

The propositions of Scheff, mentioned in Chapter 1, about the validity of stereotypes of the 'proper client' – that they are less valid and precise if the clients are marginal, if the agency is not dependent on the clients' goodwill, if the stereotypes used are not numerous, and if the agency's profession is not based on a corpus of scientific knowledge – would seem to be well supported in the field of physical disability. The agency is rarely dependent to any considerable extent upon the goodwill of sick and handicapped clients. The categorizing systems of those agencies with only a small number of stereotypes (for instance, the social security or employment systems) were thought by their clients to lack validity and match ill with the complexity of their situations. Where categorizing systems were perceived to be based on a 'substantial and scientific corpus of knowledge' – as in clearly diagnosed medical conditions – they were acceptable, but where they were based on vague concepts of 'motivation' or 'social problems' they were disliked. In any case, even the 'scientific' categories of clinical diagnosis, or of the industrial injuries system, could extend to only a limited range of conditions or areas of life. Valid categories within these systems were unlikely to be found for the marginal clients whose conditions were anomalous or indeterminate.

The practical consequences of agencies' categorizing procedures will obviously be that they determine whether or not a potential client receives a given service. But it was suggested in Chapter 1 that their consequences are wider than the immediate context, because they form a part of the complex process by which the patient comes to define his condition, his need for help, and his eligibility for services. A general category of 'disabled', carrying with it a meaningful role-prescription and a universal set of 'needs' or 'rights', meant little to the patients of this survey, as their histories have demonstrated. They might well be precisely the people for whom services had been designed, but they found 'disability', by itself, a meaningless concept: they might, because of their physical handicap, have individual difficulties in some particular area of life – in getting about, or caring for themselves, or finding a job, or supporting themselves – but their conditions were varied and their problems individual.

Few conditions or problems remained static, and the patients' definitions of themselves and their needs were continually being developed and negotiated. They did not necessarily accept the categorizations offered to them by medical and administrative agencies, of course, but whether they accepted them or reacted against them, they were bound to be influenced by their perceptions of what the categorizations were. This affected their ideas about how their problems might be solved, and so their help-seeking behaviour. The way in which they presented themselves affected, in turn, the way in which they were defined by agencies, and so a continuous process of adjustment was set in train.

One of the clearest examples of this was the history of Mr Stuart, discussed at the end of Chapter 9. This patient knew very well what his functional impairment was: difficulty with walking, and with sight, and intermittent 'illnesses' which he did not properly understand. Because he did not know that these put him into any special category of disabled person, and because the grounds of eligibility for help which he perceived were stigmatizing ones he was reluctant to use (poverty, inefficiency as a wage-earner) he had neither sought nor received effective services. Towards the end of the survey period Mr Stuart learned during an outpatient visit to the hospital (accidentally, according to his vivid account) that he was suffering from multiple sclerosis. His redefinition of his role was immediate and striking. Previously, he had looked upon his illnesses as essentially temporary, and at times when he was not working had never sought to be defined as anything but 'temporarily ill' (if his job was being kept for him) or 'unemployed' (if it was not). Now, although he still wished to go on working as long as possible, he no longer saw his 'duty' to earn a wage in quite the same way. His entitlement to N.I. benefits had been precarious because of his work record, but he had never asked for supplementary benefit although he realized that in fact he might have got more money. His reason – perfectly rational while he was regarding his illnesses as temporary – was that if he were on supplementary benefit his rent rebate would stop, and would not restart after he had resumed work again until eight pay-slips could be produced; thus, every time he restarted work he would lose eight weeks' rent rebate.

Now, however, he presented this problems to the D.H.S.S. As a man with a young family, obviously a 'well-motivated' worker, he was treated very sympathetically. He voluntarily approached the social work department for advice, and began to consider applying for a disabled person's car so that he could avoid the difficult journey to work by public transport. A major factor contributing to his distress until this time had been that he felt himself to be isolated, a medical curiosity, with no legitimation for any role he found it easy to fill; he had seen himself as simply 'inadequate'. Now he began to present himself as a member of a special group and so eligible for various forms of assistance.

This is not, of course, to suggest that the acceptance of a definition as 'disabled' is necessarily advantageous. It may well be, if the services available for the particular category of disablement match with the patient's perception of his needs. If they do not, then the acceptance of the label may prove disadvantageous.

One example of the way in which this can happen was provided by the history of Mr Hamilton, a relatively young and previously fit family man who unexpectedly found himself suffering from heart disease. Various circumstances pushed him in the direction of a self-definition as permanently impaired. His previous job in the shipping industry had been skilled and well-paid but physically hard and stressful, and he took it for granted that he would not be able to return to it. His general practitioner appeared to be exceptionally anxious to help, and contacted the Department of Employment for him. Employment officers, following the normal procedure for G.P. referrals, placed him on the register of disabled persons.

After his convalescent period, Mr Hamilton did not feel himself to be disabled in his family or social life. He was not content to sit at home in an invalid role and became very bored and depressed. Yet, having been persuaded to define himself as disabled in his working life, he found the definition accepted by others: he was offered jobs which represented severe blows to his self-respect and his standard of living. He tried one after the other (porter, garage attendant, night-watchman) leaving each because he thought it bad for his health, and he now began to speak of himself as 'disabled', though in fact he had made a very good recovery: 'Being disabled will always mean less money', 'I'll never be able to do a proper job again, with the new flexibility you need to be able to turn your hand to anything'. Ten months after his heart attack he was offered a job with Remploy (which he refused wth incredulity) and was, he said,

'Right down on the ground – can't go any lower now.' In fact, at this point it appeared that the process might start to reverse, for he made a strenuous effort and obtained a better job, redefining himself as 'not as disabled as that!'

For a long period, however, this patient had found himself in an unexpectedly devalued position, with the label of disability without the reality of severe incapacity. If he had, in fact, had a static and permanent disability he would probably, as a young and skilled worker, have been encouraged to think in terms of rehabilitation and retraining.

These two examples illustrate the importance of categories which accurately describe the individual's *needs*. To experience the reality of handicap without a facilitating label is as disadvantageous as a label which forces a change in self-concept.

One common feature of these cases, and of the other cases throughout this study where problems proved difficult to solve, was that there was a lack of congruence between the definitions of his condition that the patient found being applied to him. It was pointed out in Chapter 3 that few clear indicators could be found which would distinguish those people who had problems, within the scope of helping services, and those who did not, and between those whose problems were solved and those for whom they went unsolved. Certain obvious facts could be assumed: that those who lived alone would be more likely to have practical problems, that unskilled workers and the already unemployed would be less likely to find solutions to job problems, that those without supportive family or community networks would be likely to have problems of loneliness and isolation. There were also some less obvious patterns which appeared in connection with specific areas of life: that it was the middle-aged, rather than the young or the old, who were more likely to have job problems, that women were more likely to have problems of personal care, that problems of family relationships were more likely among the young, that relationship with the medical profession was a good indicator of the likelihood of social problems, and so on.

In general, however, only one variable could be found which distinguished those people whose problems proved difficult to solve: that the three sorts of definitions being applied to their condition – the clinical, the administrative, and their own – were not compatible. The nature (rather than the degree) of their impairment became relevant only because people with complex or ill-defined conditions, or conditions which they themselves did not understand, were very likely to be in this position. Thus, while neurological impairments or undiagnosed conditions were very likely to lead to long-lasting problems, a straightforward injury might prove equally unfavourable if there was ambiguity about its prognosis.

Conflicting definitions might arise because of inherent anomalies in the administrative system of welfare, as many examples have shown: the necessity, for administrative purposes, of a clear division between sick and well, working and unemployed, capable of work and incapable; the administrative non-existence of the housewife; the difference between the roles thought legitimate for men and for women; the definition of disability by its cause rather than its effects; the way in which being formally in or out of the labour market affects entitlement to specific welfare benefits.

Above all, conflicts may arise because the patient is faced with a system which requires him to define himself as eligible for help in so many different ways. For some services, he has first to prove himself 'in need' (which may well seem to him to be equivalent to 'inadequate') before the cause of his need, his disability, becomes relevant; for others, he has to find some official label of disablement before the question of his needs can be raised. In some cases, he may find himself, like the young man who sought to have himself removed from the register of disabled workers, trapped into a category he does not himself accept. In others, he may, like Mr Stuart, feel that he is unable to live what he sees as a normal life without assistance, and yet search in vain for a clinical or administrative category which will entitle him to help.

The focus of this study has been upon the constraints imposed by this system upon the people of the survey. But the intention has not been to show them as puppets: the relationship between agency and client is an interactive one, echoing the relationship between society at large and the continually changing system. These individuals have been shown as creating their own social reality, but not – especially in their particularly vulnerable situations – as completely free agents. They have been fettered and constrained not only by their social environment but also by the two major systems of society within which their lives were structured: the system of medical care and the administrative system of welfare, employment and social security. The situation of permanent, or chronic, or fluctuating, physical impairment is one where the individual may be especially powerless, and a crisis point may be a moment when he is particularly at the mercy of the pressures exerted by these systems. At this point he epitomizes the view of 'man, the perplexed coper', expressed by Davis:[3]

> A perplexed, somewhat anguished, yet essentially well-intentioned character groping his way among alternatives, most of which are given him by the world, and some more nearly of his own making.

No overall recipes can be suggested which will help his perplexity, or indeed the perplexity of those whose job it is to help him. Throughout this volume, matters of detail have been discussed which are obviously in need of change; services which are simply inadequate in scope or quantity, inequitable details of the system of social security, a structure of employment which is ill-adapted to the realities of physical ability, welfare provisions where the original good intentions are being frustrated by administrative procedures. In general, however, it can only be suggested that what is needed is a greater boldness in applying new principles rather than simply tinkering with the old, a clearer look at who 'the disabled' are, and a more honest choice of what the needs are that society wishes to fill.

REFERENCES

1. Mechanic, D., *Medical Sociology*, New York, The Free Press, 1968, p. 23.
2. Roth, J. A., *Timetables*, New York, Bobbs-Merrill, 1963.
3. Davis, F., *Illness, Interaction and the Self*, Belmont, Cal., Wadsworth, 1972, p.x.

Appendix
SOME NOTES ON METHODOLOGY

It was suggested in the Introduction that the 'career' perspective adopted for this study offered two advantages. Firstly, it enabled some account to be taken of the dimension of time and, secondly, it facilitated movement between the 'macro' and the 'micro', the structure and the action.

In both cases, there has to be compromise. For the analysis of structure, the sample size must be large enough to provide internal control groups (in this case, those who had problems and those who did not) and to offer sufficient numbers for comparison by broad variables (age, sex, work, type of condition). Yet the sample must also be small enough for the intensive study of each individual. Again, ideally the understanding of process requires continuous and close observation, for which a few interviews may be a poor substitute. In the end, the study may have exhibited only the faults of compromise. Nevertheless, it can be argued that these two interrelated tasks – to capture process, and to comprehend simultaneously structure and action – are the major challenges of contemporary sociological research. However inadequate it proved in practice, the methodology used in the attempt should therefore be made explicit.

This methodology tried to take into account the two major criticisms of survey research which, though typically presented from opposite sides of the ring, must both be acknowledged to be valid: firstly, that to rely on the static and pseudo-scientific 'instruments' of written questionnaires or structured 'standardized' interviews, ignoring the variable meanings that will be given to the questions by the respondents, is to render both questions and answers problematic and perhaps meaningless; and secondly, that to go to the opposite extreme and offer descriptions of individual interactions, without making clear how these are to be regarded as more than individual, and without making known and comparable the methods by which the data may be obtained, may be no more than journalism, no matter how philosophically expressed. The object must be to offer facts which may be generalizable, but which are at the same time meaningful because their relationship to the perception of the individuals concerned can be demonstrated.

Time and process

The method of repeated interview did produce evidence which sheds considerable doubt upon the validity of any single point-of-time survey. Perhaps because the subjects were in a particularly vulnerable state, and greatly influenced by their day-to-day physical condition or by a single act or statement of other people (especially the medical profession), they were apt to change their definitions of the situation disconcertingly from one interview to the next. Very vehemently expressed opinions could be reversed entirely, and worries which appeared to be felt quite desperately could be forgotten as though they had never existed. Only if such vagaries are randomly distributed, in time and among the population under study, could single interviews have produced valid results, and of course they are not: they depend upon identifiable circumstances. A limited number of interviews at intervals of, usually, months could not, of course, provide a complete record of changing attitudes, and some invalidity remains. But such a method does at least allow for the possibility of transience, and can demonstrate some of the circumstances (both of the career situation and of the interview situation) under which it occurs.

The importance of the longitudinal design was not only that it appeared to offer greater validity, however, or show more clearly the sequence of events as they happened. The intention was not simply to slice the career into cross-sections, which might show that change had indeed occurred, but would still be essentially static. Rather, it was to explore the respondent's present *in the context* of his past and future. The study began from a theoretical position owing much to Mead's treatment of social meaning as 'emergent', the elaboration of this theme by McHugh,[1] and the use of the concept of emergence by Davis. In the process of reacting to new situations, the survey patients are seen, like those of Davis, as continually engaged in a search for new definitions of who and what they are, and new interpretations of what is happening:

> This search resulted not only in perceptual modifications of the existing situation, but in unwitting re-evaluations of relevant past and impending situations as well. Thus, the actual undergoing of the process set its own conditions for further action, the conditions themselves being an existential amalgam of previously emergent responses and events.[2]

In this sense, as Mead suggested, the social present can alter chronological past and future:

> A present, then, as contrasted with the abstraction of mere passage, is not a piece cut out anywhere from the temporal dimension of uniformly passing reality. Its chief reference is to an emergent event, that is to the occurrence of something which is more than the processes that have led up to it and which by its change, continuance, or disappearance, adds to late passages a content they would not otherwise have possessed.[3]

In the situation being examined in this study, it was particularly evident that people's definition of their present situation (as a 'disabled' person or not, as in need of help or not) depended crucially upon their anticipation of the future, which in turn was an amalgam of trends, forecasts, diagnoses, events, compounded from the past. In cases where there were few innovatory events occuring (because of a long-standing and static impairment) this relevant 'past' might extend backwards for many years and the successive definitions of it could not certainly be known; in cases where a great deal was happening (whether medically, or in domestic or working life) the process of readjusting the past and the future could be demonstrated clearly, though a limited number of interviews could not explore it completely. A man who did not understand, or refused to acknowledge, the seriousness of a condition might, in the early days of convalescence, behave as if a 'normal' future were a foregone conclusion: six months later he might not only have revised this future but also altered the past, explaining his previous behaviour in the light of his present knowledge.

Objective and subjective

In trying to understand these processes, both objective data (what did he do? what happened to him?) and subjective attitudes and meanings (why did he do it? what was the significance of the happening?) are relevant. Many of the social facts with which this study is concerned are relatively 'hard', that is, they are logically falsifiable, they can be counted in numbers (if this seems profitable) and assembled in tables. 'My age is . . . ', 'I went to see my employer yesterday . . . ', 'My weekly income is . . . ', 'My leg was broken . . . ' – these are all true or false: they can be checked, and indeed if necessary and practicable they were, by cross-reference, by interview with agencies, by confirming with family members, by documentary evidence, by obtaining permission to see records.

On the other hand, an attempt was being made to obtain, by the crude method of talking to people, many social facts of a different sort; facts which are not logically falsifiable, since they are attitudes, motivations, opinions, definitions of the situation. The status of a fact such as 'My reason for my behaviour is . . . ' may be difficult to ascertain. It may be subjectively true, e.g. 'this is what I really believe,' deliberate or unconscious 'presentation', e.g. 'this is what I correctly or mistakenly believe you want to hear' or 'this is what I correctly or mistakenly think will have the effect I want to produce,' or even simple error. It may be only provisionally true, e.g. 'this is what I believe today but not yesterday or tomorrow' or 'this is what I believe at my present level of knowledge, but at any moment further information may change things.' It may also have no meaning at all, for it is insufficiently acknowledged by surveyors that it is entirely possible for people to answer their questions politely but at random.

Nevertheless, it is necessary to know what the status of these facts is. They are wanted for explanations, and explanations involve causal pathways: 'he behaved in such-and-such a way because he felt that . . . ' leads to 'people in this situation may act thus because . . . '

Throughout this study, data collection and 'analysis', in the sense of developing explanatory patterns, went on simultaneously. Each patient was approached, at each round of interviews, with a series of key questions in mind: 'what is his understanding of his diagnosis?', 'does he consider himself permanently impaired?', 'does he foresee any problems?', 'is he going back to his job?', and so on. These were not, of course, asked in this bald and unanswerable form, but constellations of simple questions were devised which would provide indicators for each of the areas of interest. The interviewers' repertoire contained various alternative patterns of questioning, not only because different indicators might be appropriate for the young and the old, men and women, but also because the patient's individual situation, and his susceptibility to worry or offence, had to be considered. As a standardized questionnaire was rejected as unlikely to offer valid results, so too was the conventional ruling that the subjects should be interviewed as far as possible under standard conditions. Rather, the patients and their family members were seen, where possible, both separately and together, and the difference – if any – between the accounts received became part of the data.

Each individual career was first viewed as a separate entity, with the process of information-gathering seen as the continuous setting-up and testing of a network of mini-hypotheses about the status of the information being received about that particular career. These were then tested by prediction (of more information or, better, of behaviour) and used to build up more comprehensive hypotheses. Before returning to any individual, the previous interview was analysed and a new set of questions prepared to test the meaning of the statements made or the validity of the impressions received. Each individual career was also continually compared with others – is it like, or unlike? why is there this pattern here, and that there? – until eventually overall patterns seemed to appear.

A simple example can be used in illustration. The question might be (though probably not asked in this over-direct form) 'does this man expect to return to work?', and the answer obtained at one interview 'he says that he does.' It is now necessary to test the status of this statement. The hypothesis which is being used is that men in these particular circumstances who expect to return to work will behave in such-and-such a way at such-and-such a contingency in their career. By this hypothesis, if he does expect to return to work then his behaviour will be so-and-so. At the relevant time, it is observed whether he does behave in this manner. If so, this tends to confirmation of the hypothesis and another is set up: now, he will do so-and-so. If not, then either there have been intervening factors and new hypotheses must be set up about these ('he feels that his condition has worsened. If so, then . . . '), or if no relevant intervening factors can be identified then the original information had a different status: it was not what he 'really' believed, but an error or presentation, and new hypotheses must be set up to test the alternative versions ('although he knew it was impossible for him to return to work, he would not admit it at that time, because . . . '). When the testing process seems to have ascertained, as far as possible, the status of the item of information, then it is possible to begin to assemble meaningful categories:

x men of a certain sort expected to return to work
y men of a certain sort did not
z men of a certain sort did not, but said they did at a certain point

and so on, either for closer examination (the reasons why they said they did) or for use with other variables.

Words were also, of course, tested against other words (at other times, or in other situations) but the major reliance was on the testing of words against behaviour. This might be presumed to imply that the 'true' status of a statement is that which is expressed behaviourally, and this would be difficult to defend as a principle. It is possible for a man to say *a* though he believes *b*, and still act in accordance with *a*. If no obvious intervening factors have occurred, then the method of analysis may be too crude to pick up such cases. However, it can be argued that it is the actions, the behaviour, that connect the attitudes, the motivations, the definitions of the situation, to the structure of the career.

There is perhaps some similarity between this method and that which Popper calls the method of logical or rational construction, or the 'zero' method, which he suggests is peculiar to the social sciences:

> The method of constructing a model on the assumption of complete rationality (and perhaps also on the assumption of the possession of complete information) on the part of the individuals concerned, and of estimating the deviation of the actual behaviour of people from the model behaviour, using the latter as a kind of zero co-ordinate.[4]

This seems to assume that one can know what action will be 'completely rational', a position which would present some difficulty. However, it seemed useful in practice to make quite arbitrary decisions about the behaviour which would be rational, without necessarily being able to regard this as an invariate fact. It may be assumed, for instance, that 'the rational behaviour of a man who is going to need an adjustment to his job (who has perfect information) is to consult his employer.' This may not be true, but at least deviations from the model raise questions about why he did not do so, and the reasons (which may seem perfectly rational) may help to revise the general model.

Presentation

Presentation of this material offers parallel problems to these difficulties of dealing simultaneously with 'fact' and 'meaning'. The intention is to weave many short strands together, in the hope that by the end patterns become apparent, but the threads are of many different sorts. It is hoped that the manner of presentation makes the distinction clear between the different kinds of 'facts'. That which is stated unequivocally may be taken as checked; quotations from the subjects may be taken as representing their true perceptions and not casual mistakes or deliberate misleadings which would have been identified during the testing procedures described (such mistakes or untruths might, of course, be labelled as such and quoted for particular purposes). Where the status of a statement is uncertain, because checks were impracticable, this is made clear by qualifying phrases. Some clumsiness of style inevitably results, but an attempt has been made in this way to avoid one of the dangers of research which primarily takes the client's point of view, that the reader to whom it is offered has no way of knowing the relative importance of the statements made, or the grounds on which they are presented as meaningful.

REFERENCES

1. McHugh, P., *Defining the Situation*, New York, Bobbs-Merrill, 1968.
2. Davis, F., *Passage Through Crisis: Polio Victims and their Families*, New York, Bobbs-Merrill, 1963, p. 10.
3. Mead, G. H., *The Philosophy of the Present*, LaSalle, Ill., Open Court, 1959, p. 67.
4. Popper, K. R., *The Poverty of Historicism*, London, Routledge and Kegan Paul, 1960, p. 142.

Index of Subjects

Index of Names